COLLECTED PLAYS

BY

STEPHEN PHILLIPS 1868-1915,

New York

THE MACMILLAN COMPANY

1921

Norwood Press
J. S. Cushing Co. — Berwick & Smith Co.
Norwood, Mass., U.S.A.

PREFACE

I REMEMBER my father as a big man, with a
beautiful, but rather sullen face, and eyes full
of strange, sad melancholy, as if the soul were
always dreaming and yearning, and reaching
for heights unattainable.

He had about him a presence of mystery and
of power; that sense which one may feel to exist,
but which one may never describe in the language
of words.

To strangers he was cold, impassive and re-
served, which gave to him an aspect of sombre-
ness, but to those whom he knew to be in sympathy with his greatness of thought he became
at once a being of quite natural impulses, and
on these occasions, when he felt at ease, the light
of genius that burned unwaveringly within him
would burst into visibility with a power and
wonder that could not fail to impress.

Often, under the midnight stars, he would

pace the ground, giving utterance to those beautiful ideas, in a loud, vibrating voice, full of the intensity and clearness, the spiritual tone and exquisite charm, of which he alone was the master.

He was passionately fond of music and the haunting strains of some old song, or refrain, would sometimes awaken a beautiful thought within him, and while he was transmitting it to paper, he would ask for the particular piece to be played again, and perhaps again, until he had finished and was content.

Strangely enough he preferred the most simple music, especially an old song if it were at all sad, or had an air of dreaminess about it.

He had a magnetic personality. When once one had heard him reciting some lines in his remarkably expressive voice, one invariably wished to linger to hear more, if one had a sense of the beautiful or the divine.

Poetry was his chief and most constant companion, for he was not a mere conjuror of words or phrases, as a workman carves mechanically at his bronze, but a spirit of wild passion, calm

philosophy and sometimes of deep sadness, as
the mood took him.

And very often he had periods of such sadness,
when he could write only of sorrowful things,
and these, I think, contain some of his best
work.

It would be hard to find a more beautiful lyric,
in regard to its sadness and trance-like simplicity,
than this:

> "Beautiful lie the dead,
>   Clear comes each feature,
>   Satisfied not to be,
>   Strangely contented.
>
>   Like ships, the anchor dropped,
>   Furled every sail is;
>   Mirrored with all their masts
>   In a deep water."

The clearness, the directness and the appeal
of every word goes straight to the slumbering
soul and awakens it to the delight, the fragrance
and joy, which has, for the moment, eluded it.

Then, too, the quality of his tragedy was almost supreme. Just a few lines, taken at random, from "Paolo and Francesca"

> "What rapture in perpetual fire to burn
> Together! — where we are in endless fire.
> There centuries shall in a moment pass,
> And all the cycles in one hour elapse!
> Still, still together, even when faints Thy sun,
> And past our souls Thy stars like ashes fall,
> How wilt Thou punish us who cannot part?"

As a poet, dealing with the quietness and constancy of sorrow, or with the temperamental fires of tragedy, he was, I believe, standing, with firmly planted feet, upon a pinnacle of the mountains, where the fickle storms of criticism could not reach him.

It seems that now, after the turmoil of war, during which there was no leisure for Art, the time has arrived when his work should be placed before the reader once more, so that he or she may have an opportunity of judging its excellence, for although he was not the greatest of poets, he deserves a little niche, even a partially secluded one, in the eternal framework of immortality.

STEPHEN PHILLIPS, JUN.

ASHFORD, MIDDLESEX,
   ENGLAND.

TABLE OF CONTENTS

AYLMER'S SECRET

A PLAY IN THREE SCENES

BY

STEPHEN PHILLIPS

CHARACTERS

AYLMER

THE CREATURE

MIRANDA, *Aylmer's Daughter*

A PLAY IN THREE SCENES

SCENE. — AYLMER'S *Attic in* SOHO

TIME. — *The Present*

AYLMER'S SECRET

SCENE I

SCENE. — *Soho, London.*

TIME. — *The Present.*

A room fitted up as a laboratory, filled with mortars, batteries, etc., and other scientific instruments. (Body of CREATURE *at back, hidden by curtains.) Window at back. Curtain drawn before window across room. Lamp burning on table.*

[AYLMER *seated at table, alone. Nightfall.*

AYLMER. [*Agitated — rises and goes to window.*

It comes, it comes! At last the night comes on

That I so long have looked for : I have lived

But for this night.   To-night I bring to trial,

Put to the *test*, the labours of a life.

As I look back upon the years, I see

One long, one mad pursuit.   But is it mad?

This night shall prove.

> [*Walks restlessly up and down.*

The study of the stars,

Of stones, of plants, of creeping things, of all

This visible world sufficed for other men —

They left me still unsatisfied.

> [*Pauses in his walk — stands still.*

I sought

For that which lay behind all sciences —

For that without which they are cold, dead

things —

The very principle and breath of life,

Which God first breathed in Adam.

> [*Pauses, then sits, throws himself back in chair.*

                            And this thing

Possessed me like a passion, strong as love

Or hate!   Men came to me and said:

"Beware! for there are limits set for man

Beyond which if he goes he sins."   I see

No limit set to knowledge.   Who shall say,

"Thus much it is permitted thee to know, —

No more"?   Or where doth Nature stay her

    hand?

So, like a dreamer standing on the edge

Of some vast precipice, as he looks down,

The very depth and terror of the place

Draws him to leap, and lose himself in air;—

So I, long gazing, felt the wild impulse

To plunge in the unknown. Here, in this
  room,

I lived alone, above the streaming life

And roar of London, which has pass'd me by,

Still mingling chemistry with chemistry,

  [*Rises and holds lamp to the different in-
    struments lying in the room.*

Until at last I wrung from *cylinders*,

Batteries, mortars, engines, crucibles,

This awful fire, *this very breath of life*,

This secret, first of secrets and the last.

  [*Goes up and draws curtain, disclosing
    body of the* CREATURE.

Here lies a human frame, which I have toiled

And toiled on, year by year, that it might be

A fitting mansion for so high a guest.

Look on him, Nature, scan him, search him
well,

Created bone for bone and vein for vein

Like thy first Adam.   Look on him again. —

What is there lacking?   Where doth he fall
short?

In muscle, organ, tissue, fibre, nerve?

[*Goes, holding lamp, up to high shelf, and
reaches phial.*

And thou dost hold a mightier secret yet —

Or all my life is vain; — an essence pure,

Which shall have power upon those lifeless
limbs

That they shall rise and stand and walk to me,

Here, in this very room. Ah! Why do I

    shudder?

Why have I hidden here, away from men,

Like an assassin — bolted out the world

As from a solitary crime?   Not dared

To ask Heaven's blessing on my enterprise?

Long years have I looked forward to this night,

And now this night has come,

           [Puts down lamp on table.

                I fear: and why?

           [Holds up phial, and looks at it.

'Tis but the last of all discoveries.

Galileo, Newton, Herschel trod the same

Path that I now tread; I but bring their seed

To harvest.   Has not Nature, has not God

As He led them, led me, too, by the hand,

And shall I now draw back? Surely, to doubt

Were greater blasphemy than to defy Him.

[MIRANDA'S *voice is heard outside.*

Listen!

[*Stands listening.*

My child's voice! Is it hers? or

that —

Who knows? — of a better angel? And it

seems

To call me back from what I was about

To do.

[*Sees phial in his hand. Shudders, and
slowly retreats to shelf and puts back
phial, still listening, face towards sound.*

Let me put back this phial.

[*Voice ceases.*

Ah!

Now it has ceased! I feel in me again

The longing I have felt before, to leave

For ever this unnatural life, to dash

That phial to the ground, and to return

Once more to *human* love, to *human* life,

And lay this fevered head in my child's lap.

MIRAN. [*Heard off.*] Father! Father!

AYLMER.   She calls me!

VOICE.   [*Outside.*]   Father, may I come in

a moment?

AYLMER.   My child, I have forbidden you

to come in here.

Leave me for this night to myself.

VOICE.   Only a moment, father!

[AYLMER *draws curtain back, concealing*

body. Unlocks door. Enter MIRANDA.
*She stands a moment, looking round;
shudders, and then comes to* AYLMER,
and puts arms round his neck.

MIRAN. Father, when will you leave this
dreadful room, with all these ugly instruments, which make me shudder even to look
at them? What is it you work at here, all
alone? Can't I help in some way? I am
sure that I could. You used to be glad to
have me with you, and now I scarcely ever
see you. I only hear you pacing up and
down this room night after night, and mutter-
ing to yourself. I am so lonely by myself.
And whenever I speak to you, it is always,
"Some other time — some other time."

[*Rises petulantly.*] I was your daughter once — long ago — but now you have another daughter whom you love much more — Science.

AYLMER. Science, my child, is an exacting daughter.

MIRAN. She exacts too much! Oh, father, is it right for you to be so much alone? Perhaps I am not like other girls, who care only to be loved. But I should be quite happy if you would let me watch over you. Then I should be content. But now, my life is so vain. I have this great need at my heart — something to love, something to cherish. Let me love *you*, father! Let me be near you, as I used to be. You do still care for me, father, don't you?

AYLMER. Care for you! You are the only thing I love; and, after to-night, the old days shall come back. I have one more great experiment to make before dawn, and then I will seal up this chamber for ever, and we will be together, with nothing to part us any more.

[*They embrace.*

MIRAN. This shall be the last night, then?

AYLMER. The very last. To-morrow, early, I will wake you, and we will go out together, and look on Nature at her sunniest. And now leave me. And yet, why should you leave me? No, no! Stay by me, stay by me, child. I am better when I am with you. Save me — save me! Do not leave me to myself to-night!

[*Sinks wildly into a chair.*

MIRAN. Ah, you are ill. Let me lead you out of this hateful room, and never enter it again. Come!

AYLMER. No. It was only a passing weakness; I am well again now. [*Rises, mastering himself.*] I am strong. [*Aside.*] I will not go back nor falter. [*Aloud.*] This night I must spend alone, for on this night I either succeed in the labours of a life — or I fail.

MIRAN. [*Reluctantly.*] Well, if it must be so — good night. But this is the last night you will sit up alone, is it not, father?

AYLMER.   The last.

MIRAN.   [*At door.*]   Remember, you prom-
ised!   To-morrow I claim you for myself.
Good night.

[*Exit.*

[AYLMER *locks door, walks slowly back to
table and sits down.*

AYLMER.   I am a man again!   I feel, I
love!
And this unnatural and feverish fire
Leaves me, and a more sober glow comes
back.
And yet I must go on.   The night is spent.
I must to work.

[*Draws curtain.*

Were it not for the sake

Of future ages, I should pause before

I wakened thee, thou still, inanimate clay.

Thou art at peace as yet.   How many men

Groaning beneath intolerable lives,

Had they been offered choice — to lie for ever,

As thou liest now — would have refused this
    gift

Of feverish life I give to thee?   'Tis *we*,

We who have *lived*, who envy thee thy sleep.

Yet, why do I dream here?   The morning
    comes

Upon me, and I must to work.   Oh, why —

Why do I still draw back?   O, Thou great
    God,

Who hast made life, and given life to me,

If Thou art wroth, — or if I now usurp

Thy high prerogative — or if I go

Beyond the boundaries Thou hast set for man ;

If there be worlds forbidden, regions sealed

To us Thy creatures, where to breathe is sin, —

Then, ere it be too late, consume me !   Let

The lightning, flashing like Thy unsheathed
    sword,

End me, now, where I stand in very act

To babble Thy holy secret to the world ;

For, if I live, I must go on.

                         [Pause.

                Nothing !   Nothing !

Why, I am raving !   To what end these cries ?

'Tis but the last of all discoveries,

And I shall make it.

    [Reaches down phial and stoops over body.

Then drink thou down this.

How my hand shakes!

[Pause — rises.

I must be calm, take breath.

Now I am master of myself.

[Again stoops over body.

Once more,

I pour into thy veins the fire of fires.

[Long pause, after placing phial to CREA-
TURE'S *mouth.*

Motionless still!

[Starts back.

Ah! Am I going mad?

I see a faint flush on his face! Is it the light

Thrown from the lamp?

[Brings lamp and looks at body.

No, no; I see it still!

[Throws himself in chair by table.

I dare not look again.

[Pause.

Was that a sigh?

[Pause.

Again a shuddering sigh!

A moment more, and he will move — will
  live! . . .

I'll slay thee, ere it be too late.   To slay thee

Ere yet thou art alive can be no crime.

[Advances again to body.

I will not have thy life upon my hands.

No! It is now too late! He stirs — he stirs!

And if I kill him now, I smother life.

[Pulls blind aside.   Dawn enters chamber.

The dawn — the dawn! The world wakes,
    and thou, too,

Art waking! Waking! Is it pain to thee

To live? And costs it such a struggle then?

Thou comest into life with agony,

Imploring to be left alone, — to sleep

On, as thou hast slept. Strange!

                          [More light.

                    The sun is up!

And come, thou rising sun, rise, too, on him

As upon other men. Why thy bright rays

Search him. He shall not flinch before thy
    light.

If he be false — counterfeit man — a dream,

Then find him out; let him dissolve and melt

Away before thy beams — a midnight vision.

No! He shall live, and shall rejoice in thee!

[CREATURE *slowly rises. He comes and kneels before* AYLMER. *As he kneels,* AYLMER *drops phial with crash on ground.*

                      O, great God,

What have I done? Kneel not — kneel not
    to me!

O God, forgive me! Kneeling before me!

This is a sin — idolatry! I am no God,

But man, as thou art. Rise, I conjure thee;
    rise.

[CREATURE *slowly rises and sinks on chair. The dawn floods the chamber. Blinded with the light,* CREATURE'S *head sinks on his hands.*

[AYLMER *retreats with eyes still fixed on him to door and exits.*

[*As he locks door outside, Curtain descends.*

SCENE II

SCENE. — *The Same.*

Three months are supposed to elapse between Scenes I and II.

TIME. — *Evening.*

[AYLMER *seated at table.*

AYLMER.   Three months have passed since this Creature whom I created broke out of this dim room — how, I know not.   When at last, I dared to enter here again to look on him, I found him gone.   Then I breathed freely, and thanked Heaven, which, in its mercy, had lifted this burden from me, and suffered this haunting vision to depart. To have kept him imprisoned here for ever would have been impossible, and yet, if I had suffered him to pass this door, he might — who knows? — have met my child. Ah, Heaven, save me from that! Three months have passed, and he has not returned. And now, how should he? No, they can never meet. How will it fare with him out yonder in the world? Even now, perhaps, he is lying cold and stiff on some bleak London pavement — or, if not dead, he is lost in this vast city. He is gone! And I feel once more at peace. He is gone — and with him is gone the former life, solitary, feverish, unnatural. Earth wins me back again from those unhallowed toils to the arms of my child — to the life all men should live — loving and being loved. What is this Creature to me now but a vision? — a vision of the night — that night when I had well nigh lost my reason to see him kneeling before me, and —

[*Enter* MIRANDA, *carrying flowers*

Ah, Miranda!

MIRAN. Look, father! Do look at these flowers. You have shut yourself up here so long, you have almost forgotten there were such beautiful things as these springing all the time in the world outside. Smell them.

AYLMER. Yes, they rebuke me. Shut up

here, alone, brooding over those instruments, all my life I have let the beautiful fresh world go by. These smell of rain and earth.

MIRAN. Yes. [*Begins to arrange flowers about room, then stops in dismay.*] Oh, I could do nothing for this room till those instruments were cleared away. Do you know, I have a new idea. I mean to make this my special room, and —

[AYLMER *shudders.*

— have my piano in here. We are to be together now; and this old fortress where you had entrenched yourself so long, I have stormed.

AYLMER. Well; have your way. I have surrendered to you.

MIRAN. Ah, father! you shall never be lonely again.

AYLMER. My child, you need have no fear. That old, sinful life is gone. I cannot even look at those instruments without loathing. No; that night was the last, as I told you. I and Science took leave of each other then for ever.

[*They embrace and exit* AYLMER.

MIRAN. What a new man father is! In that one night, he broke with the associations of a life-time, and said farewell to Science for ever. Did he succeed that night in his great discovery? I suppose not; and now he has resigned himself to tranquillity and — *me*. Well, he shall not return to his old, lonely life again, if I can help it. No; he has shaken that off for ever. [*Walks round room, arranging flowers.*

[*The door opens and the* CREATURE *appears in entrance.*

CREA. This is the room where I first saw light; but it is changed. Ah! who is that beautiful being? Will she despise me as all others do?

[MIRANDA *turns and sees him at door.*

MIRAN. Who are you? Who told you to come here? Who directed you?

CREA. I have been here before.

MIRAN. Before?

CREA. Yes.

MIRAN. When? But it is cruel to ask

you questions. Sit here a moment. I will bring you some wine.

[*Exit.*

CREA. [*Looking round.*] Once more within the room where I was born! There, on that floor I struggled into life. Life? Is this life? To be despised and shunned by all! Yet *she* has not turned from me.

[*Re-enter* MIRANDA.

MIRAN. Now, drink this. It will give you strength.

[*Pause, in which he drinks.*

Can I help you?

CREA. You help me by speaking to me. I could bear my life if I might hear a word of pity now and then.

MIRAN. Is your life, then, so wretched?

CREA. There is little I can tell you. My past life I cannot remember. All that I feel is in the present. I have never heard, till now, the sound of one kind word.

MIRAN. How strange!

CREA. I have wandered up and down the pavements of this vast city. I have begged food from door to door, and been repulsed and cast out, again and again, till sheer misery drove me to speak the language those about me spoke. I cannot tell you why, but men seemed to shrink from me as from a man apart from other men. Even the homeless beggars with whom I crouched in some dark archway, to escape the wind and rain, turned from me. Even those houseless wanderers, whose misery should have made them my companions, never spoke to me. Were we not all exiles together? Together at war with the world? And should not this have made us friends? But, no! I have seen them leave the door in whose shadow I took refuge, and face the wild weather, trust themselves to the pitiless skies rather than to me. The rest I had borne — the weakness, the hunger, the blows — these I had borne as I saw others round me bearing them. But *that* I could not bear — I could not bear!

MIRAN. They shunned you because you could not help them. Beggars are like the rich in this.

CREA. It was not that. It was not that.

MIRAN. It was that, and that alone. But tell me more.

CREA. Then, at last, this great loneliness wrought on me so that I said, I will go back to this room, and ask shelter of him who owns it. *I have some claim on him,* I think. He will not let me die.

MIRAN. Let you die! Why, do you know who owns this room? My father!

CREA. *Your father!*

MIRAN. Yes. He will not turn you away. He is all kindness and gentleness.

CREA. He must not find me here with you. I will go.

MIRAN. Stay, stay! You shall not go. You have some claim, you say, on my father. You know him, then?

CREA. Yes. All my life I have known him. Never were two so closely bound together.

MIRAN. You fear him? Is it not so? He has seemed to you cold, stern. For a long time even I, his daughter, thought of him as you do; but lately he has given up that lonely, studious life in which you knew him. He has given up his scientific studies, which made him seem cold and hard. I think he failed, one night, in some great experiment.

CREA. [*Aside.*] He did fail.

MIRAN. And after that night, he gave it all up. Men have no business to shut themselves up, away from those who love them, prying and peering into what Heaven never meant them to know. But all that is over now. Oh, you will find him changed. If you have any claim on him, stay here and I know he will help you.

CREA. Will *you* plead for me, if I stay?

MIRAN. I will.

[CREATURE *sighs in happiness.* He has known what it is to be lonely. He will feel for you all the more because he has felt.

CREA. Ah, *you* do not know what it is to have this great need at your heart — this continual crying out for love, and never to find it.

MIRAN. Yes, I have felt a little what you feel; when my father was wrapt up in his studies — and I would have given worlds for a look now and then, to show I was not quite forgotten.

CREA. Ah! Do not speak of your father. Tell me of yourself. You, too, have felt, you say, this great desire. Have pity then on me. I am in this great world, I know not why. Alone I have wandered through the streets, alone have lived. Alone, alone for ever!

MIRAN. Ah! do not say that.

CREA. Tell me — tell me, why do men

shrink from me? It seems there is a great gulf fixed between me and all mankind. A gulf I cannot pass. I see them on the other side — those human beings I love, but who love me not; I see them, but I cannot reach to them. Oh! will there never come a day when one of them will look across and see me — on the other side! Oh! shall I ever hear a voice out of the world of men saying, "Come," or shall I ever feel a hand stretching across to lift me over the wide gulf and set me there as a human man with human men! Ah! might I dare to think that *you* — you have not turned from me — you do not start from my touch — you do not loathe me, — pity me, pity me a little!

MIRAN. Loathe you! Why should I?
I pity you from the bottom of my heart.

CREA. Now, I have found what I had
sought so long! At last — at last I am
pitied, I am loved a little! Oh, let me have
one to speak to, one to whom I can cling. Do
not forbid me now! I only know that I was
scorned, and I am pitied; I was loathed, now
I am loved; I was lonely, now I have a
friend! I *must* love you or I shall die.

[MIRANDA *makes a movement.*

If I have hurt you, forgive me. Now I would
live on. Life to me now is beautiful. Now, let
the great world go by for ever. I am happy!

[*A step is heard.*

Ah! he is coming! I know his step, and

tremble at it. He will tear me in pieces!
Hide me — hide me from him!

MIRAN. Be still! Be still!

CREA. He will send me away from you.
I shall lose you.

MIRAN. Whoever it is, he shall not hurt
you. I will stay by your side. Why, it is
my father's step. Come; take my hand.

[*Enter* AYLMER.

AYLMER. Come back! Come back!

[CREATURE *throws himself at* AYLMER'S *feet.*

MIRAN. Rise, rise. No need to kneel.
Father, here is a poor outcast. He says he
has some claim on you.

AYLMER. None. Miranda, leave us together. Leave him to me.

CREA. Your promise! Stay by me!

AYLMER. Miranda, leave him at once, and for ever. Let go his hand. You know not what you do. And you who have crept back here, I banish you from this room. I command you never to see or hear her voice again. Back — back into the streets which you have left.

MIRAN. Father! You surely would not cast him out. He has suffered so much.

AYLMER. So have thousands; but they suffer on. I tell you, I had rather see you in your grave than holding *his* hand, as you do now. Quit this — creature whom you see cowering on the ground before me. For you to see him, to touch him, is pollution.

MIRAN. Ah! you are cruel.

AYLMER. Am I to be obeyed, or not?

MIRAN. I owe you all duty. That I know. But I have other duties. I am a woman born into the world to pity and console, by a right divine as your command. I told you, and I tell you now, I have felt a want all my life — something to shelter, something to protect. I had hoped it might be your old age; but you drive me from you by these cruel words. You have left me alone all this while to think for myself — to teach myself — while you sat apart, deep in science. Well, I have lived this life. I have learned to think for myself, and I feel — I *know* that I should pity this poor outcast.

AYLMER. Then, hear me! I demand that you leave his side.

MIRAN. Why? Why?

AYLMER. I will not tell you why. I will not tell you more than this. Is it not enough? I *command* you to leave him.

[MIRANDA *slowly and reluctantly leaves* CREATURE, *and crosses to door, where she stands during the rest of speech.*

As for you, you have no claim on me. You have left me, and I will not shelter you. Yes, you have come back, like the fiend to the haunted man. But I will cast you from me. I have awakened, and I see a new life opening out before me — a life of love, of peace, at last; and you shall not stand between me and my hopes. Hence, thou plague — thou monster! Hence out into the streets, and die! Die quickly!

CREA. Oh! Oh!

MIRAN. I cannot bear this! I *will* stay by you!

[MIRANDA, *who has been standing at door, at* AYLMER'S *last words comes to* CREA-TURE *and stands by him.* AYLMER *sinks despairingly down.*

END OF SCENE

SCENE III

[CREATURE *sleeping at back. Enter* AYLMER *with a light.*

AYLMER. He sleeps; and he must not wake. Even now

He has divided me from all I love.

My child has turned from me.   He must not
  live.

It is no sin for these my hands to strangle

What these my hands created.   God Himself

Slays every day what He Himself created,

Haunted, perchance, as I, even in His heavens,

By cries and wild upbraidings of His creatures,

Which follow Him and will not let Him rest.

He takes the life He gave : then, why not I ?

O wretched, paltry end !   That this my work,

For which alone I lived : my dream, my
  goal —

Cries out for death, to be unmade, undone !

That these same hands must shatter what
  they shaped !

Yet he must go. It is not me alone

He menaces, but he has touched my child

With his pollution. Anything but that!

Yet, if I slay him, am I quit of him,

Therefore, for ever? That if this faint spark

Of life that I have lit — if this survive

Beyond the grave, how will it be hereafter?

Will he not meet me in that other world,

With those imploring eyes entreating me

A place of rest? In which of you, ye stars,

Appointed homes for spirits, into which,

If he ask shelter, will he be received?

Will he not wander on for evermore

From world to world, as here from house to

house,

A stranger looking in upon a feast?

Shall I not see him, alien that he is,

Cast out, a lie, a lone, unnatural thing,

Counterfeit coin rejected at God's mint,

Not with His image stamped, as other men?

Will he not then come back to me, and I

Be forced to cherish him *there*, even as here?

Heaven grant this fire of life, in rashness lit,

May die out here for ever! Else I see

No end, no limit to my folly. *Space*

Will cast him back on me. *Eternity*

Consign him to my keeping evermore.

He wakes!

THE CREATURE. [*Waking.*]

Give me thy hand. Art thou not near me?

    No,

She is not here; and *thou* hast parted us.

Ah! was it not enough, thou hard creator,

To force me into life, unripe and harsh,

Not coming like a flower thro' the earth,

Eased with a thousand dews and many rains,

But dragged into existence?   To what end?

That thou might'st be a god.   Shall I forget

The pain, the agony of hearing still

That strong, o'ermastering voice that called

   to me

To *live*, still fighting to be left alone?

Shall I forget the pangs of being born?

When every sense was forced upon me, till

I was compelled to see, to hear, to feel,

And burning life came in my veins like fire.

And to what end?   That thou might'st be a

   god.

But was not this enough?   At length I lived.

I stood before you, and you quaked and fled

From your creation, leaving me alone.

From that dim casement I looked down and
   saw

Life streaming on below me, and I chafed

At this my prison, and broke out of it.

I wandered forth into the world of men.

My heart went out to them: I sought their
   love,

Prayed for it, as a beggar prays for bread.

I found no mercy and no pity.   Cast

Out like a dog from every door, the rain

Beat on me, and the night made me afraid.

All loathed me, and all started from my touch,

As, by an instinct all too true, they felt

My being was not *theirs*, my *birth* not *theirs*.

At last, outworn and faint, I crept again

Back to this room ; thinking at least thy *pride*

Would not permit the life thou gav'st to fail.

And then I found, oh ! at the last I found

One that would not reject me, knew not how

To scorn. She shrank not from my touch,

    and she —

She, out of all the hurrying, heartless crowd —

Turned back, and spoke to me. They were

    the first

Soft words my ears had heard. She made me

    feel

That there was no great bar, no mighty gulf

Set between me and all mankind alive.

Long had I yearned to love and to be loved,

And now, as in a moment, it had come.

I loved her, and she seemed to feel for me.

Then, as I sobbed and kissed her hand, I
     heard

Thy step far off — I heard, and knew at once

Thee, my creator.   And I trembled then

Even to behold thy face.   I knew that I

Had been too happy, and thou, striding in,

With that same voice which called on me to
     live,

Forbad'st me *love*.

AYLMER.   Control thyself.

CREA.   What is

Control?   Thou gav'st me no control, but life.

And without love I cannot live my life.

O my creator, pity me a little!   [*Kneels*.

AYLMER.   Rise from your knees.

CREA.   Or, if I may not love,

May not be loved; if thou hast given me life,

And then deniest me that on which life lives,

Then slay me now.   Oh, send me back again

To the darkness whence I came, and to the

    blank

From which thou formed'st me.   Nothing is

    alone

Save me.   I only go companionless.

AYLMER.   I will not hear!   Thou askest

    love of me

Thou lucky mingling of dim chemistries,

Thou monster, bitter fruit of impious years,

To breathe with thy composed, unnatural

    breath

Upon her face, pure as the face of Heaven!

Oh! horrible!

CREA. Slay me, then. Let me not thus
    linger on,

Living, yet gasping for the breath of life.

AYLMER. I will not slay thee. For thou
    art the crown

And flower of all my life; the end, result

Of long, laborious years. Weak as thou art,

Suffering and wretched, yet art thou a *man*

As other men, perfect in every sense.

From the four winds I gathered thee together.

The dews, the saps, ay, the great Sun himself

Have I made minister to thy creation. All

My life without thee is a waste, a blank.

For thy sake I am old before my time.

I have sold sleep for thee, that thou might'st stand

Before me, as thou standest, perfect man

And thou art dear to me.

CREA.   Must I live on?

AYLMER.   I will not slay thee.

CREA.   Then, let my lonely life

Be near her and lie round about her path.

Ah, let me see her, catching but a glance

To treasure up and feed on by myself.

AYLMER.   Thou shalt not see her. Find some other out.

Thy ways and hers are parted evermore.

CREA.   Can'st thou deny me? May'st *thou* one day feel

As I feel! May the God who gave thee life

Make it a fever in thy veins, to cool

At one touch only, only at one voice,

And may that touch thou yearnest for, that
    voice

Be unto thee a thing forbidden, dead!

May He look down out of His terrible
    Heavens,

And say, "As thou forbadest thy creation

To love, so I forbid thee!"   May'st thou pray

To die, and death shall be denied thee!
    Then,

When love is to thee what it is to me,

Then shalt thou turn, and cursing thy Creator,

Execrate Him as thee I execrate,

Casting thy life back in His teeth, as I

Cast mine back upon thee!   [*Falls.*

AYLMER. What ails you? Say

CREA. I am dying of thy cruelty. I am
failing!

Oh! call her. Let me see her. Call her quick.

[*Enter* MIRANDA.]

MIRAN. I am here.

AYLMER. He has called for you. He is
dying — failing fast.

CREA. Ah, you have come! I cannot
linger on

In life, since love I may not have; and now
I am dying.

MIRAN. But *I* love and pity you.

CREA. It may not be. Ah! were it not
for you,

I could almost believe this were a dream —

This little feverish life that I have lived —

A dream that I could gladly shake from me,

And sleep again.   But *you* have made it real,

Too real!   and I have felt too much to think

This were a vision.   I could have forgot

The agonies of birth, the wanderings;

But this I cannot put away — forget,

As I came into life with agony,

So I am leaving it with ease.   I seem

To ebb away, and you are growing dim.

Yet I still cling to life, for you are here.

Give me more life !   Ah !   let me not sink back

Into a place where she is not — a blank !

Give me the torture and the loneliness;

Give me the burning sun, the world of men,

The cursed, forbidden life, but only *you* —

I cannot lose you!

[*Appeals to* AYLMER, *who sits silent.*

You will not let me die?

To die while *you* are living at my side!

To have seen you, and to lose you! Oh, can this

Be possible! Is torture such as this

Permitted? This grim life I would not leave,

For you have made it dear to me.

AYLMER. [*Comes to him, much moved.*]

Forgive me, poor lone being! I have brought

This agony upon you; I have made

You feel: have put you on the rack. O God!

I have brought more suffering into Thy world.

CREA. It had been better had you let me rest.

I have known sorrow, which I had not then.

But I shall never see you any more,

Nor you — nor you ! —

MIRAN.   We have a faith which says

That, in another world, we yet may meet

Those whom we loved, and see them face to

    face.

CREA.   Ah ! but your faith is not for me.

I am

A thing apart.   Your beautiful promises

I have no share in.   Others — others may

    meet

But I no more shall see you.   Never more !

    [*He dies.*   AYLMER *and* MIRANDA *hanging*

    over him.

MIRAN.   Father, what was he to you ?

AYLMER.   He was — my child !

CURTAIN

ULYSSES

A DRAMA IN A PROLOGUE & THREE ACTS

BY
STEPHEN PHILLIPS

ULYSSES

CHARACTERS

ON OLYMPUS

ZEUS (*Jupiter*), with thunderbolt.

POSEIDON (*Neptune*), with trident.

HERMES (*Mercury*), with caduceus and winged sandals.

ATHENE (*Minerva*), with spear, shield, and ægis.

APHRODITE (*Venus*), with roses and doves.

ARES (*Mars*), with spear and shield; APOLLO, with lyre; HEPHÆSTUS (*Vulcan*), with hammer and pincers; DEMETER (*Ceres*), with cornsheaf, wreath, and veil; HESTIA (*Vesta*), with veil and sceptre; ARTEMIS (*Diana*), with bow and quiver; GANYMEDE, cupbearer to the gods.

ON EARTH

ATHENE.

HERMES.

CALYPSO, the Nymph of the Island Ogygia.

ULYSSES.

PENELOPE, his wife.

TELEMACHUS, his son.

EURYCLEIA, his old nurse.

ANTINOUS (young, insolent, splendid)
EURYMACHUS (mature, politic, specious) } Chief Suitors to PENELOPE.
CTESIPPUS (elderly, rich, ridiculous)

EUMÆUS, a swineherd.

7

MELANTHIUS, a goatherd.

PEIRÆUS, a steward.

PHEIDON, a gardener.

MELANTHO
CLYTIE   } handmaidens.
CHLORIS

ELPENOR   } sailors.
PHOCION

SUITORS, HANDMAIDENS, ATTENDANTS, SEA-NYMPHS,
SAILORS, ETC.

IN HADES

ULYSSES.
HERMES.

GHOSTS OF PHÆDRA, EURYDICE, SUICIDES, LOVERS, AND
CHILDREN.

CHARON.

GHOST OF TEIRESIAS (a prophet).

GHOST OF AGAMEMNON.

GHOST OF ANTICLEIA (the mother of Ulysses).

FURIES, TANTALUS, SISYPHUS, PROMETHEUS.

PROLOGUE

PROLOGUE

ULYSSES

PROLOGUE

The curtain rising discloses the summit of Olympus, an amphitheatre of marble hills in a glimmering light of dawn: where the hills fall away, a distant view of the world, with countries and rivers, is seen far below. Near the front are the seats of the gods, cut in an irregular semicircle in the rock. As the scene progresses the morning light grows clearer, descending gradually from the mountain summit over the figures of the assembled gods. In the centre, ZEUS, with the empty seat of HERA beside him; to his right ATHENE, APOLLO, ARTEMIS, HERMES, and HESTIA ; *to his left* POSEIDON, DEMETER,

ARES, APHRODITE, *and* HEPHÆSTUS.

ATHENE. [*Comes forward with outstretched

   arms.*] Father, whose oath in hollow hell

   is heard ;

Whose act is lightning after thunder-word ;

A boon ! a boon ! that I compassion find

For one, the most unhappy of mankind.

   ZEUS. How is he named?

   ATH.   Ulysses.

      [POSEIDON *starts forward, but is checked

         by* ZEUS.

                              He who planned

To take the towered city of Troy-land ;

A mighty spearsman, and a seaman wise,

A hunter, and at need a lord of lies.

With woven wiles he stole the Trojan town

Which ten years battle could not batter down :

Oft hath he made sweet sacrifice to thee.

ZEUS. [*Nodding benevolently.*] I mind me of

the savoury smell.

ATH. Yet he,

When all the other captains had won home,

Was whirled about the wilderness of foam ;

For the wind and the wave have driven him

evermore

Mocked by the green of some receding shore ;

Yet over wind and wave he had his will,

Blistered and buffeted, unbaffled still.

Ever the snare was set, ever in vain ;

The Lotus Island and the Siren strain ;

Through Scylla and Charybdis hath he run,

Sleeplessly plunging to the setting sun.

Who hath so suffered, or so far hath sailed,

So much encountered, and so little quailed ?

ZEUS. What wouldst thou ?

ATH. This! that he at last may view
The smoke of his own fire upcurling blue.

POSEIDON. [*Starting forward with menacing gesture.*] Father of Gods, this man hath stricken blind
My dear son Polyphemus, and with wind,
With tempest and a roaring wall of waves,
I fling him backward from the shore he craves.
Sire! if this insolence unpunished go
We soon shall lack all reverence below;
It will be said, 'The arm of Zeus doth shake,
Let none henceforward at his thunder quake!'

[ZEUS *moves uneasily.*

This man is mine! [*Strikes trident on ground.*]
By me let him be hurled
From sea to sea, and dashed about the world!

ATH. Hath not Ulysses through such travail trod

As might appease even anger of a god?

Monarch of monstrous rage —

> [*With furious gesture at* POSEIDON.

Thou who dost launch

The crested seas in streaming avalanche!

Lord of the indiscriminate earthquake throe,

Of huge and random elemental blow,

Thou who dost drink up ships, and swallow down

Alike the pious and the impious town,

Whose causeless fury maketh men mistrust

If there be gods, or if those gods be just;

Thy rancour is eternal as thy life,

Thy genius ruin, and thy being strife!

Pos. [*Tauntingly.*] And thou, demure de-
fender of chaste lives,

Smooth patroness of virgins and of wives,

I'll pluck from thee the veil thy craft doth wear,

The secret burning of thy heart declare.

Thy marble front of maidenhood conceals

Such wandering passion as a wanton feels.

What is thy heavenly sympathy but this,

To find occasion for Ulysses' kiss?

I will proclaim thee to Olympus—

    [POSEIDON *and* ATHENE *start forward, threat-*

        ening each other with trident and lance.

ZEUS.   Peace,

Children, and from your shrill reviling cease !

Do thou, Poseidon, for thy part, revere

The dower of her divinity severe :

And, daughter, gird not at his gloomier might,

His spoil of morning wrecks from furious night.

Endowed is he with violence by that law

Which gives thee wisdom — and thy father awe.

  ATH. Of reverence speak'st thou? Then Ulys-

    ses urge

Back to his home irreverence to scourge ;

There weeps his wife Penelope, hard driven

By men who spurn at law and laugh at heaven.

A swarm of impious wooers waste his halls,

Devour his substance and corrupt his thralls:

They cry about her that her lord is dead,

They bay around her for the marriage bed —

    ZEUS. [*Solemnly.*] Ulysses shall return !

    POS. [*Starting forward.*]   Cloud-

    gatherer, stay !

    ZEUS. Yet canst thou work him mischief on

    the way.

In thy moist province none can interfere ;

There thou alone art lord, as I am here.

Where bides the man?

    ATH.   Calypso this long while

Detains him in her languorous ocean-isle,

Ogygia, green on the transparent deep.

There did she hush his spirit into sleep,

B

And all his wisdom swoons beneath the charm

Of her deep bosom and her glimmering arm.

Release him, sire, from soft Calypso's wile,

And dreamy bondage on the Witching Isle.

ZEUS. [*Oracularly.*] Go, Hermes, and unweave

    her magic art.

Then let him choose; to linger, or depart.

Yet ere he touch at last his native shore

Ulysses must abide one labour more.

ATHENE. Say! say!

ZEUS.   The shadowy region must

    he tread,

And breathing pace, amid the breathless dead,

The track of terror and the slope of gloom,

To learn from ghosts the tidings of his doom.

ATH. O spare him, Father, spare him —

ZEUS.   He must go

From dalliance to the dolorous realm below.

ATH. Remember, sire, she snared with spells

his will,

But his deep heart for home is hungering still.

HERMES. [*Mischievously, pointing at* APOLLO.]

And, sire, remember, we are gods, yet we

From human frailties were not ever free.

If even immortals genially stray,

Shall we be merciless to mortal clay?

But lately the sun-god himself was seen

Snatching at Daphne's robe upon the green.

APHRODITE. [*With soft insinuation.*] And even

thou, O Father — in thy youth —

Didst feel, at least for mortal women, ruth.

To Leda, Leto, Danaë, we are told,

Didst show thee on occasion tender —

[ZEUS *thunders softly. General suppressed*

laughter among the gods. ZEUS *thunders*

loudly: all the gods abase themselves.

ZEUS.   Hold !

'Tis true that earthly women had their share

In this large bosom's universal care,

That Danaë, Leda, Leto, all had place

In my most broad beneficent embrace :

True that we gods who on Olympus dwell

With mortal passion sympathise too well.

                              [*Sighs deeply.*

But, daughter, 'tis not I that do impose

Upon Ulysses this the last of woes.

I to no higher wisdom make pretence

Than to expound eternal sapience.

It is that power which rules us as with rods,

Lord above lords and god behind the gods ;

Fate hath decreed Ulysses should abide

More toils and fiercer than all men beside :

Heavily homeward must he win his way

Through lure, through darkness, anguish, and delay.

ATH. Yet swear he shall return!

ZEUS.   If he can dare

Through shadow of the grave to reach the air.

ATH. Then swear it by the Styx!

ZEUS.   I swear it.

         [*Rolling thunder is heard beneath.*

HERM.   Hark!

'Tis ratified by rivers of the dark!

ATH. I'll to Telemachus his son, and fire

His heart to prove him worthy of his sire.

[*To* HERMES.] Thou to Ogygia in the violet

    sea,

To touch Ulysses and to set him free.

               [*Exit* ATHENE.

Pos. And I, Ulysses, will thy bark waylay!

And though thou must return, thou shalt not say

Thou wast afflicted lightly on the way.

             [*Exit* POSEIDON.

ZEUS. [*To* HERMES.] Hermes, command Calypso to release

Ulysses, and to waft him over seas ;

Yet she shall not forewarn him that his fate

Permits him homeward but through Hades' gate.

[*Exit* HERMES.

[*To* GANYMEDE.] The cup, bright Ganymede !

Ah, from the first

The guiding of this globe engendered thirst.

[ZEUS *drinks :* OLYMPUS *fades.*

ACT I

ACT I

ACT I

SCENE I

Forecourt of the palace of ULYSSES *at Ithaca, with stone seats disposed around it. Towards one side, the front of the palace, with portico and pediment richly decorated in the Mycenæan style. Separated from this, a building containing the women's apartments, from a gallery in which a flight of stairs leads down into the court. A boundary wall encloses both buildings: in the interval between them, the mountains of Ithaca are seen above the wall. To the right a low colonnade, over which appear the trees of the orchard — apples, pears, figs,*

25

etc., with a great vine trailing into the court.
In the court, a scene of wild laughter, uproar,
and prodigal confusion: some of the SUITORS
dancing in abandonment with the HANDMAIDENS,
while others pour out of the central door of
the palace to join the rout. TELEMACHUS *is*
seen sitting moodily apart. At last the dance
ends in breathless disorder.

ANTINOUS. Come, Clytie, I have no breath left,
sit on my knee and drink from this cup! No!
I'll have fresh wine. [*Pours it on floor.*] A
fresh jar.

CTESIPPUS. Now may the Lady Penelope defer
her answer so long as she pleases. This way of
life suits me. [*A* HANDMAID *empties cup of wine*
over him.] Fetch up fresh jars from the cool
earth !

MELANTHO. [*Entering from door in wall to left of house, and holding up key.*] I have the keys of the great wine vault.

PEIRÆUS. Ah! you have stolen my keys! How shall I meet Ulysses!

[*Everyone laughs.*

MEL. Come with me, some of you, and bring up fresh jars.

[*Exit* MELANTHO *with three* SUITORS.

Enter three HANDMAIDS, *loaded with flowers and branches of fruit — figs, apples, pears, grapes, pomegranates, followed by* PHEIDON.

CHLORIS. See! see! we have stripped the great orchard. Here! here!

[*They fling fruits and flowers over* SUITORS.

PHEIDON.   Princes,   princes!   Years   and
years   have   I   tended   these   plants   and   trees,
and   in   a   moment   they   are   torn   up,   and   all   the
fruitage   of   the   summer   squandered.   Ah!   if   my
master   should   return!

CTES.   That   need   not   trouble   you.

> [*All laugh.*

> [*A wild scene of flinging fruits and red,
> white and purple flowers ensues.*

Re-enter MELANTHO *and* SUITORS, *rolling
fresh jars of wine.*

ANTIN.   Break   off   the   necks,   and   let   the   wine
run   on   the   floors — I'll   cool   my   feet;   and   drench
this   wreath   again!   Ulysses   is   dead,   or   if   he
live,   we   are   masters   here   to-day.

> [*Jars are broken, wine flows on floor.*

ALL.   Ha!   Ha!   Ha!

Enter EURYCLEIA, *the old nurse, followed by two faithful* HANDMAIDS *bearing work-baskets, etc.*

EURYCL. O, you vile handmaidens! that sit on princes' knees and drink the wine of your master who was ever kind to you.

GIRLS. La! la! la! la! la!

EURYCL. Oh! may you never come to a husband's bed! but wither unwooed to the grave!

ANTIN. The old dame is envious! Here, Ctesippus, you still lack a damsel. Take her and comfort her! Kiss her, kiss her, Ctesippus!

EURYCL. Wiser to let her be!

[*They drag* CTESIPPUS *to* EURYCLEIA *and push him towards her.*

CTES. Her time is past — young lips for a man of my spirit.

MEL. Men reach not for withered apples!

CLYT. Parchment face!

MEL. You skin hung in the wind to dry!

ALL. Ha! ha! ha!

EURYCL. O! when Ulysses shall return—

ALL. Ha! ha! ha!

EURYCL. For return he shall—

ALL. Ha! ha! ha! ha!

EURYCL. O! then may he not spare you, women though ye are, but strike you down with the men—fools! wantons! thieves!

MEL. [*To faithful* HANDMAIDS.] Why slave under that bitter hag when you can have the kisses and the gold of princes?

ANTIN. What would he do—one man amongst us all?

EURYCL. Kill you! kill you! kill you! Ulysses! Ulysses!

[*She is hustled off.*

Enter other SUITORS *dragging in* EUMÆUS,
the swineherd.

SUITOR. Here is the man who sends us the lean swine.

ANTIN. Bring him before me!

EUM. Princes, I am but a serving-man and have respect unto my lords. Shall I serve up a dish that would poison the great princes?

ANTIN. Poison us?

CTES. [*Turning pale.*] What does he say?

EUM. My lords, a fever is fallen upon the swine! To eat them were death.

CTES. Ah! ah!

A SUITOR. What, what, Ctesippus!

CTES. Ah! the pain! the pain! I am poisoned!

[*All laugh.*

Do I swell? do I swell already?

Suitors. [*With mock solemnity.*] Farewell, farewell, Ctesippus, thy death is on thee!

Ctes. Help me within doors! Ah! ah!

[*Exit* Ctesippus, *supported by* Hand-

maidens.

Antin. [*To* Eumæus.] This is a lie!

Eum. There are but two left of the whole herd, and already I like not the countenance of one of them!

Antin. It is a lie to keep us from our food!

Melanthius. [*Obsequiously.*] Believe him not, most noble Antinous! But I, it is my pleasure to bring you what I have; fat kids; sweet morsels for my noble lords. He hath hidden the swine away, most mighty Antinous.

Antin. Go, drag him out, and drive in the swine.

Suitors. Come, come: show us the swine!

Eum. And so I will. [*Aside.*] But not the fat ones. [*Exeunt* Eumæus *and* Suitors.

Antin. [*To* Servants *within.*] A fresh feast, and swiftly!

[*To* Suitors *and* Handmaids.]

Meantime a brief sleep, for the sun bears heavily on us. Come, Clytie, my head on your lap.

A Suitor. And you with me, Melantho.

[*The* Suitors *lie down in various attitudes with the* Handmaidens.

Re-enter Ctesippus, *who starts in horror.*

Ctes. Ah! they are dead already.

Antin. Cease, old fool, and sleep awhile.

[Ctesippus *lies down.*

Athene *appears, and stands by* Telemachus.

Athene. What man art thou?

c

TELEM.   O goddess bright !

ATH.   Be still ;
Where is Ulysses' son?

TELEM.   I am he.

ATH.   Thou he !
Where is Ulysses' son? Gone on a journey?
Or dead, that this is suffered in his halls?

TELEM. Nay, goddess ; I am he ! [*Buries his
face in his hands.*]

ATH.   Art thou his son?
Art thou the child of the swift and terrible one?
Could he who shattered Troy beget thee too?
What dost thou here, thy head upon thy hands,
While all the floor runs with thy father's wine,
And drunken day reels into lustful night?
What more must these men do to make thee wroth?
How scratch, how bite, how wound thee to find

       blood?

O, should Ulysses come again, how long,

How long should strangers glut themselves at

    ease?

Why, he would send a cry along the halls

That with the roaring all the walls would

    rock,

And the roof bleed, anticipating blood,

With a hurrying of many ghosts to hell

When he leapt amid them, when he flashed,

    when he cried,

When he flew on them, when he struck, when

    he stamped them dead!

Up! up! here is thy Troy, thy Helen here!

  TELEM. Goddess, I am but one and they are

    many.

  ATH. Thou art innumerable as thy wrongs.

Hist! how they sleep already like the dead!

               [ATHENE *disappears.*

TELEM. How would my father find me should

    he come !

Weak, weak ! How have I raged and fumed in vain,

And pondered on the doing ! Now to do !

                        [*He starts up.*

    [*During the ensuing speech of* TELEMACHUS,

        the SUITORS *gradually awake and rise,*

        some stretching themselves and yawning.

Antinous and Eurymachus, and the rest !

Too long have I borne to see you snatch and spoil,

And eat and swill, and gibe and ravish. Now,

Now from this moment I'll stand master here ;

Lord of my own hall, ruler of this hearth.

I'll flit no more a phantom at your feasts,

Discouraged and discarded and disdained.

I am the son of him whom all men feared,

And if he live I hold his place in trust ;

If he be dead I stand up in his room.

Now on the instant, out! out at the doors!

[ANTINOUS *yawns loudly.*

CTES. Are we awake, or do we all still dream?

TELEM. Take wing, you vultures that too long

have perched!

Hence, hence, you rats that gnaw my father's

grain.

EURYM. I rub my eyes: is this Telemachus?

TELEM. I'll have no tarrying! Out, out ere

ye wake!

The spirit of my sire descends on me,

And 'tis Ulysses that cries out on you;

You by the throat, Antinous, I take.

[*He makes towards* ANTINOUS, *who still holds*

CLYTIE *in his arms, while she laughs*

impudently at TELEMACHUS.

ANTIN. Softly, sir, softly! Clytie, do not laugh,

This is your lord!

CTES. I like to see such mettle!

EURYM. Be not too rough with him, Antinous!

ANTIN. A moment, sir, before you cast us out —

[*He laughs, as do the others till he recovers himself.*

Before you cast us out — as easily

Doubtless you could!

A SUITOR. We are helpless and o'ermatched!

EURYM. Sad Ithaca, when such a tyrant rules!

CTES. Reach down thy father's bow and shoot us dead!

TELEM. [*To himself, while* EURYMACHUS *and other* SUITORS *at back are consulting in whispers how to deal with him.*]

Fool, fool! I have but made myself a jest:

It was not thus Athene meant. Fool, fool!

EURYM. [*Coming forward to* TELEMACHUS *from others at back.*] One word! You say that

we devour your halls,

That we are vultures, rats. Yet answer this,

Do we bide here, then, of our own inclining?

We come to woo your mother — are your guests,

And we would have an answer ere we go!

   ALL. An answer, yes!

   ANTIN. [*Starting up.*] An answer from her lips,

Which one of us she chooses for a husband.

Have we not seen moon kindle after moon

And still she puts us by! How long, how long!

   TELEM. Eurymachus, I have blustered windy

threats;

But 'tis a grievous office thus to sit

A master and no master in my halls:

And still I say you do me injury,

Devouring thus the substance of my sire!

ANTIN. Then let your mother make her choice

of us!

Would she have strength and splendour of the limbs,

Sap of the body and youth's burning blood,

I little doubt on whom her choice will fall.

EURYM. Nor I — would she have prudence in

her lord

And craft.

CTES. And I say nothing, but I know

A woman before prudence chooseth gold.

ANTIN. [*Striking table.*] And till she answer,

none, not Zeus himself

Nor all the gods shall turn me out of door.

EURYM. Come, drink, Telemachus; we wish

thee well.

'Tis difficult for thee: I'd be thy friend.

Come, lad! [*Putting his arm about* TELEMA-

CHUS.]

TELEM.   I'll not drink with you.   What to do?

EURYM.   Now that this little tempest is o'erblown,

Sing to us, minstrel, and chase wrath away.

Come and sit near to me, Telemachus.

CTES.   [*In lachrymose manner.*]   Sing, minstrel,

    sing us now a tender song

Of meeting and parting, with the moon in it;

I feel that I could love as I loved once.

                [*Sighs deeply.   All laugh.*

MINSTREL.   O set the sails, for Troy, for Troy

    is fallen,

    And Helen cometh home;

O set the sails, and all the Phrygian winds

    Breathe us across the foam!

O set the sails unto the golden West!

    It is o'er, the bitter strife.

At last the father cometh to the son,

    And the husband to the wife!

[*During this song* PENELOPE *has softly de-*
scended, accompanied by two HANDMAIDS,
and stands listening unnoticed. She
holds her veil before her face.

And she shall fall upon his heart

With never a spoken word —

PEN. [*Dropping veil.*] Cease, minstrel, cease,

and sing some other song;

Thy music floated up into my room,

And the sweet words of it have hurt my heart.

Others return, the other husbands, but

Never for me that sail on the sea-line,

Never a sound of oars beneath the moon,

Nor sudden step beside me at midnight:

Never Ulysses! Either he is drowned

Or his bones lie on the mainland in the rain.

[*The* SUITORS *gather around her admiringly*
and importunately.

ANTIN. Lady, he sang to chase away our wrath.

Thy son, Telemachus, upbraids us all

That we stay here too long, and cries, ' Out !

out !'

But we await your answer, still deferred :

Deferred from day to day, from month to month.

I, I at least no longer will be fooled,

Whose pent and flooding passion foams at bars.

Choose one of us, and they — the rest — will go !

PEN. Ah ! sirs, remember that I but delay

To choose till I have woven at the loom

A shroud for old Laertes.

MELAN.   O my mistress !

How canst thou stand and lie to noble men ?

O Princes, I have spied on her, and she

At night unravels what she wrought by day.

Ye'll wait a long time if for this ye wait.

PEN. Melantho ! I was ever kind to you.

ANTIN. We are tricked then!

ALL.   We are duped!

EURYM.   O she is subtle!

PEN. Princes, you drive me like a hunted thing
To feint and double thus.

CTES.   A game they play!
The mother fools us and the son reviles us.
She thinks us asses, and he calls us rats.
Am I then like a vulture or a rat?

  TELEM. Mother, 'tis true I did upbraid them
      all;
I am called master here, but am no master;
Lord, but I rule not! smiled at and passed by,
A shadow while these men usurp my halls.

  EURYM. [*Going to* TELEMACHUS, *and laying
      hand on his shoulder*.] Lady, indeed your
      son hath much excuse,
And for his sake I'd urge you to make answer,

For his sake and the sake of this dear land,

Which lies now with defenceless coast, a
rabble

Leaderless, laws and altars overturned.

Let then your son rise in his father's room.

CTES. Let the boy take the reins and drive:
but thou

Depart with one of us; and better sure

A live Ctesippus than a dead Ulysses.

EURYM. [*Pointing to* TELEMACHUS.] Thy duty
points thee to thy son that lives!

PEN. Is it so, child, this brooding on a dream

Hath kept thee from thy kingdom? I am wrapt

So in my husband I forget my son.

TELEM. Mother, although my office here is
hard,

Yet would I rather lie out by the door,

Cursed, spat on, offal thrown to me for food,

Than any grief of mine should hasten you
To answer with your lips but not your heart,
Or be the cause of your departing hence.

  PEN. And yet I see 'tis so, and that dear
    ghost
Excludes the living child : forgive me, son.
[*To the* SUITORS.] Yet, sirs, I cannot on the in-
    stant choose :
I lose your faces in the thought of him.
Not on the instant — give me a brief space !
Then will I choose as husband one of you.

  CTES. Though she looked straight before her
    didst thou see
How her eye wandered toward me?

  EURYM.   She looked not
On me : that argues in a woman love.

  ANTIN. See, the young moon hath not begun
    to quicken,

And on the evening hangs awaiting life.

We'll give thee time till yonder moon is full:

Then shalt thou choose from us. Till then!

   No more.

PEN. I will do so.

TELEM.   Mother, think not that I —

PEN. My child, I have no blame for you at all.

EURYM. [*To* SUITORS.] Thy answer, then, when

   that faint moon is full!

ANTIN. I challenge any here to hurl the quoit:

To the market-place.

EURYM.   Haste, then, ere it grow dark.

    [TELEMACHUS *again comes forward to*

        PENELOPE.

PEN. Go with them, child! Nay, thou hast

   done no wrong.

   [*Exeunt all but* PENELOPE, *who stands stretching*

     out her arms in the darkening twilight.

Where art thou, husband? Dost thou lie even now

Helpless with coral, and swaying as the sea sways?

Or dost thou live, and art with magic held

By some strange woman on a lone sea isle?

Yet we are bound more close than by a charm;

By fireside plans and counsel in the dawn —

Like gardeners have we watched a growing
    child.

Thy son is tall, thou wilt be glad of him;

All is in order; by the fire thy chair,

Thy bed is smoothed, but now these hands have
    left it.

Thou knowest the long years I have not quailed,

True to a vision, steadfast to a dream,

Indissolubly married to remembrance;

But now I am so driven I faint at last!

Why must my beauty madden all these wolves?

Why have the gods thus guarded my first bloom?

Why am I fresh, why young, if not for thee?

Come! come, Ulysses! Burn back through the
world!

Come, take the broad seas in one mighty leap,

And rush upon this bosom with a cry,

Ere 'tis too late, at the last, last instant — come!

[*Again the* MINSTREL'S *song is heard as the
scene changes.*

SCENE II

*The shore of Ogygia with the sea-cave of Calypso.
A vine full of fruit trails over one side of the
cave, and round about it grow whispering
poplars and alders, from under which rillets of
water run to the sea. Beyond, a verdant shore,
with thickets of oleander, etc., and the ship
of* ULYSSES *lying beached. Within the cave
a fire burning gives out the smell of sawn*

D

cedar and sandal-wood. The sun behind is sinking, and the water is golden, while over all broods a magic light. A chorus of OCEAN-NYMPHS *is discovered dancing and singing on the sands.*

Enter along the shore ULYSSES *and* CALYPSO.

CAL. Art thou content then, utterly content?

ULYS. I'll drift no more upon the dreary sea.

No yearning have I now, and no desire.

Here would I be, at ease upon this isle

Set in the glassy ocean's azure swoon,

With sward of parsley and of violet,

And poplars shivering in a silvery dream,

And smell of cedar sawn, and sandal-wood,

And these low-crying birds that haunt the deep.

CAL. Thy home, then? Hast no thought of it at all?

ULYS. It seemeth to me like a far, faint place.

CAL. Rememberest thou thy wife ?

ULYS. [*Dreamily.*]   As through a mist :

And dim she seems, and muffled, and away.

Those crimson lips again ! O eyes half-closed,

That closing slowly draw my soul from me !

Thou fallest back, thy hair blows in my face,

And all the odour goeth to my brain.

CAL. Come !   I would have thee sleep upon

  this bank

Till the first star shall light us to our couch

Of o'erblown roses and of fallen leaves.

  [*She leads* ULYSSES *out and he lies upon a
    bank.*

Thy purple cloak, wilt have it so, or so?

Now sleep, my love : thou canst not go from me.

  [*She returns and passes within the cave.*

  [*Calling the* NYMPHS *about her :*

The golden shuttle and the violet wool:

And all ye nymphs sing to me while I spin.

NYMPHS. [*Singing.*] From the green heart of

the waters

We, old ocean's daughters,

Have floated up with mortal men to play;

Out of the green translucent night

Up to the purple earthly light,

To dance with creatures of a day.

For alas! we have seen the sailor asleep

Where the anchor rusts on the ooze of

the deep,

But never, never before

Have we seen a mortal dance on the long seashore.

HERM. [*Appearing, unseen by* CALYPSO *and her
nymphs, and standing over* ULYSSES *where he
lies asleep.*] Ulysses, thralled by passion this

long while,

I lift from thee the glamour of this isle.

Olympian wisdom bids thee waken free

Of white Calypso's glimmering witchery.

Behold, I raise from thee the magic woe:

[*Touching him with caduceus.*

Now lies it in thyself to stay or go.

[HERMES *stands aside and watches* ULYSSES,
*who, slowly awakening, begins to gaze
and stretch out his arms over the
sea.*

NYMPHS. [*Watching* ULYSSES *from the mouth
of the cave and singing.*]

See, see Ulysses, weary and wise.

Sing low, sing low with downcast eyes;

For he rouses at last,

And his eyes are cast

To the land where his spirit would be,

Over the violet sea.

Alas for the arms that yearn !

Alas for the eyes that burn !

Ulysses — Ulysses — ah !

[*They all start up as* HERMES *steps suddenly amongst them.*

CAL. Hermes, I know thee, though too rarely seen ;

What is your will with me? Art thou from Zeus?

Some word of Zeus thou bringest; let me hear.

HERM. Lady, who sitteth there upon the shore?

CAL. It is Ulysses. Ah, 'tis not of him?

HERM. There sits the man of whom I came to speak.

CAL. Say then !

HERM. Thus Zeus commands : that you set free Ulysses.

Cal.   Ah !

Herm.   And waft him on the deep,
If in his heart he hungers for his home.

Cal. He is most happy and forgets his home.

Herm. Yet if he shall desire at last his
    hearth —

Cal. He will not — no ! —

Herm.   Then shalt thou waft his sails.

Cal. He shall not go !

Herm.   But Zeus commands.

Cal.   I say
He will not care to go, doth not desire ;
To leave me hath not entered in his heart.
Yet will I set him free if he so choose ;
But I am sure of him.

Herm.   And he shall have
More peril being gone, down into hell
Must pass, and view the hollow night of things.

Cal. This will I tell him.

Herm.   No! for Zeus forbids.
Farewell, Calypso — linger I may not.

                              [*Exit* Hermes.

Cal. I cannot doubt thee, and the spell was
strong.

[*She goes to the door of the cave and calls*
     Ulysses *three times. At last he hears*
     and rises, then comes slowly down to
     her rubbing his eyes like one awakening
     from a trance.

Cal. Art thou Ulysses that so slowly comest?
Who hath bewitched thee that thou gazest past me?
And thou wert wont to rush into my arms!

[*She leads him within the cave —* Ulysses
     still seeming numbed and changed.

Ulysses, there hath been a god with me,
A messenger from Zeus. Come from the shadow,

That I may see your face. Thus Zeus commands :

'If sad Ulysses yearns to see his home—'

      [He starts and gazes again seaward.

Ah! you would go then! back the bright blood

   comes,

And to your eyes the sea-light!

   ULYS.   Goddess — I —

   CAL. 'If sad Ulysses burns to see his home,'

Then Zeus commands me that I let you go.

Ah! set your teeth upon your lips : but still

I hear wild music at your heart.

   ULYS. [*Beginning to recover and realise.*]

                     O whence

Comes this release—or—this command of Zeus?

   CAL. O spoil it not! then thus comes this

   release.

The gods have pity on you, seeing you

Unwillingly beguiled by cold Calypso.

And more; I am to swell your aching sails,

And breathe you with a breeze over the deep:

Only if you desire — 'tis in your will.

Well! well! Why do you gaze so in my eyes?

ULYS. I have learned to dread what cometh
    suddenly,

And sniff about a sweet thing like a hound:

And most I dread the sudden gifts of gods.

CAL. Gifts!

ULYS.   I would say commands — this
    is some lure.

Swear suddenly 'tis not! [*Harshly and quickly.*

CAL.   Is this thy voice?

Put me upon my oath, and I'll swear false.

I tell you out of a sad heart the truth.

ULYS. [*Still hesitating.*] Who bore this mes-
    sage down?

CAL.   Hermes.

ULYS. **A most**

Garrulous god!

CAL. He came from Zeus himself.

ULYS. And Zeus himself I trust not over-far.

Hurler of bolts! I speak it reverently.

[*Seizing her arm.*

I will not loose you, till you swear by Styx,

River of hell, the dreaded oath of gods.

CAL. I swear to you by Styx, river of hell!

ULYS. [*Breaking away.*] O then the ship, the

ship!

CAL. [*Detaining him.*] A moment yet!

Kiss me, dear guest! My love for you is deep,

But ah! not deep enough to wish you home.

ULYS. The gods command : we mortals but obey.

CAL. Why will you leave me? I must let you

go,

But not without a reason : must I? Speak!

I do but ask the why of what must be.

[He kisses her absently.

Is this Ulysses' kiss?

ULYS.   Goddess, this news

Makes me forgetful.

CAL.   Worse and worse !

ULYS.   Again

[Kisses her.

CAL. This out of gratitude?   And when you
   gaze

Into my eyes you see a world beyond.

[He again moves to go.

Yet stay ! I do not ask for the old look,

Or to lie nearer in the deep of night :

That's ended like a song. But I will know

Why you so burn to sail ; why suddenly

I touch these arms of stone, this hand of flint,

Why suddenly your eyes peer seaward, why

All in one moment you are mad for home.

Is it your wife whom you at last remember?

Penelope? — doth she not drag her feet

A little as she walks? — slow — but how chaste!

If I could see her, I would understand.

  ULYS. I'd not compare Penelope with thee.

  CAL. I have shown you amorous craft, tricks

    of delay,

Tears that can fire men's blood; you must for-

    get

These, and return to simple husbanding.

Hath she the way of it? all the sweet wiles?

The love that shall not weary, must be art.

  ULYS. She hath no skill in loving — but to love.

  CAL. And are her eyes dark; dark, yet with

    lightning?

Never a blue eye held a man like thee.

  ULYS. I have forgot the colour of her eyes.

CAL. Patient and fair and comfortable? yes?
Stands she as I do? Is her head so poised?

ULYS. How should a mortal like a goddess stand?

CAL. And can she set a rose in bosom or hair?

ULYS. She hath a wisdom amid garden flowers.

CAL. Doth she sing sweet?

ULYS.   The songs of my own land.

CAL. [*Suddenly.*] She hath forgotten thee, so
   long away.

ULYS. I would remind her with what speed I
   can.

CAL. Remember, she is mortal: she must die.

ULYS. Therefore I flee the faster to her side.

CAL. O what an end! You two will sit in
   the sun,
And challenge one another with grey hairs.

ULYS. And so to spare your eyes I would be
   gone

Ere this my head to such a greyness grow.

   CAL. How shall my heart contend against your

     brain?

Now by that time I thought eternity,

By long sea-evenings when all words would

     cease,

By all the sad tales of thy wandering,

Sad tales which will be happy to remember,

Tell me the reason of this haste to go.

'Tis she, I know; I want no words to tell me.

But is it she? And now I do recall

Even in your wildest kiss a kiss withheld,

Even in abandonment a something kept;

When veil on veil fell from you, still a veil.

When you so poured your soul out that a

     woman,

Even a woman, had in her heart said 'now!'

I felt in all that sweet a something stern.

ULYS. Why harp upon my wife? You being
woman
Too much exalt the woman: a thousand calls
Are ringing in my ears: my mother pined —
   CAL. When did a lover heed a mother's
      woe?
ULYS. My father desolate or dead: my son —
CAL. No father nor no son could launch that
      ship.
ULYS. My comrades, then!
      [ULYSSES' *comrades meanwhile are wander-*
         ing at back.

                     Whatever my inclining,
They still have homes which I must think upon
Who took them far.

   CAL.   Friend hath killed friend for love.
   ULYS. My empty throne and my neglected land:
Duty —

CAL. O! hath it come to duty now?

Duty, that grey ash of a burnt-out fire,

That lies between a woman and a man!

We fence and fence about: tell me the truth.

Why are you mad for home? I'll have the truth,

Once and once only, but the living truth.

ULYS. [*In a wild burst.*] Then have the truth;

I speak as a man speaks;

Pour out my heart like treasure at your feet.

This odorous amorous isle of violets,

That leans all leaves into the glassy deep,

With brooding music over noontide moss,

And low dirge of the lily-swinging bee, —

Then stars like opening eyes on closing flowers, —

Palls on my heart. Ah, God! that I might see

Gaunt Ithaca stand up out of the surge,

You lashed and streaming rocks, and sobbing

crags,

E

The screaming gull and the wild-flying cloud : —
To see far off the smoke of my own hearth,
To smell far out the glebe of my own farms,
To spring alive upon her precipices,
And hurl the singing spear into the air;
To scoop the mountain torrent in my hand,
And plunge into the midnight of her pines;
To look into the eyes of her who bore me,
And clasp his knees who 'gat me in his joy,
Prove if my son be like my dream of him.

   We two have played and tossed each other
     words;
Goddess and mortal we have met and kissed.
Now am I mad for silence and for tears,
For the earthly voice that breaks at earthly ills,
The mortal hands that make and smooth the
   bed.
I am an-hungered for that human breast,

That bosom a sweet hive of memories —

There, there to lay my head before I die,

There, there to be, there only, there at last!

    [CALYPSO *weeps*. ULYSSES *comes and touches*

      her softly.

Remember, Goddess, the great while it is,

How far, far back, alas how long ago!

    CAL. [*Clinging about him*.]   Now wilt thou

      leave me, now, close on the hour

Of silent planets luring us thro' dew,

And steady pouring slumber from the waves,

Wave after wave upon the puzzling brain?

    ULYS. My wife, my wife!

    CAL.   And, mortal, I will breathe

Delicious immortality on thee.

Stay with me, and thou shalt not taste of death.

    ULYS. I would not take life but on terms of

      death,

That sting in the wine of being, salt of its feast.

To me what rapture in the ocean path

Save in the white leap and the dance of doom?

O death, thou hast a beckon to the brave,

Thou last sea of the navigator, last

Plunge of the diver, and last hunter's leap.

CAL. Yet, yet, Ulysses, know that thou art going

Into a peril not of sky nor sea,

But to a danger strange and unimagined.

ULYS. I'd go down into hell, if hell led home !

CAL. [*Resignedly.*] Call up your comrades !

Bid them hoist the sails !

ULYS. Comrades ! [*He lifts his arms and cries to his followers, who come running to him, leaving the* NYMPHS *on the shore.*]

Great hearts, that with me have so long

Breasted the wave and broken through the snare,

Have we not eaten and drunk on magic shores?
Your hands here!

> [*They crowd round him eagerly, some clasping, others kissing his hands.*

COMRADES.   O great captain!

ULYS.   Have we not
Heard all the Sirens singing and run free?

COM. Lead! lead!

ULYS. Close, close to me! have we not burst
Up from the white whirl of Charybdis' pool?

COM. Storm-weatherer! mighty sailor!

> [*They clasp his knees.*

ULYS.   What say you?
Shall we put forth again upon the deep?

COM. We will go with thee even into hell!

> [*They raise a great shout.*

ULYS. Then Zeus decrees that we again set forth
And break at last the magic of this isle.

Com. Yet whither — whither?

Ulys.   Would ye see at last
Gaunt Ithaca?

Com.   Ah, God!

Ulys.   Would ye behold
The bright fires blaze and crackle on your
    hearths?

Com. Torment us not!

Ulys.   Would you again catch up
Your babes?

Com.   Have pity!

Ulys.   And clasp again your
    wives?

Com. Cease! cease!

Ulys.   Then homeward will we
    sail to-night.

Com. [*With amazed cries.*] Home? Home?

        [*A wail of* Nymphs *is heard on sands.*

Ulys.   Now lay the rollers under her,
And you make taut the ropes, you, hoist the sails,
And run her down with glee into the deep!

Com. [*Rushing off in various directions.*] The
ship! the ship! Ithaca! Praise the gods!

Cal. [*Coming out with cup.*] The cup, Ulysses! Drink to me farewell!

Ulys. [*Taking cup.*] First unto Zeus that
would not have us die,
But suffered us to see our homes again.
Farewell, Calypso, the red sun half way
Is sunk and makes a firelight o'er the deep.

Cal. Remember me a little when thou comest
To thine own country. Say farewell to me,
Not to the thought of me!

Ulys.   I will not. See!
The ship moves! Hark, their shouts! She
moves! she moves.

Hear you the glorying shingle cry beneath her?

She spreads her wings to fly upon the deep!

> [*The cries of* ULYSSES' *crew are heard as the
> ship is shoved down and they climb in.*
> ULYSSES *springs in and stands in the
> stern.*

MEN. We float! we float!

ULYS.   Now each man to the oar

And, leaning all together, smite the sea!

For it is fated we shall see our homes!

> [*The ship puts off, and the wind raised by*
> CALYPSO *fills the sails.*

CAL. I breathe a breeze to waft thee over sea!

Ah, could I waft thee back again to me!

> [*The ship gradually disappears, the joyous
> chorus of* ULYSSES' *boatmen dying off as
> the wailing of the* NYMPHS *becomes
> louder. A cloud gathers over the scene.*

[*The curtain descends, but rising again discovers the ship, now a black speck on
red sunset, and* CALYPSO *standing alone
looking after it across the sea.*

[*Wailing of* SEA-NYMPHS.

CURTAIN

ACT II

ACT II

ACT II

Scene I

*A gloomy barren shore, with black broken cliffs
and a few cowering trees: at the back the
entrance to a vast cave. Enter* ULYSSES
*slowly, armed and carrying a hunting spear;
he gazes about him.*

ULYS. A dark land and a barren! Hither

    urged

By strange and cold compulsion of the sea,

What hope for us of shelter or of food?

A grassless, fruitless, unsustaining shore!

I have outpaced my comrades. [*Calls*] Phocion!

Elpenor! The gods lied to me who swore

That we should see our homes again. Yet now,

77

What breathèd sweetness as of blended flowers?
Nearer and nearer still!

Enter ATHENE.

Athene! Thou!

Preceded by the fragrance of thy soul.

ATH. Ulysses, know'st thou to what land thou
art come?

ULYS. I know not, but I know the gods did
lie

Who swore that I should see at last my home.

ATH. The gods lied not, for thou shalt see
thy home.

ULYS. [*Eagerly.*] Ah!

ATH. If thou hast but courage to descend
Thither; to gather tidings of thy land
There, in the dark world, and win back thy
way.

ULYS. What world?

ATH. Doth not the region even now

Strike to thy heart? These warning cypress

trees,

This conscious umbrage cowering to the ground,

The creeping up of the slow fearful foam;

Rocks rooted in the terror of some cry

That rang in the beginning of the world:

All nature frighted into barrenness.

Lo, mortal, here the very gate of death,

And this no other than the door of hell!

[ULYSSES *falls on his face.*

Swoonest thou down, Ulysses? Wouldst thou see

Thy home?

ULYS. My home, alas!

ATH. Thither! Wouldst thou

Catch to thy breast thy wife?

ULYS. My wife, my wife!

ATH. Thither!

ULYS. [*Rising wildly.*] Who should endure

 this? Back to the sea !

Back to the wild sea ! Farewell, Ithaca !

To the wild winds ! Penelope, farewell !

       [*Makes to go.*
ATH. Ulysses !

        [*He stops.*

    Hast thou that in thee which I

Have vaunted of thee 'mid the mighty gods,

And have stood surety for thee in high heaven?

ULYS. Hast thou no pity?

ATH.   More than ever a woman ;

But as my pity, so my pride in thee.

ULYS. Why unto me, to me alone, is heaven

For ever cruel? Have I not borne enough,

Cyclops and Sirens and Charybdis' whirl,

Ogre and witch and dreadful swoop of winds,

That hell now stands between me and my

 home ?

ATH. The Power that is behind the gods decrees

To make a fiery trial of thy spirit.

ULYS. Is there no other way?

ATH. Thither alone,

Led by cold Hermes, who alone of gods

May pass that portal. Now, Ulysses, learn

What first must be encountered, and o'ercome.

Right in the threshold Hunger stands, and Hate,

And gliding Murder with his lighted face,

And Madness howling, Fear, and neighing Lust,

And Melancholy with her moony smile,

And Beauty with blood dripping from her lips.

Then shalt thou view the inmost house of woe,

And all the faint unhappy host of hell.

If these thou canst endure and pass, thou shalt

Hear tidings of thy home and of thy wife,

Emerge and come at last to thine own land.

F

ULYS. The gods lay on me more than I can bear.

ATH. Thy native shore!

ULYS.   The darkness and the dead!

ATH. Thy warm fire-blaze!

ULYS.   The grave and all the grief!

ATH. Voice of thy wife!

                              [*Faint wailings from the abyss.*

ULYS.   That crying from the deep!

ATH. Dare, dare it!

ULYS.   Is it sworn I shall return
Upward and homeward?

ATH.   In thy will it lies.
Thou, thou alone canst issue out of hell.

ULYS. Then? Then?

ATH.   Thou shalt return. Zeus
give thy voice.

                              [*Thunder.*

ULYS. I go!

ATH.   Now thou art mine!

[*She vanishes.*

COMRADES. [*Heard off.*]   Ulysses! Where?

Enter COMRADES.

ELPENOR. We have found thee, captain!

ANOTHER.   Does this land give aught
That we can eat?

ANOTHER.   Or drink?

ANOTHER.   O good roast flesh!

ANOTHER. Even bread were something.

ANOTHER.   Great Ulysses, speak!

   [ULYSSES *remains with fixed gaze on the en-*
      trance of the cave.

ANOTHER. What hast thou speared for supper,
hunter fleet?

   [ULYSSES *slowly turns and looks on them.*

ULYS. Listen !

[*A sound of cries, at first faint, rises. They*
     all come round him fearfully.   Three
     times the cries arise, each time louder.

PHOCION. Who are they that cry up from the
     earth ?

ULYS. The dead !

COM.   The dead !

PHOC.   And this?   What
     is the place?

ULYS. We now are standing at the door of
     hell !

[THEY *shudder away from him in silence,*
     all but PHOCION.

PHOC. Come ! come away !

ULYS.   No ! for I must
     descend.

Thus only can we reach our homes again.

PHOC. In every peril have I been with thee :
Let me be with thee here !

ULYS. [*Tenderly.*] My Phocion !

ELP. I am an old, old man ! am long forgotten

Even by my dearest. Let me go with thee !

ULYS. It may not be : leave me, and say no
word !

[*They gradually disappear.*

[ULYSSES *advances and peers into the dark.
A long solitary cry causes him to reel
back, and he seems to hesitate, when
again* ATHENE *stands opposite him
smiling. After a mute appeal to her
for help, she vanishes. He again advances, but recoils as from some terrible sight.*

HERM. [*Within.*] Ulysses !

Com. [*From a distance.*] Ulysses!

[Ulysses *after a moment's pause gradually
and fearfully descends.*

Scene II

*The descent into Hades. As the stage is dark-
ened wailings are heard and a sound of
moaning wind which ceases as Scene II. discloses a world of darkness with all things im-
palpable, save for a precipitous descent dimly
seen, and at its foot a livid river flowing, a
black barge floating on it. There is a continual
movement as of wings and flying things. A
sudden flash of* Ulysses' *armour discovers him
beginning to descend warily with* Hermes *in
silence.*

Ulys. Darkness!

Herm. Descend!

ULYS. Thy hand! I fear to fall.

HERM. Thou, thou alone canst downward tread.

ULYS. But this!

Is it ocean, land, or air? I grope down, down!
[*Pauses.*] A whist world! but for whirring as of
wings.

[*He looks down intently.*

Is that a forest yonder, that sways and sighs
With a vast whisper? yet no trees I see.
And there, what seems an ocean: yet no wave!
The wonder of it takes away the fear.

[*They descend further.* ULYSSES *pauses as a
faint cry is heard.*

Listen!

[*Again the cry comes, nearer. Again, and
nearer.*

What cry, so feeble and so frail?

HERM. It is the cry of children that died
young.

The glitter of thy armour lures them toward thee.

[*The* SPIRITS *of* CHILDREN *flit about him with
wistful cries.*

ULYS. Little bewildered ghosts in this great
night !

They flock about me —

HERM. Wandering on their way
To banks of asphodel and spirit flowers.

ULYS. Ah, a girl's face ! A boy there with
bright hair !

He is new come and is not listless yet.

And thou dost make a little prattling noise
And hast not learned to speak !

A CHILD. O the bright armour !

ANOTHER. O father, bring us to the place of
flowers !

ANOTHER. We have lost our way! Show us
the grassy fields!

[ULYSSES *makes appealing gesture to* HERMES,
who stands silent.

ULYS. I cannot bring you, children, to those
flowers.

[*The* CHILDREN *flit away with wistful cries.*

ULYSSES *starts forward.*

And 'tis not from the prattle of dead babes
I shall have tidings of my home, my wife.
Down and yet down!

[*Again they descend.*

[SHAPES *of* FURIES *appear circling in the air.*

Hermes, I am pursued,

But O by whom? As sharks to him that
drowns,
They make toward me, sidelong swimming
shapes!

I'll draw my sword.

[*He draws his sword and thrusts vainly
at the* SHAPES.

HERM.   What use to strike at phantoms?
The Furies these, who hurrying to the earth
To scourge the wicked, scent thee in mid-flight.

ULYS. [*In terror.*] Over and over me! and
    round and round!
They'll search the guilt out in my secret soul,
Their eyes go through my body to my heart!
I am but a man! I am all black within!
They leave me, they lift their faces to the
    wind!
Upward they rush!

HERM.   A sudden scent from earth!
                [*They again descend.*

ULYS. More and more difficult — yet down and
    down!

And now I seem to wade, and now to part

Entangled branches, now pass through a cloud.

[*He pauses.*] Hermes, a sighing near my feet,

    as of reeds.

And now about me phantoms, men and women.

    [PHANTOMS *of* SUICIDES *rise about him.*

One hath a scarred throat, and that woman

    holds

Poison as in a phial — what are ye?

  FIRST PHAN. [*To* ULYSSES.] Thou, thou hast

    life in thee, and flesh and blood.

See, see the man is in the body yet.

  ULYS. What are ye?

  SECOND PHAN. Spirits of those who cast away

Sweet life and slew ourselves with violent hands.

    [*The* PHANTOMS *circle about him.*

  FIRST PHAN. In madness I !

  SECOND PHAN.   And I in jealousy !

PHAN. OF PHÆDRA. Me! Me! Knowest thou

not me? Phædra was I,

The queen that burned for cold Hippolytus,

Who scorned me till I knotted here the noose.

ULYS. And art thou Phædra?

PHÆDR. Give me back the sun

And all the scorn again! Only the sun!

FIRST PHAN. Seest thou that glimmer? there

still gleams the world!

PHANTOMS. [*Together.*] Back: take us back!

How soon these wounds would heal!

ULYS. O ye that being dead, so love the

light!

Yet is there not some dear and favourite

field,

Some holiest earth where each of ye would be?

PHANTOMS. [*Wheeling round.*] Ah, ah!

ULYS. Doth one of you perchance remember

A windy land that stands out of the sea

Gull-haunted, and men call it Ithaca?

[*The* PHANTOMS *float away with sad cries.*

A pause.

No ! not from babes nor these who slew them-

selves

Wring I one word of that which I would know.

Ah ! bring me to that ghost that shall reveal !

[*Again they descend, but* ULYSSES *pauses.*

HERM. Why tarry we, Ulysses?

ULYS.   Hermes, this world

Begins to grip my heart with gradual cold !

O how shall I descend in flesh and blood

Unready and unripe? I have not died :

Therefore I fear ! You gods, first let me have

The pang, the last sweat and the rattling throat,

The apparelling and the deep burying,

And die ere I descend amid the dead.

HERM. 'Tis in thy will. Remember Ithaca.

ULYS. [*With effort.*] Down, down! Yet terror
hath ta'en hold on me.

[*The burning forms of* LOVERS *suddenly
surround him.*

O what are ye? What fire consumes you still?

FIRST PHAN. We are the spirits of lovers who
still love.

ULYS. Did not the cold grave all that burning
quench?

SECOND PHAN. No! for that fire did eat into
our souls.

PHAN. OF EURYDICE. Look upon me! I am
Eurydice

That for one moment was so near the day,

When Orpheus backward looked, and all was night.

O lay me on his heart again!

[*The* PHANTOMS *wheel about him.*

PHAN. OF PROTESILAUS.   Ah ! come,
Laodamia !

PHAN. OF PHYLLIS. [*Woman.*] O Demophoön !

ANOTHER. O fire that dies not with our death !

ANOTHER.   Alas !

ULYS. Do I not burn for a breast unreachable,
And languish for one voice I may not hear?
For her that weepeth by the rolling sea,
Penelope !

        [PHANTOMS *disappear with wailings.*

        No answer still, no word !
That oath was hollow as this hollow world
Which said I should hear tidings of my home.
Where is that spirit that shall tell me?

HERM.   Lo !
The foot of the descent !

ULYS.   Have I then come
Thro' hell at last: now surely — now to hear.

HERM. No, for the river waits thee and the
barge.

ULYS. What river?

HERM. See! the creeping Stygian stream,
The mournful barge in which thou must embark
And drift thro' more tremendous torments, ere
Thou shalt have tidings of thy home and wife.

ULYS. [*Wildly*.] Is't not enough to have de-
scended hither
Breathing and in the flesh? Now must I drift
Upon the dreadful river? Spare me, Zeus!
Athene, who didst never leave me yet,
Athene! hearken!—even she forsakes me.
O Hermes!

HERM.   None can aid thee but thy will.

ULYS. [*With a cry*.] On, Hermes, on, even to
the river of hell!

[*They approach the river, and* HERMES *enters*

the barge, but as ULYSSES *is embarking*

CHARON *starts forward oar in hand.*

CHARON. Stay thou ! The flesh still clings
about thy limbs,

The blood runs in thy veins ! Rash fool, forbear !

Here is no passage save for spirits ! Back !

Back to the earth or fear some monstrous doom.

    [*He thrusts* ULYSSES *aside.*

HERM. Charon ! by heaven's permission comes
this man.

Take thou thy oar and urge us down the
stream.

    [*They begin to drift, and now they pass the*
    woe of TANTALUS *and the fruit.*

Lo ! Tantalus in his eternal thirst

Still reaching at the fruit he may not grasp.

See how the wind carries the branches from him.

G

ULYS. Ah! Tantalus, do I not reach and grasp
not?

[*They pass the woe of* TANTALUS *and drift
onward, when suddenly on the bank*
TEIRESIAS *the Seer starts forward.*

TEIR. Ulysses, art thou come, then? Is no
toil
Too hard for thee that thou must drift thro'
hell?

ULYS. Teiresias, prophet true! of all men thee,
Thee do I thirst to hear, now shall I know.
Shall I return unto my home at last?

TEIR. Thou shalt return.

ULYS.   O Zeus!

TEIR.   Yet with sheer loss
Of all thy comrades under tempest crash.

ULYS. Alas!

TEIR.   And to a home of strife and storm;

To deadlier peril even than here in hell;

To danger and to darkness shalt return.

ULYS. And she, Penelope — doth she still live?

TEIR. She lives.

ULYS.   O thou kind heaven! and holds
she true?

TEIR. She lives.

ULYS.   O if thou hast a heart, though dead,
Thou wilt not leave me thus.

TEIR.   She lives: farewell.

[*The* SHADE *of* TEIRESIAS *disappears; again*
they drift onward.

ULYS. 'Lives' and no more is worse to me
than 'dead.'

Would that I had known nothing! onward — on!

This fire he hath put in me I must quench!

[*They pass the woe of* SISYPHUS *and the*
stone.

HERM. See Sisyphus that in his anguish rolls

Upward, ever, the stone which still rebounds.

Mark how the sweat falls, and what whirl of dust!

ULYS. Ah, brother, such a stone I roll in vain!

There is no torment here that is not mine.

> [*They pass the woe of* SISYPHUS, *and again*
>
> *drift on.*

ULYS. Is there not one of all these ghosts that

throng

The bank, one only, that can tell me truth.

Hermes! yon spirit lordlier than the rest

With something in his pace familiar:

See how he cometh thro' the other shades

With such imperial stride and sovereign motion.

HERM. [*To* SHADE.] Stay thou!

> [*The* SHADE *turns, disclosing the form*
>
> *of* AGAMEMNON.

ULYS.   Ah, mighty Agamemnon! king!

O royal 'mid the dead as in the light!

I am Ulysses: often we took counsel

Under the stars, in the white tents, at Troy.

Now speak to me: a living man I come

Amid the dead for tidings of my wife

Penelope. Doth she hold true to me?

AGAM. Ulysses, fear thy wife! Fear to return.

ULYS. What? What? O speak!

AGAM.   Thy wife awaits thee now

Coiled like a snake to strike thee with her
    fangs.

ULYS. Unthinkable!

AGAM.   She weaveth death for thee!

ULYS. Horrible!

AGAM.   Look on me, me whom my wife

False Clytemnæstra lured unto the bath

And struck me here where now thou see'st the
    wound.

I that first night did bathe in my own blood,

The first night, the sweet night of my return.

ULYS. [*Bowing his head.*] O Agamemnon!

AGAM.   She while I did fight

About Troy city for Ægisthus burned,

She snared, she slew me, then with him she slept.

ULYS. Penelope! I'll kiss thee and fear not.

AGAM. Never so sweet was Clytemnæstra's kiss

As on that night, her voice, never so soft.

[*The* SHADE *of* AGAMEMNON *disappears, and
          again they drift onward.*

ULYS. Are these the tidings, these for which I
     dared

This darkness and the very river of hell?

I'll not believe it. O for some fresh voice!

On, on! I cannot hear worse words than these.

[*They pass the woe of* PROMETHEUS *and the
        vulture.*

HERM. Behold Prometheus, who stole fire from

    heaven;

Now at his heart the eternal vulture eats.

  ULYS. Prometheus, on this breast too anguish

    feeds,

And on this heart swoops down the eating fear:

The fear lest I should find her false at last,

False, false after such sea, after such storm;

False tho' I stumble toward her out of hell.

You gods, impose some limit! Now to know,

To know if she be true, to know, to know!

    [*They pass the woe of* PROMETHEUS, *and again*

      drift onward.

  SHADE OF ANTICLEIA. [*Unseen.*] Ulysses!

  ULYS.   Ah, who calls me by my name?

  ANTI. Ulysses!

  ULYS.   And the voice, tho' faint it comes,

Is yet the voice of one that was a woman.

ANTI. Ulysses!

ULYS.   And it goes through all my

blood.

Hermes, there is one near me whom I loved:

A flitting shadow, and it comes and goes,

It stretches out its arms — the face — the face!

'Tis gone! Come nearer or come not at all!

Again! the first face that on earth I saw,

The shining eyes and the remembered smile!

Mother!   [*He leaps on to the bank.*

          Here to this breast, here to this heart!

    [*He makes to clasp her but the* PHANTOM

        eludes him. Again he seeks to embrace

        her but in vain.

ANTI. Thou canst not touch me, child.   I

cannot fold thee

For all my yearning. O to have thy head

Again upon this bosom! but alas!

I now am but a shade and a shadow that glides.

ULYS. Mother, thy kiss!

ANTI.   These were the lips
 that kissed thee,

This was the very breast which gave thee milk,

And this the voice that sang thee into sleep.

ULYS. What brought thee to thy death?

ANTI.   Waiting for thee,

Waiting and weeping, and long wondering.

ULYS. Alas, alas! and mother, she? she lives —

But stays she true to me?

ANTI.   Child, I have come

But lately to this place, and when I died

Still was she true to thee, and knew not time.

ULYS. At last, at last the word that lighteth hell!

One word! and thou alone, mother, couldst
 speak it!

Thy voice alone: thine out of all the dead!

ANTI. It seems no farther off than yesterday

That she and I were standing hand in hand

Looking for thee across the misted sea.

[ULYSSES *weeps.*

But child, tho' lately I did leave her true,

What hath befallen since? Ulysses, home!

I am aware of tumult in thy halls,

Confusion and a roar of hungry voices,

And peril closing round Penelope:

Fierce peril, child! O hasten!

ULYS.   Ah! what peril?

ANTI. I know not: but the time is short: she

     hath

Swift need of thee: haste, haste! tho' how I yearn

To keep thee for a little comfort! yet

Home, get thee home!

ULYS.   Farewell, mother — farewell!

[*The* GHOSTS *begin to surge about him.*

ANTI. Speed, speed !

[ULYSSES *rushes to the foot of the descent, and
        stumbles upward, a multitude of* SHADOWS
        swarming with cries about him.

ULYS.   She lives, and she is true to me.
But she hath need of me ! Up to the earth !

[GHOSTS *wheel about him with cries.*
O whirling dead ! And a great swirl of souls.
Wife ! wife ! I come.

[*Cries.*

Ithaca ! Ithaca !

[*Fiercer cries.*

I gasp and fight toward thee ! Still endure !
Think me not dead ! O hear me out of hell !

[*Fiercer and louder cries of the whirling
        dead.*

Ah ! shall I reach that glimmer? Upward, up !
Faint not, Penelope : faint not, endure !

ACT III

ACT III

ACT III

SCENE I

*The seashore of Ithaca veiled in a sea-mist, the
pent-house in front of the hut of* EUMÆUS *the
swineherd dimly visible up stage.* ULYSSES, *aged
by suffering and exposure, is lying asleep under
a tattered sea-cloak ; on one side of him stands*
ATHENE, *on the other* POSEIDON.

ATH. [*With outstretched arm.*] Depart, Posei-

    don ! Thou canst vex no more

Ulysses, who now sleeps on his own shore,

By hunger withered and by tempest wrung,

From toil to toil, from hell to shipwreck flung.

Here let thy buffetings and fury end !

Pos. He shall not rest! Even here his limbs
I'll rend:
Back to the foam-path shall the man be hurled,
To plunge and tumble on the watery world!

Ath. Let Zeus then from Olympus give a sign,
And thunder answer to my prayer or thine.

Pos. [*Raising his hands.*] Father of gods! to
me be vengeance given,
That none henceforward mock the might of
heaven.

Ath. Father, permit the man peace in his home,
And lift at last the wandering curse of foam.

[Zeus *thunders*, Athene *makes gesture to*
Poseidon.

Pos. Highest, I hear thy thunder and obey!

[*Going.*

Woe to all ships I meet upon my way.

[*Exit* Poseidon.

ATH. [*Bending over* ULYSSES.]   At last I ease

    thy bosom of its sighs,

And close the tribulation of those eyes.

Soft as a sister over thee I bend,

Mortal, and move as an immortal friend.

There is no earthly burning in this breast,

No fever, but this love is rich in rest ;

The wistfulness of women I may feel,

And mine the faithful smile, the hands that heal ;

But what in them is passion falls from me

Only as dew doth in benignity.

Yet once more will I try thee, to make clear

If yet thy wit is nimble ; and appear

As a young goatherd from the pasture near.

              [*Turning before she goes.*

Hath the wave rusted thee, or damped thy

    skill?

Of all thy tasks the fiercest waits thee still,

H

Ere I restore thee, at the destined time,

To armèd splendour of thy manhood's prime.

[Exit ATHENE.

ULYS. *[Dreaming of past labours.]* Ah, loose

    me to that music ! Cut these cords !

Hark ! breakers thro' the gloom ! Reef, reef the

    sail !

[He wakes and gazes about him.

Some god hath cast me forth upon this land ;

And O ! what land? So thick is the sea-mist,

All is phantasmal. What king ruleth here?

What folk inhabit? — cruel unto strangers,

Or hospitable? The gods have lied to me

When they foretold I should see Ithaca.

This is some swimming and Cimmerian isle,

With melancholy people of the mist.

Ah ! Ithaca, I shall not see thee more !

[He sits down in dejection

Enter ATHENE *disguised as a young goat-herd with a cloak and a staff.*

ULYS. Sir, I pray you tell me what land is this?

ATH. First tell me, sir, of yourself, and from what country you are come.

ULYS. [*With rapid affable mendacity.*] My name is Neleus and in Crete was I born; my father Melampus, and my mother Arcite. But I, sir, have a man's blood on my hands and therefore am fugitive, and seek refuge here if any may be found.

ATH. [*Aside in delight.*] He hath his tale on the instant!

ULYS. But now tell me what is this shore on which I am cast up?

ATH. Hast heard men speak of Ithaca?

ULYS. [*Repressing sudden joy.*] Ithaca!
Somewhere have I heard the name, but where?
And is this Ithaca?

ATH. Even so.

ULYS. Is it an island or part of the mainland?

ATH. An island surely. And hast thou heard
never of our king? He is far-famed.

ULYS. How is he called?

ATH. Ulysses.

ULYS. Ulysses! Did he not sail with other
chiefs against Troy city?

ATH. Even so. But now we know not if he
be alive or dead.

ULYS. I fear that he is dead.

ATH. Hast any certain news?

ULYS. None certain, but I much fear that he
is drowned in the salt sea.

ATH. [*Delightedly.*] Yet might his wife entertain thee kindly.

ULYS. His wife — [*checking himself*]. Ah! had he a wife?

ATH. Surely — her name Penelope.

ULYS. Penelope! and it seems to me that her name too I have heard.

ATH. O! well said, Ulysses. Thou art never wanting.

ULYS. [*Starting.*] Stranger!

ATH. I am Athene, and have taken this shape but to try thy wit.

ULYS. Goddess, how shall men know thee? And yet while thou wast speaking I was aware of a tone more sweet than mortal; but would not betray thee.

ATH. O excellent Ulysses, who standest there and fearest that thou art dead! I have more

joy in thee than before, for thy craft is in no
way abated.

ULYS. But ah! I am fooled again! Goddess!
Is this Ithaca indeed — this very earth?

ATH. Behold!

[*The sea-mist slowly unrolls, discovering the
land.*

ULYS. Slowly the mist fades! Ah! the cypress
tree
I was so proud to plant as a boy! and there
The cave forbidden which I therefore loved!
Brighter, more bright! The crest of Neriton!
The rustling glade there where I killed the boar.
Now all the land gleams: look you there! the
ridge
Where the young laughing babe Telemachus
First clapped his hands at sight of the sea:
and O!

Yon holy winding path where last I kissed

Penelope, who toward me swayed and spoke

    not.

I came there down the slope most lingeringly,

And turned by the myrtle tree, and turned and

    turned.

Goddess, I cannot see for the great tears.

There! there! the very peak to which she

    climbed

Waving a sea-farewell with helpless hands!

O verdure to the sea-man that's come home!

O light upon the land where I was born!

O dear, dear Earth, thou warm mother of me,

Art glad, art glad in thy brown bosom; here

I kiss and kiss thee: here I fling me down

And roll and clasp and cover me with thee!

                    [*Starting up*

Ah! 'tis a dream: O God, it is a lure!

Incredible that ever I can rest!

I am fooled by the old sea-magic: my home
   trembles:

An apparition of the glassy deep,

A fading island that we come to never!

Is it rooted, rooted fast and cannot fly?

I shall go mad if I am fooled! Speak! speak!

Is this the earth, the earth where I was born?

   ATH. Ulysses, 'tis at last, 'tis Ithaca!

   ULYS. Ah! [*Sobs, overcome by emotion, then
      slowly*] I have been but a little while away
      then,

And suffered the great sea as in a dream.

But she, Penelope? She lives, I know,

And she holds true: but peril closes round
   her—

What peril?

   ATH. Up, Ulysses, from the ground!

Art broken down? Fury, not tears, I ask!

Up, up! thy wife by suitors is beset

Who waste and strip and drink away thy home:

She is hard driven and on the point to yield.

ULYS. Dogs! Dogs!

ATH. Wilt thou not rush upon them

straight

And slay them? smite, and on the instant?

ULYS. No:

I'll crouch before I spring, spy ere I leap.

ATH. O wise, still wise! Now have I tried thee

sure,

Rage doth not make thee rash! No more I

doubt.

Now bow thy back! and cast on thee that

cloak.

Thou art so marred with the sea misery

That none will know thee: lean thee on this staff,

And as a beggar knock at thy own door,

And weave in thy own halls these wooers' doom.

[*Going.*

ULYS. Now dost thou leave me, in so fierce a
pass?

ATH. I'd see thee stand alone; 'tis sweet to
those

In heaven at seasons to withhold their aid.

But I am ever with thee, unto the end.

Strike not, Ulysses, till I send the sign.

ULYS.   What sign ?

ATH.   A lightning flash : till then forbear.

ULYS. [*Assuming his disguise and recognizing
the hut of Eumæus.*] Ah ! the old swine-
hut : lives Eumæus yet?

[*Exit* ATHENE.

[*He walks slowly towards the hut.* EUMÆUS
is heard within : ' G-r-r. Antinous, in

Eurylochus, g-r-r Ctesippus.'. EUMÆUS
comes out to the pent-house in front of
the hut, carrying a pointed stick.

EUM. Away, old beggar! Here are no leav-
ings for you!

ULYS. Sir, but a handful of husks that the
swine have left.

EUM. Out! These are Ulysses' swine: they
leave nothing.

ULYS. Sir, I fall with hunger.

EUM. And so perhaps even now does my master.

ULYS. I have tidings of your lord Ulysses.

EUM. That's an old tale with you beggars—
you have all seen Ulysses, and then you are well
fed by his queen Penelope. [*He begins making
a mash for the swine.*] One saw him in Troy-
land, another in Crete, another saved him from

drowning, another saw him drown but could not save him. One hath a lock of his hair, another the string of his sandal. Dost carry anything of his about thee?

ULYS. I do.

EUM. And what?

ULYS. His hunger.

EUM. Away, you saucy beggar, or I'll loose his dogs on you : yet no. His wife will be wroth if any are turned away who can tell of Ulysses. Is thy lie ready, is it a good lie?

ULYS. Sir, I beseech you, food !

EUM. Come in, then, and earn thy supper. I am not fooled like a woman : fill that jar with water, and pick up these fallen acorns. [ULYSSES *obeys.*] Where hast thou seen him then? There is but one place where he has not been seen—

ULYS. What place is that?

Eum. In hell: I recommend hell to thee: no beggar hath yet bethought him of hell.

Ulys. But this would not please his wife?

Eum. No, but 'twould set her mind at rest concerning him. Here's a piece of fat chine for thee.

Ulys. Humbly I thank you.

Eum. His swine are well kept still—

Ulys. And for that I thank you.

Eum. [*Prodding swine outside.*] G-r-r-r Antinous, Ctesippus; in Eurymachus.

Ulys. Are swine so called.

Eum. I name these three after the chief suitors, and when rage swells to bursting, I strike them so: a poor vengeance, but ready at all hours. Ulysses! Ah! year after year have I been faithful to thee, master, and of each of thy swine can I give account!

ULYS. But he being far off, thou hast no need to be over-careful.

EUM. I have the greater care because of the smaller need.

ULYS. But if he be dead!

EUM. I'll not believe that till I hear it from his own lips.

ULYS. But this Ulysses — so I have heard — was but a careless ruler, and little beloved.

EUM. Old man, hast a mind to finish thy supper?

ULYS. I have indeed: for my hunger is no whit abated.

EUM. Then let no ill word escape thee of Ulysses, or thou wilt go hungry away!

ULYS. And his queen, Penelope?

EUM. She, poor lady, is so driven by the rascal wooers that this very night is she to choose one of them for husband.

Ulys. This night?

Eum. Yea, indeed, for this night the moon is at the full.

Ulys. Take me to her, even now : my hunger is gone from me.

Eum. Come, then, for the sky pales toward twilight ! [*A sound of running is heard.*]

Hark !

Ulys. A sound of running, and the feet run across my heart. [*Aside.*]

Eum. Back ! 'tis Telemachus, Ulysses' son, rushing hither ; and see, men pursuing him to take his life. Ah ! that spear grazed his neck. Master, master !

Enter Telemachus *breathless, faint with running.*

Telem. Eumæus, let me die here in this faithful spot ! I am pursued by men set on by the wooers; I cannot turn; from each bush they start. I'll die here with my face to them: but you — ah, old man!

EUM. An old beggar with the old tale of your father.

> [*The pursuers appear: two or three hang back, and two follow to the door of the hut.*

TELEM. Fly, old man.

EUM. They are upon us.

TELEM. Father, let me die as thy son should.

ULYS. [*A beating at the door.*] Stand back! Within, both of you! I will speak with them.

TELEM. Wilt die then?

ULYS. I do not intend so. In! I'll have my way.

> [ULYSSES *from entrance of hut approaches the foremost of the two pursuers.*

ULYS. Sir, sir, I die of hunger — I pray you.

FIRST MAN. Out of my way, old dog ! Pylas, in !

ULYS. Thus do I clasp your knees, and entreat.

FIRST MAN. Loose me, rags !

[ULYSSES *tightens his grip.*

ULYS. I will not loose you till you give me food.

FIRST MAN. Help, Pylas, help ! his arm holds like iron ! Help, help, he pulls me down like a hound at my throat.

[ULYSSES *hurls him down and springs at his throat.*

TELEM. Take not his life : he is a hired thing. Who set you on to murder me?

PYLAS. [ULYSSES *suffering him to rise.*] Eurymachus.

TELEM. Ah, he whose arm is ever around my neck.

[ULYSSES *releases* PYLAS, *who limps away.*

I

Second Man. I'll fly a land that breeds such

beggars as this.

Telem. Thou hast saved me — me, who am

not of thy blood.

Thou hast o'ertasked thy strength and tremblest :

lean

On me : give me thy hand.

Ulys. [*Aside.*]   I fear to touch it.

Telem. Still thou art trembling. Come !

[*Again holds out his hand.*

Ulys.   Suffer me, sir,

To kiss this hand.

[*He kisses* Telemachus' *hand and bows

over it.*

Telem. Sorrow not thus, old man ! Lift up

thine eyes.

Ulys. I cannot yet : thine arm !

[Telemachus *leads him a step or so*

There hath been a time
When I had led thee thus, ay, step by step.

TELEM. Thou hast not looked into my face once.

[ULYSSES *looks slowly up into his face, laying*
both hands on his shoulders : he looks
long on him, then bows his head.

ULYS.   Ah !
Thou art the son of Ulysses, art thou not?

TELEM. Ay, of Ulysses, him that comes not
back.

ULYS. I saw thy father on a lone sea-isle
Once, and he spoke thy name.

·TELEM.   O what said he?

ULYS. Only thy name.   He looked o'er the
wide sea,
And softly said, ' Little Telemachus.'

TELEM. [*Dashing tears from his eyes.*] Thou
hast seen him ! art the nearest thing to him.

Ulys. And I had a sacred word from him to
.thy mother.

Telem. Come tell it to her now, ere 'tis too late;
Suitors like wolves about her howl; and she
Must choose this very night of the full moon.

Ulys. Haste, haste!

Eum. [*Coming out.*]   Old man, a cup of
wine for thee,
Thou'lt have no further need of any lie.
Thou hast saved her son, and thou art sure of
supper.

Ulys. [*Drinking.*] Is this Ulysses' wine?

                              [Eumæus *nods.*

                    'Tis a good wine.

[*He sets cup down suddenly, pointing to
the sky, in which the full moon has
become faintly visible.*

The moon, the moon: come.   [*He starts to go.*

Eum.   How didst thou guess

That way leads to the palace?

Ulys.   I came here

Once as a boy, long since : my father brought me.

[Eumæus *retires again within the hut.*

Young sir, a moment : and this way — apart.

We two are going into mighty peril,

And the end who knows? now lest we meet no
    more,

Wilt thou not kiss this grey head once?
    may'st thou

Never such sorrow know as I have known!

[Telemachus *bends over* Ulysses' *head
    and kisses it.* Ulysses *is shaken.*

From here thy palace roofs can we descry :

See'st thou that upper chamber looking south?

There wast thou born upon a summer night.

Telem. But thou then?

ULYS.   I stood by the door in fear.

[*He throws back the tattered cloak and
        raises himself to his height.*

Child, I begot thee.

TELEM.   Father, art come home?

[*He falls in* ULYSSES' *arms.*

ULYS. Askest thou proof?

TELEM.   I feel that thou art he:
I know it in every vein and drop of blood.
Thou art ragged?

ULYS.   But to weave these wooers' doom.

TELEM. Eumæus, hither! my father is come
    home.

EUM. [*Appearing at door.*] Hast no likelier
    tale for me than that?
Call me not from the pig-mash.

TELEM.   Hither and see.

[EUMÆUS *comes down.*

Dost thou not know him?

Eum. [*Gazing at him.*] Sir, I know you not.

Ulys. You that are human know me not : and yet

If Argus my old hound should see me now,

Though he were dying he would wag his tail.

Eum. [*Confusedly.*] Argus, old Argus !

Ulys. And for further proof,

The scar made by the boar in yonder glade !

[*He bares his knee.*

Eum. [*Embracing his knees.*] O master, O my

man of men — at last !

Ulys. Rise, 'tis no time for tears. Ye'll go

with me?

Eum. To death.

Ulys. Yet I mistrust ye.

Telem. Father !

Ulys. Not

Your love : I doubt your wisdom and your craft.

When ye shall see me buffeted, reviled,

Ye will forget I am a beggar man.

EUM. We will revile thee more and taunt thee

worse.

ULYS. Can ye be very patient? for I know

not

As yet what I shall do : I wait the sign

From her, that goddess who hath brought me

hither.

TELEM. We will be very patient till the end.

ULYS. Come then : but I will enter last, alone.

Remove you every weapon from the hall,

But leave three spears, three shields, upon the

walls

That we may snatch them when our need is

come.

Now haste —   [*They start to go.*

Yet stay ; if any ask of you

Why ye have thus removed the spears and shields

Have ye bethought you of your answer?

TELEM. No.

ULYS. Then say ye have removed them lest
the smoke

Should tarnish them !

EUM. Master, I know thee now.

Thy old craft !

[*The full moon at this point shines forth
brightly.*

ULYS. Lo, the moon already bright !

[*Exeunt.*

SCENE II

Interior of the banqueting-hall in ULYSSES' *palace.
The walls richly decorated and encrusted with
coloured patterns, bosses and friezes of ani-
mals, etc. Two columns plated with bronze*

sustain the roof, the central part of which is raised so as to admit the light. On a wall hang the three spears and three shields as ordered by ULYSSES, *and in another place his bow in a richly-decorated case. The hall is lighted by lamps held by* ATTENDANTS. *The main entrance from without is through a doorway with a raised threshold in the centre of the stage at the back: this door stands open to the vestibule and the moonlight: a staircase on the left leads up to another door opening into the women's apartments. A daïs extends along the back of the hall: on this and on the floor to right and left are disposed the tables and couches where the* SUITORS *are discovered revelling, with the faithless* HANDMAIDENS *interspersed among them and drinking from their cups, and* ATTEND-

ANTS *standing by and serving.* TELEMACHUS *sits at the head of one of the tables. In the centre of the hall is an open space, with a fire burning on the hearth in the midst, and beside it the chairs of* PENELOPE *and the Minstrel, the former unoccupied.* PHEMIUS *the Minstrel is seated in his chair by the hearth, singing —*

Great is he who fused the might

Of the earth and sun and rain

Into draughts of purple light,

Draughts that fire the heart and brain :

Let us praise him when the goblets flash in

light

And the rapture of the revel fills the brain.

What were revel without wine ?

What were wine without a song ?

Let us hymn the gift divine

With a music wild and strong,

With a shouting for the god who gave the

wine,

And a guerdon to the minstrel for his song.

Blest is he who strikes the lyre

At the feast where princes quaff:

Higher mounts the mirth and higher,

Loud and louder peals the laugh —

[PHEMIUS *breaks off suddenly, gazing on the*

SUITORS *in horror while a dim mist*

comes down on the hall and the moon-

light is obscured.

ANTIN. What ails thee, man?

EURYM.   Why dost thou stare on us?

PHEM. O wretched men! What doom is

coming on ye?

What mist is this that overspreads the world?

Shrouded are all your faces in black night!

[*They laugh together softly and sweetly.*

See how the feast is dabbled o'er with blood,

And all your eyes rain tears, and though ye laugh

Sweetly on me, ye laugh with alien lips!

[*Again they laugh sweetly upon him.*

And a voice of wailing arises and all the walls

Drip fast with blood, yea, and with blood the roof!

[*They laugh again.*

And the porch is full and full is the court of ghosts

And spirits hurrying hell-ward in the gloom,

Yea, and the light hath perished out of heaven!

Laugh not so idly on me with your lips,

But arise and flee! your doom is at the doors.

[PHEMIUS *hurries out of the hall. The mist clears and* ULYSSES *is seen standing on the threshold in the central doorway unobserved by any.*

ANTIN. Madness is come upon him!

EURYM.   O, a poet!

CTES. He hath taken from me all desire for food.

And there! is that blood there?   Eurymachus!

Am I not rosy and round as ever I was?

EURYM. You are, Ctesippus.

CTES.   And I see no ghosts.

ANTIN. He hath drunk o'ermuch : hence all this mist and blood.

EUM. [*To* TELEMACHUS.]   O master, see you that old beggar man?

Say, shall I put him from the door?   Out, out!

[*With exaggerated roughness.*

ULYS. [*Coming down into the hall.*] I crave

a word, sir, with Ulysses' son.

Which is he?

EUM. There !

ULYS. [*Approaching* TELEMACHUS *humbly.*]

Suffer me, sir, a word !

I bring you tidings of your father.

TELEM. [*With simulated harshness.*] O !

The old tale !

ULYS. [*Cringingly.*] Sir !

TELEM. Out with thee !

EUM. Out !

TELEM. Or stay !

Thou shalt have leave to limp from guest to

guest

And eat what thou canst beg. As for your

tale,

My father is long dead.

ULYS.   Then first from you
I beg a crust of bread, or sip of wine.

TELEM. Here's for thee.

> [*Tosses him bread.*

ULYS.   Humbly, sir, I thank you.

> [*He passes from guest to guest.*

A SUITOR. Here.
> [*Pushes wine-cup to him.*

CTES. My appetite is fled: take what you
will.

EURYM. Here is a gristly morsel for old gums.

MEL. [*To* ANTINOUS, *as* ULYSSES *approaches.*]

Antinous, keep the old man far from me!
He'll soil this robe; and hath a smell of swine.

ULYS. I would not soil you, lady; but you, sir—

ANTIN. You louting beggar, I have nought
for you!

From me!
> [*He strikes him on the mouth.*

EURYM.   He stood thy buffet like a rock!

ULYS. O my deep soul, endure!

TELEM. [*Starting up.*]   Antinous,

I'll have no beggar struck within my halls!

ANTIN. Oho! And did I strike one of thy blood

Or of thy guests? Thou filthy beggar, off!

[*Strikes him again.*

ULYS. Athene, patience!

EUM.   All my blood boils up.

[*Throws log savagely on fire.*

ULYS. [*Coming near to* ANTINOUS.] O noble

sir, of all who feast around,

Tall men and fair, thou art the fairest far,

And splendid in thy youth and in thy strength.

But I am old and many have I seen

So fair, so strong, fallen into misery,

Princes whom in their pride the gods laid low.

Remember in thy strength the evil days.

K

ANTIN. [*Starting up.*] This dismal beggar I'll
    endure no more,

Who gibbers at the feast of evil days.

Away with him or I will hurl him forth.

CTES. A sad feast this—the minstrel first sees
    blood :

And now this beggar croaks to us of age.

CLYT. Since he came in we are all grown
    miserable.

MEL. Sirs, drive him forth, that we may laugh
    again

SUITORS. [*Rising from the tables.*] Out with
    the old crow ! cast him out : away !

    [*They come round* ULYSSES *and hustle him
        to the door.*

TELEM. I say the old man shall not be thrust
    forth.

[*Aside to* ULYSSES.] Is it now, father, is it now?

Eum. When, when?

Suitors. [*Hustling* Ulysses.] Out with him!

Handmaids. Spit on him!

Suitors. Unloose the dogs!

Ctes. [*Interposing*.] A word, a word! thy

mother still delays:

Let us beguile the time; leave him to me,

And we'll wring laughter from this kill-joy yet.

[*To* Ulysses *with mock deference*.]

Give me your hand, old man!

[*To* Suitors.] These beggars all

Were princes once. Now hearken! Sir, I see

Behind these rags and filth what man thou art.

Tell us — and now I look on thee I mark

A something noble in thy air — thou hadst

A palace once, and riches, hadst thou not?

Ulys. A palace and great riches had I once.

[*General laughter.*

CTES. [*To* SUITORS.] What said I ? Yet in
rags the great are known.

Wast thou not in old days thyself a king?

ULYS. In the old days I was myself a king.

[*All laugh heartily.*

CTES. [*To* SUITORS.] Hush !

[*To* ULYSSES.] Look around ; even such a
hall hadst thou.

ULYS. [*Gazing slowly around.*] Once did I
feast in some such hall as this.

CTES. Not by thine own fault (ah ! I know it
well)

But by some anger of the gods thou art fallen.

ULYS. The gods, the gods have brought me to
this pass.

ANTIN. Impudent liar !

CTES. And thou didst leave behind
A wife most beautiful, a queen of women !

TELEM. How long will he endure?

EUM. O for a blow!

MEL. He is grown cautious, he'll not speak to that.

CLYT. His wife! Some addled hag that tendeth swine!

MEL. Was woman found to mate her with such mud?

TELEM. His spirit is dead in him.

EUM. Thou art broken at last!

CLYT. He speaks not! See, the old fool's eyes are dim.

MEL. [*With mock caress.*] O shall I kiss thy tears away, my love?

CHLOR. Thy wife is old: wilt thou have me, fair youth?

CLYT. O wouldst thou take me, bridegroom, to thy halls!

EURYM. Cease, cease! Ye all mistake. He
hath come here
A suitor for Penelope.

ANTIN. [*Throwing cup at him.*] Then take
This gift to aid thy suit.

A SUITOR. [*Throwing a bowl.*] And this.

CTES. [*Throwing a scrap from the feast.*] And
this.

OTHERS. [*Casting things upon him.*] And
here: and here.

CTES.   Now up and urge thy suit!

TELEM. [*To* EUMÆUS.] Why wait a word that
never comes? The swords!

EUM. Stay, stay: he looks on us, and his eye
burns.

Enter PENELOPE *down staircase from the*
upper chambers; she walks slowly and
sadly to her chair beside the hearth in
the centre of the room.

SUITORS. [*Making way for her and then gath-*
ering to right and left of her in the central
space.] The Queen, the Queen!

ANTIN. Now be the bridegroom chosen!

EURYM. Lady, this is the night when thou

shalt choose.

Grave is thy mien: here's that shall make thee

smile.

Bring forth this wooer lordliest and last.

CTES. These rags are but a guise: a noble

man!

PEN. [*To* TELEMACHUS.] Child, knowest thou

this old man whom they mock?

TELEM. Mother, it is an old poor beggar man

Who says that he brings tidings of my father.

Wilt thou not hear him, mother, ere thou choose?

EURYM. Art thou still eager, lady, for new lies?

ANTIN. Art thou not weary of these beggars'

tales?

PEN. I have been too oft deceived : now my

still heart

I bare no more to every beggar's eye :

Sacred shall be this hunger of my soul

And silent till the end —

[*To* TELEMACHUS, *who makes signs to her.*]

What wouldst thou say?

TELEM. [*Taking her apart.*] Mother, a word ;

but a word.

ANTIN. [*Interposing.*] Stand back, young sir !

There shall be no more plots between you two.

[*Murmurs of assent,*

Nor beggars weave another web — of lies.

The moon is full! Now shalt thou choose at
  once.

TELEM. Mother!

ANTIN.   An end of tricks!

SOME SUITORS.   Thy word, thy word!

OTHERS. Now answer!

OTHERS.   Now no more delay!

ALL.   Choose, choose!

  [*They all crowd about* PENELOPE *to hear
    her decision,* ULYSSES *in the meantime
    crouching in the ashes by the hearth.*

ULYS. Goddess, hast thou forsaken me at last?

TELEM. [*To* ULYSSES.] A moment, and too
  late!

ULYS.   I wait the sign!

PEN. Speak any then who will: I'll answer
  him.

Ctes. I claim to speak the first.

Eurym. By right of age.

Ctes. Lady, I cannot speak as a raw boy,

But as a man of comfortable years;

Though in my youth more terrible was none

To foemen; and I like not to remember

The blood that I have spilt. Behold me now

A man not old, but mellow, like good wine,

Not over-jealous, yet an eager husband.

This figure something of Apollo lacks,

But though I might not catch the eye of a girl,

Still a wise woman would consider well,

Ponder by nights ere she would let me go.

Yet I would urge less what Ctesippus is

Than what Ctesippus has the power to give.

[*To* Attendants.] Now hold up to the moon

    that glimmering robe;

Turn it this way and that; this coffer now,

With armlets of wrought gold, brooches of price,

And golden bowls embossed with beasts and
    men ;

These draught-boards, ivory inlaid with silver,

That glistering tire and these enamelled chains.

Lo, whatsoever woman can desire

I'll give thee without pause and without stint,

Wilt thou but suffer me to lead thee home.

   PEN. Ctesippus, not the glory of gems or gold

Can move me : hath the sea a pearl so rich

As dead Ulysses which it treasureth

Far down, far from these eyes? Rather would I

Possess some rag of him drawn up perchance

By nets of seamen hauling 'neath the moon

Than all these jewels glistering at my feet.

How couldst thou think to please me with these
    toys,

When in that chamber I have garnered up

Garments more rich to me, faded and dim,

Old robes and tarnished armour lovelier far?

Those hadst thou seen, thou couldst not offer
   these.

   EUM. [*To* CTESIPPUS.] Now thou hast leave
   to go —

                              [*Murmurs.*

                    Your pardon, princes.

   EURYM. Lady, I bring no gauds of pearl and
   gold,

I know thou art not this way to be lured.

I share thy grief for him who now is dead:

Noble was he, a wise man and a strong.

O were he here, I first would clasp his hand.

A moment till my voice return to me.

          [*He bows his head on his hands.*

But she who sits enthroned may not prolong

The luxury of tears; nor may she waste

In lasting widowhood a people's hopes,

So hard is height, so cruel is a crown.

Thou art a queen: a moment then for grief;

Then for the people what remains of life.

I offer thee the comfort of high cares,

And consolation from imperial tasks:

To share with me the governance of a land

And bring thy woman's insight to the state,

The touch that's gracious, deft, and feminine.

  Sea-gazing consort of a hero dead

Reign thou with me; and find in rule relief!

That thou no longer art a girl, and green,

Troubles me not; rather I prize thee more

For that long suffering and sleeplessness

And the sweet wisdom of thy widowhood.

Thou hast caught splendour from the sailless

    sea,

And mystery from many stars outwatched;

Rarer art thou from yearning and more rich.

Humbly I would entreat you for my answer.

PEN. Sir, could I list to any, 'twere to thee :

Fair were thy words, and such as women love,

And thou hast found my brain, but not my
    heart,

Feigning a ruth I felt thou didst not feel.

Ask me not to forget in public good

This solitary, dear, and piercing loss.

Rather would I remember one dead man,

Wasting the years away, and yet remember,

Than rule a living kingdom by thy side.

Alas ! I am a woman utterly !

ANTIN. Enough of jewels, and enough of
    thrones !

Would these men lure thee ?   I by thee am
    lured.

For thee, O woman, thee alone, I thirst.

Time, that doth mar us all, and dims, and
    damps,

Ashens the hair and scribbles round the eye,

Weareth not thee, thou miracle, away,

Ever in beauty waxing without wane.

No more I'll toss upon a burning bed,

Leap out at midnight on a smouldering floor,

Pacing, pacing away the aching night.

Thou, thou didst light this fire, and thou shalt
    quench it.

  TELEM. [*Aside to* ULYSSES.] Dost thou hear,
    father?

  ULYS.   Goddess, now the sign!

  ANTIN. Or, if thou will not, I'll compel thee.

                        [*Murmurs.*

                           O!

I care not for your murmurs: I risk all!

Come now away! or on the instant I

Will catch thee in these arms up from the
ground

And fling thee o'er my shoulder, and run with
thee

As from a house aflame.

TELEM. I'll spill thy blood.

ULYS. Unleash me, goddess, let me go.

EUM. Up, up!

ANTIN. For what dost thou still wait? For
whom, for whom?

Thy husband? he is dead, drowned in the
ooze:

The fish are at him now in the deep slime.

PEN. O!

TELEM. [*To* ULYSSES.] Art thou tame?

ULYS. I bite these
bloody lips.

ANTIN. Or if he be not dead, what is he now?

A shambling shadow, a wrecked, mumbling
   ghost,

A man no more : no better than yon beggar

That huddles to the fire : so bowed, so worn,

So ragged and ruined, and so filthy and fallen !

Look on that beggar ! There thy husband see !

  PEN. Splendid Antinous, I tell thee this ;

That if my husband on this moment came

In by that door even as yon beggar man,

So bowed, so worn, so ragged and so fallen,

Him would I rather catch unto this heart

And hold his holy ruins in my arms,

Than touch thee in thy glory and thy strength.

  ULYS. [*Starting up.*] O nobly spoken !

                           [*Uproar.*

               Suffer an old man !

  ANTIN. Now answer.

  EURYM.   Lady !

   L

Ctes.   Bring those robes
again !

Pen. [*Bewildered.*] Sirs, but one moment,
will you give me leave?
Then do I swear by all the gods to choose.
A womanish last request — a silly favour !

Antin. O !

Eurym. [*Fawning on her.*] Lady, I will not
refuse thee.

Pen.   'Tis
That I may satisfy me if this beggar
Perhaps doth bring me tidings of Ulysses.

Antin. This but to put us by !

Eurym. [*Still fawns.*]   Suffer her, sirs :
[*The* Suitors *retire sullenly up.* Penelope
*comes back to her seat at the fire beside
which* Ulysses *crouches. As she approaches him he trembles.*

PEN. Old man, wilt thou deceive me yet again'
Be not afraid : there's nought in me to fear.

ULYS. I'll not deceive thee, lady : nearer draw
And motion all away !

    [PENELOPE *signs to all to move away*
        Canst thou endure
The shaft of sudden joy, yet make no cry?

PEN. Though I shall fall I'll not cry out : say, say.

ULYS. Ulysses lives — thou art gone white —
 be still !
Grip fast thy chair and look upon the ground ! —
And he is very near to thee even now.

PEN. Where, where ?

ULYS.   This night is he in Ithaca ;
Perchance even now is rushing to his halls ;
Might at this moment come in by that door.

PEN. How shall I trust thy tale? If thou sayest true
Thou ne'er shalt beg again.

ULYS.   I come from him.

PEN. What is thy name?

ULYS.   Idomeneus from Crete.

He charged me with these tidings—and this ring.

PEN. This would he not have given : O this
     was pulled

From his dead finger !

ULYS.   Lady, if I lie,—

If on this night Ulysses comes not home, —

Then give me to thy thralls to slay me here.

PEN. Ah ! they will kill him.

ULYS.   Fear not ; he is wise.

Only do thou each moment still delay

Thy answer.

PEN.   Yet what plea ?

ULYS.   Propose to them

Some simple trial whereby thou mayst choose.

PEN. What, what ?

ULYS.   The bow : is that Ulysses' bow ?

PEN. Cherished and daily suppled by these
hands.

ULYS. Say thou wilt choose whoe'er shall bend
his bow.

But still to interpose some brief delay,

Call you some woman forth to bathe my feet.

PEN. Melantho, bring clear water hither and bathe
This old man's feet.

MEL.   I ? I'll not touch his feet,
For I can touch the lips of better men.

ULYS. Lady, some woman that hath seen much
sorrow

As I have.

PEN.   Eurycleia, bathe his feet.

[EURYCLEIA *brings water in a brazen vessel
to* ULYSSES ; *as he lifts his robe she
sees the scar and drops the basin.*

Eur. The scar there.

Ulys. Wouldst thou slay me?
hold thy peace.

Pen. What ails thee, Eurycleia?

Eur. O my mistress !
These old hands tremble even at such a task.

Antin. [*Advancing.*] Now, lady, now ! This
is delay enough !

Hast thou at last heard tidings of thy lord?
Doth he come home to-night?

Pen. Alas, alas !
He is drowned, and from his finger, lo ! this ring.

Antin. Thou'rt satisfied at last?

Suitors. Now answer :
choose.

Pen. No one of you I like above the rest,
Yet have I sworn to choose : so I will put
This matter to a simple trial.

SUITORS. What ?

PEN. See where behind you hangs Ulysses'
bow.

He that can bend his bow and loose a shaft,
Him will I take as husband from you all.

[*They rush to take it.*

SUITORS. The bow !

PEN. [*Staying them.*] My son alone shall reach
it down,

After such time shall be the first to touch it.

[PENELOPE *retires down to watch the trial.*
TELEMACHUS *brings down the bow and
a sheaf of arrows.* CTESIPPUS *advances,
and after much groaning and panting
fails to string it.*

CTES. Easily in the morning could I bend it,
But I have supped !

[EURYMACHUS *essays to string it and fails.*

EURYM.   Lady, wilt choose a husband

For brutish force? what play hath the mind here?

[ANTINOUS *fails to string the bow.*

ANTIN. If I can bend it not, no man can
bend it.

PEN. [*To* OTHERS.] And will you not essay?
or you?

OTHERS.   Not we.

ANOTHER. Where craft and strength have failed,
what use for us?

PEN. I will wed no man till he bend that bow.

[*Angry murmurs among the* SUITORS.

[*Lightning flashes;* ULYSSES *recognises by the*
sign that the moment for action has come.

ULYS. [*Rising.*] Lady, and princes, but to
make you sport,

I will essay to bend Ulysses' bow:

[*Loud laughter.*

To make you sport — for I have supped full well.

ANTIN. Impudent rags ! Thou shalt not vie
with us.

TELEM. The beggar shall make trial : come,
old man !

CTES. The old man ! excellent !

ALL. [*Laughing loudly.*]   The beggar man !

EURYM. Come forth, thou wooer lordliest and
last.

ANTIN. Here is a broad mark for thy shaft,
old man.

PEN. Ah, mock him not !

ULYS.   Sirs, but to make you sport.
            [*He totters towards the bow.*

Athene, strength ! O if my might should fail me !
    [*He takes the bow, and after simulated
        faltering, strings it amid the amazed si-
        lence of the* SUITORS. *He springs to his*

*height, and appears in his own likeness,
his rags falling from him, and disclosing him armed and in the full glory of
manhood.*

Dogs, do ye know me now?

PEN. [*Rushing towards him.*] Ulysses!

ULYS.   Back!

SUITORS. [*Amazedly amid themselves.*] Ulysses!
is it he? Is it he — Ulysses?

[ULYSSES *shoots, killing* ANTINOUS, *who falls.*

ULYS. Who is for me? The swords there and
the shields!

TELEMACHUS *and* EUMÆUS *snatch down the
weapons, and arming* ULYSSES *and themselves, stand by him.*

EURYM. [*Coming over fawningly from among
the* SUITORS *towards* ULYSSES.] Hero restored,
I'll stand by thee for one!

ULYS. [*Striding out and spearing him.*]
Would'st fawn on me? go fawn among the dead.

[EURYMACHUS *falls. The* SUITORS, *finding no
weapons on the walls, crowd waveringly
together.*

CTES. [*Encouraging them.*] We are ten to
one : crush, crush them by sheer weight.

[*The* SUITORS *make a headlong rush upon*
ULYSSES *and his companions, but are
stayed in mid rush by thunder, lightning,
and supernatural darkness, followed by
the apparition of* ATHENE *standing by*
ULYSSES.

SUITORS. The gods fight for him. Fly! we are
undone.

[ATHENE *and* ULYSSES *with* EUMÆUS *and*
TELEMACHUS *fall on them, and they are
driven in fierce brief medley, visible by*

*flashes of lightning, and with noise of
groans and falls, out headlong through
the door. Sounds of slaughter con-
tinue to be heard from the court without. The darkness lifts, discovering
ULYSSES standing on the threshold at
the upper end of the hall, ATHENE still
at his side. He turns, laying by sword
and shield, while PENELOPE gazes in
passionate uncertainty toward him from
the corner of the hall.*

ULYS. [*Solemnly.*] First unto Zeus and to
    Athene praise !

Go all of you apart ! even thou, my son,

And leave me with Penelope alone.

ATH. Thou art come home, Ulysses ! Now
    farewell !

For violated laws are here avenged,

And I, who brought thee through those bitter
  years,
Those bitter years which make this moment sweet,
I, even, in this moment have no share.

> [ATHENE *disappears.*

> [ULYSSES *and* PENELOPE *slowly approach each
> other across the hall, with rapt gaze,
> hesitatingly. Then she is folded to his
> breast in silence, while the voice of the
> Minstrel is heard without, repeating the
> words of the song from the first Act,*

> > And she shall fall upon his breast
> > With never a spoken word,

> *and the fire on the hearth, which has
> burnt low throughout this scene, leaps
> up into sudden brightness.*

CURTAIN

NOTE BY THE AUTHOR

THE methods and limitations of epic and drama differ completely : and in attempting to write a play on the story and character of Ulysses, as they are known to all the world from the Odyssey of Homer, the first thing needful is to sacrifice five-sixths at least of the episodes which give that poem its enchantment. Some writers who have made the attempt have even judged it best to omit the entire tale of the hero's wanderings, and to treat only those of his actions which take place after his return to Ithaca. Both M. Ponsard, in a lyrical drama written to Gounod's music, and Mr. Robert Bridges, in his poetical play, 'The Return of Ulysses,' have followed this plan.

As the reader has perceived, I have gone farther back in the story, and taken in two of Ulysses' earlier trials, the sojourn with Calypso and the visit to Hades, which seemed to me to afford matter for telling dramatic presentment and dramatic contrast. And I have tried to weave these adventures, together with the return to Ithaca and the final discomfiture of the suitors, into the fabric of a properly-knit play ; with what measure of success it must be for readers and playgoers to decide.

For the rest, the scholar will have found in the foregoing scenes some things strictly according to Homer, and some loosely so : but others not according to him at all, as for instance the stay with Calypso made to precede the descent among the dead instead of following it ; Calypso herself endowed with some of the attributes of

Circe ; Hermes, the chartered escort of the dead, given as a guide to Ulysses through Hades ; Hades itself conceived on lines which are Virgilian rather than Homeric ; the action at the swineherd's hut, and that in the palace at Ithaca afterwards, re-arranged, re-imagined, and above all unsparingly accelerated and cut down. In the author's mind all these liberties were an essential part of his dramatic scheme ; nor can the need for similar liberties be well escaped by any practical playwright who chooses to work upon materials supplied either by history or by epic.

As to the material presentment of the play, my warmest thanks are due to Mr. Tree for an enthusiasm and a generosity which have admitted no obstacle in the attempt to realise on the stage the best conjectural picture of the Homeric world which could be devised. The attempt is

M

new, and the result is a spectacle richer, more barbaric, many-coloured, and full of fantasy than could have been obtained by adopting the conventional classical costumes and familiar building styles of later Greece. The architecture and its decoration, designed by Mr. W. R. Lethaby, have been based on recent discoveries of the Mycenæan age. For the dresses (since the Mycenæan costume, so far as it is known to us, would be ill suited to the stage) Mr. Percy Anderson has gone back to the very earliest Greek sculpture, and to vases of the sixth and seventh centuries B.C. Both these gentlemen, as well as the author and manager and their valued helper Mr. Lionel Hart, have been greatly aided in their work by the zeal and learning of Dr. A. S. Murray, Mr. Sidney Colvin, and other friendly authorities of the British Museum.

S. P.

Printed in the United States of America.

THE SIN OF DAVID

BY
STEPHEN PHILLIPS

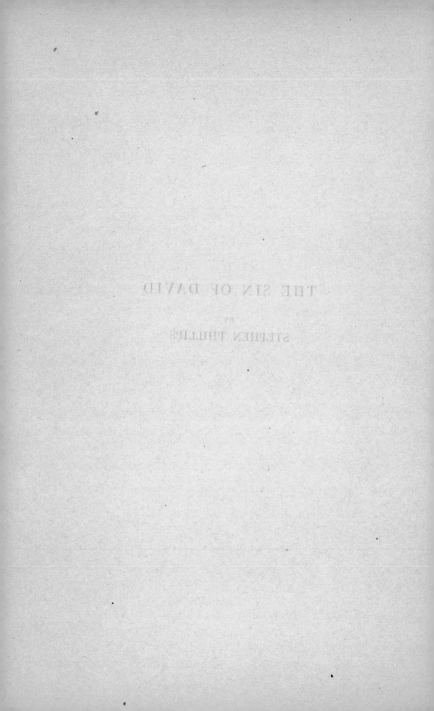

ACT I

CHARACTERS

SIR HUBERT LISLE, { *Commander of the Parliamentary forces in the Fenland.*

HUBERT, { *The child of Lisle and Miriam in Act III.*

COLONEL MARDYKE, { *Of the Parliamentary army, owner of Rushland, the headquarters of the army.*

COTTON,
FINCH,
MARSH,   { *Officers of the Parliamentary army.*
CRABLOVE,
IRON,

JOYCE,   *A lieutenant.*

A DOCTOR.

RATCLIFFE, { *Servant of Mardyke; afterward of Lisle.*

MIRIAM, { *Wife of Mardyke; afterward of Lisle.*

MARTHA,   *Sister of Mardyke.*

OFFICERS, NURSES, SOLDIERS, *etc.*

The period of the play is that of the English Civil War between Charles I and the Parliament.

THE
SIN OF DAVID

ACT I

TIME. — *Summer of* 1643, *the first year of the war: noontide.*

SCENE. — *Hall of Rushland House, the headquarters of the Puritan army in the Fenlands. On the left a flight of steps leading up to a turret-chamber. A door on either side, on the right communicating outward, on the left inward. At the back, a door flanked by recessed windows opens on a terrace beyond, with foliage of poplars and alders, and a distant view of the Fens.*

Various military officers are standing in

silence, with bowed heads and folded hands,

as in prayer, around a table covered with

papers. MARDYKE *stands at the head of*

the table.

MARDYKE. [*After a pause.*] Now, sirs,

that we have sought the Lord in prayer,

Each one in silence, will we hear and
judge,

Knowing ourselves His mortal instruments.

All we with clean hearts unto judgment
come;

Yet in Thy sight no human heart is clean;

And if we punish others, we ourselves

Are ready to abide Thy punishment.

[*They slowly seat themselves.*

Read, Captain!   Who is charged with
    mutiny,
With plunder or with harryings or with
    flame,
Making God's army of the Fenland mocked,
A hissing and abomination, yea,
A laughter sweet unto the Philistine,
And all our fire, our kindling, and our zeal,
As ashes fallen, and as the greyness of
    ashes?
Read!

COTTON. [*Rising with papers in his hand.*]

There is nothing here of mutiny,
Nor here is any charged with drunken rage,

With plunder or with harryings or with
flame,

To make God's army of the Fenland
mocked.

But one among us is of carnal crime

Loudly accused: 'tis charged against him
here

That he by violence hath a maid undone.

[*Murmurs.*

His name Lieutenant Joyce: who on this
cry

Arrested and close-guarded waits without.

FINCH. Is this already public in men's
mouths,

So noised we cannot overpass it, sir?

If not, 'twere well to mingle policy

With zeal, and hush it for the larger good.

MARSH.   Publish it not, lest we be pointed

at.

Such is our cause a little smirch undoes

it,

By its own virtue the more vulnerable :

Greatness hath often by a whisper crashed.

COTTON.   The thing is public and the

wayside talk ;

The clucking housewife hath it, and the

crone

Mumbles it sitting half-out in the sun.

MARDYKE.   Public or no, I palter not

with heaven.

The sin is sinned ; and if we punish not,

Then stand we here partakers of the sin.

CRABLOVE. Doth Joyce deny this? Let

us hear him speak.

[MARDYKE *motions to bring in* JOYCE.

COTTON. Freely he hath confessed and

bides the issue.

Enter JOYCE, *guarded*

MARDYKE. Lieutenant, publicly you stand

accused

Of a young maid's enforcement: what say

you

In answer?

JOYCE.   I make answer, "It is true."

MARDYKE. None here can come be-

tween thee and thy God.

Yet in mid-madness didst thou not recall

That thou wert more than Joyce: an officer

In this our righteous warring; that you
brought
This holy host into derision? Speak.

JOYCE. Her face was close to me, and
dimmed the world.

Yet have I fought, and in the front of all.

Shall one mad moment all those hours
outweigh?

Who being human is for ever sure?

MARDYKE. [*Rising.*] God needs not thy
polluted arm henceforth.

He asks not Captain, no, nor man-at-arms
Of heart unclean: thou shalt not fight for
Him.

Take him away! thy punishment with us.

[*Exit* JOYCE, *guarded.*

Now, sirs, he hath confessed, his sentence
    lies

With us.

  FINCH. You, sir, who fought with Eng-
    lish Vere

At Heidelberg, at Mannheim and Ostend,

Where'er the persecuted faithful fell,

Whose fame still clings about the vines of
    France,

How dealt ye in those camps with carnal
    crime?

  MARDYKE. Our cause, as now, required
    our spotlessness,

And we on grave occasion visited

Such sin with death!

    Enter RATCLIFFE, *with letter*

RATCLIFFE.   A letter, sir, post-haste.

MARDYKE.   [*After glancing at letter.*]

Summon your mistress and my sister

here.

[*Exit* RATCLIFFE.

This letter, sirs, concerns us all — I'll

read.

"I, Sir Hubert Lisle, being appointed by

the Parliament to the command of their

levies in the Fenland, where, as I hear,

there is much need of enkindling, do pro-

pose, by your leave, to make Rushland

House my headquarters. I know that your

zeal will not refuse me this if it be any

way possible; but I pray you excuse me

to your lady for so sudden demand on her

B

kindness. I follow hard on this letter, and am minded to stir up such a fire in this region as shall not easily be put out.

"HUBERT LISLE."

[Animated murmurs.

Sirs, with my wife I must have speech
 forthwith,

And make such preparation as I may.

 [*The officers retire in eager dis-
 cussion on to the terrace at back,
 and from time to time they are
 visible conversing together during
 the scene which follows. Meanwhile* MIRIAM *and* MARTHA
 enter. MIRIAM *stands submis-
 sively before* MARDYKE, *who, intent*

on letter, does not observe her for

a moment.

Mistress, you must prepare, and instantly,

For entertainment of Sir Hubert Lisle,

Sent hither to command our Fenland host.

Learn then what manner of man is he who

    comes ;

One sprung to arms from England's

    chivalry,

Despising lure of courtier or of priest,

To fight the fight of freedom and of God :

In foreign battle nursed, yet not as we,

Stricken and bowed, but in his flush of

    strength ;

Quickly provide, then ! Stand thou by his

    chair

And bring with thine own hands the cup
    of welcome:

See he lack nought thou canst bestow.

    But hither!   [*She turns to go.*

Miriam! heed well that you displease him not

By silly gaud on bosom or in hair,

Lest he account thee light, a daughter of
    Gath.

I'll strip this chain from thee; these
    wanton beads,

Meshes of Satan, grind I into dust.

    [*He snatches chain roughly from her
        and tramples it under foot.*

You, Martha, with a graver thought assist

My wife. Receive this guest as from the
    Lord!   [*Exit* MARDYKE.

MIRIAM. [*Trembling.*]   Am I not as that
    chain, trod underfoot,
Chidden and checked even more than when
    a child?

MARTHA.   My brother sternly broods, but
    loves you still.

MIRIAM.   Why, Martha, why could I not
    ever stay
His daughter?   So my dying father left me,
When side by side they fought at La
    Rochelle;
And as his daughter grew I up submiss;
Why must he then make me his wife?

MARTHA.   Perchance
To shelter you, and comfort his grey
    heart.

MIRIAM. I am no wife to him; and the
    waked woman

Within me cries against the yoke and
    loathes it.

  MARTHA. Why to so loathed a marriage
    did you yield?

  MIRIAM.   How could my orphanhood
    withstand his will?

Did I not owe him all, refuge and bread,

And sheltering sustenance? Could I take
    all,

And then refuse that petty price "myself,"

Sole price which he who gave so much
    required?

Well I have paid to the full! He starves
    my soul,

He locks my spirit up and keeps the
key.

MARTHA. Say not there is some other —

MIRIAM. No one. No.
My misery is faithful to him.

MARTHA. Child,
What is't you sigh for, whither would
you fly?
I cannot understand.

MIRIAM. Nor I myself;
And 'tis the very blindness of this beating
That makes of me a creature so unhappy,
And unto thee a plague.

MARTHA. Never, my child.

MIRIAM. O thou dear Martha, living
without sin,

And reputably rusting to the grave,

Thou vacant house moated about by
          peace,

Thou shadow perfect, and thou blameless
          ghost,

I cannot feed my soul on "Thou shalt
          not."

I'll fight 'gainst numbness, wrestle against
          rust.

There's the arch-foe of women! this doth
          kill us.

Not pain, nor secret arrow of the mid-
          night

That quivers till the bird-song, ended
          faith,

Mortal surprise of marriage, nor the dawn

Of golden-vista'd children clouded quite,

Nor fallen loneliness where love hath been.

These, these are understood, wept o'er and

    sung.

But worse, ah, worse the folding of the

    hands,

The human face left by the tide of life,

The worm already at the human heart.

  MARTHA. Sooner the worm than guilt

    within the heart.

  MIRIAM. No! I would rather drench my

    soul in sin

So I might feel this fire and grip this

    glory,

The colour and the bloom and the music

    of life!

MARTHA.   Miriam! no more I'll listen to

you.   Know

That He who gave us life ordained us

law.

MIRIAM.   Law!   And is law then but to

bind and freeze?

By law the lightning spurts, and the earth

quakes,

And the spring surges thro' a million buds;

And law is filled with rushings and with

thunder.

MARTHA.   You must endure.   Thy an-

cestors and mine

Went for their faith to torment and to fire.

MIRIAM.   Ah, for their faith! I hope

my blood is theirs,

And I would splash the flames about my
head

Gladly as in a bath for splendid death,

But for this life no life I was not born.

MARTHA. When there shall come a
child —

MIRIAM.   Ah, speak it not!

A child of him! I sicken, I quake at it;

My very flesh doth shiver. Think you I

Could squander upon any child of him

The brooding balm and wistful riches, all

The holy longing that on summer evens

Arises homeless in my silent heart?

Babes that we love, we must have loved
ere birth.

[RATCLIFFE *enters behind and beckons to*

> *the officers outside.   As he passes*
> MIRIAM, *he picks up chain and*
> *gives it her.   She gives him her*
> *hand, which he kisses.   She smiles*
> *sadly on him.   He goes out.*

MARTHA.   See, they return.   Come, then.
Give me the keys!

MIRIAM.   Ah! might this tumult find at
last a goal!

> [*Exeunt* MARTHA *and* MIRIAM.

*Reënter slowly military officers, who seat
themselves at the table.   Lastly enter*
MARDYKE.   *He sits at the head*

MARDYKE.   Do Thou, O Lord, direct a-
right our minds,

And our decision be unto Thy glory!

Your judgment, sirs, upon Lieutenant Joyce!

Shall we but cast him from us as unclean?

Or shall we punish carnal crime with death?

FINCH. Purge we our army of the sin-

 ner; yet

See we deter not by too fierce a doom

Others that waver still from taking sword.

IRON. If outrage be not punished the

 whole land

Rising in wrath against us will take sword.

COTTON. My voice also for death; when

 war begins,

Mercy at first is cruelty at last.

MARSH. Break him, but leave him lei

 sure to repent.

CRABLOVE.　Enough we cast him straightway from among us.

MARDYKE.　For death my voice; else
every one of us
Will into holy battle go unclean.

FINCH.　[*Rising.*]　The vote is even!

MARSH.　　　　　What shall now decide?

[Trumpet heard.

Enter RATCLIFFE, *hurriedly*

RATCLIFFE.　Sir Hubert Lisle, sir, ridden
furiously.

MARDYKE.　[*Rising.*]　Lisle, our commander: his the casting vote.

[They all rise.

FINCH.　On him alone the burden and
the issue.

Enter LISLE, *spurred, and spattered with mud.* MARDYKE *advancing,* LISLE *takes him by the hand, and they stand looking at each other for an instant*

LISLE. God save you, sirs, what busi-

ness of the camp

Presses; what labour from the Lord awaits

me?

MARDYKE. [*Motioning* LISLE *to head of table.*] This on the instant then:

Lieutenant Joyce,

Of this God's army, charged with carnal

crime

In that he hath enforced the innocent

And brought a young maid into public

shame.

This he denies not. Now three voices
here

Cry that we purge this holy host of him,

So satisfied; and three that he shall die.

With thee the casting vote. The Lord
speak through thee.

LISLE. [*Rising.*] Sirs, in no common
quarrel are we up,

Nor to a slight fray have we girded us,

But are embattled for dear liberty,

Dear liberty to righteousness affianced,

That each man on our English soil henceforth

Shall live his own life out beneath the sun,

Master of his own conscience, his own
soul,

And answerable only to his God:

For this and no less thing rise we in arms.

For this the noble hath disdained his ease,

For this the gentleman forsworn his hearth,

For this the yeoman left his glebe un-
ploughed,

For this doth brother clash with brother,
friend

With friend, and father smiteth his own
son:

For this have we preferred, rather than
reap

A servile tilth, to trample the sown field

And springing pasture to incarnadine.

But vain the father's and the brother's
blood,

c

Pasture ensanguined and abandoned hearth,

And worse than vain our liberty at last,

If we have builded it with hands defiled.

[*Murmurs of admiration.*

Therefore I show no mercy on this man.

Death! Let him die.

MARDYKE. Bring in Lieutenant Joyce.

Enter JOYCE, *guarded*

LISLE. Lieutenant, for the sake of that

high cause

For which we are embattled, and which

thou

Hast stained, I sentence thee forthwith

to death.

JOYCE. Death!

LISLE. To a soldier 'tis a little thing.

JOYCE. I do not count death as a little
thing.

I cannot go out of the warm sunshine

Easily; yet I am a gentleman

And I can die.

LISLE.   Hast anything to say?

JOYCE. Thou who so lightly dealest death
to me,

Be thou then very sure of thine own soul!

LISLE. I fear not that; and less do I
fear death.

[LISLE *dismisses* JOYCE *and guards.*

[*Drawing his sword.*] And judge me, Thou
that sittest in Thy heaven,

As I have shown no mercy, show me
none!

Deal Thou to me what I have dealt to him.

Nay, more; not the mere death that he
  shall die,

Strike at the heart, the hope, the home
  of me,

If ever a woman's beauty shall ensnare

My soul unto such sin as he hath sinned.

> [MIRIAM *has entered with wine and
>   stands waiting.* LISLE, *lowering his
>   sword, sees her before him and
>   stands motionless.*

MARDYKE. Sir Hubert Lisle, my wife!
  To her I leave you.

> [*Exit* MARDYKE *and others.* MIRIAM
>   *pours out wine and proffers* LISLE
>   *the cup.*

LISLE. [*Taking cup.*] Lady, I thank

    you, and must ask your pardon

For breaking in on you so suddenly

And so disordered — I would say — but you,

You are not of our country?

MIRIAM.   No, of France,

And I was born in the sun's lap — will

    you

Not rest awhile?

        [*She moves as if to conduct him.*

LISLE. [*Hesitating.*] You are then of

    that land

Where flows the crimson wine that now I

    drink?

Is't not so?

MIRIAM.   Even so.

LISLE. [*Holding up the wine.*] And in
  such glory
Have you fared hither to us over sea.

MIRIAM.   Will you not rest? [*Again
  moving.*]

LISLE. [*Going, then again hesitating.*] I
  thank you.

MIRIAM.   See — this way.

LISLE.   And you — how long since is it
  that you left
Your southern vines?

MIRIAM.   I came here as a child;
My father died at La Rochelle.

LISLE.   Alas!

MIRIAM.   Committing me to Colonel
  Mardyke's care,

Who was his comrade then.

LISLE.   And who is now

Your husband?

MIRIAM.   Yes. Your room, sir,

eastward lies.

LISLE. I will come with you — and

these glimmering fens,

Do they not pall after the southern glow?

MIRIAM. I am grown used to them.

LISLE.   And yet it seems

Strange in the drear fenland to light on

you.

MIRIAM. How still the air is: scarcely

can one breathe.

A storm approaches — [*Hesitating.*] Will

this war soon end?

LISLE.   Not till we triumph — or —

darker it grows.

This leads us to the garden? See how

still

That poplar, conscious of some heavy

fate!

That breathless alder! Like to guilty

souls

Against a coming judgment.

MIRIAM.   [*Hesitating.*]   Is there aught

Wherein I still can serve you?

LISLE.   [*Coming toward her.*]   No, I

thank you.

MIRIAM.   I have made all ready —

[*Hesitates.*]

LISLE.   Every bird doth cower.

MIRIAM. [*Going, but returning.*] I have

laid some books within your room —

you read

Much — so they say — I thought — how the

air faints

As though beneath some suffocating

clutch!

LISLE. Darker and darker yet — what

books are dear

To you?

MIRIAM. Old histories.

LISLE. That mandolin —

You touch it in the twilight?

MIRIAM. Not with art.

How the air sighed then! Nearer comes

the storm;

A moment and 'twill break above our
heads.

LISLE. [*Coming close to her.*] Sweet
after battle must thy music be.

[*A sudden sound of musketry heard
without.*

MIRIAM. What sound was that? That
was no thunder-peal.

LISLE. Lieutenant Joyce of this God's
army, shot
By my command!

MIRIAM. What crime hath he
committed
That you take on you God's prerogative
Of death?

LISLE. How can I name it to you! He

Hath sinned against a maid.

MIRIAM.   But such a doom!

LISLE.   No doom too harsh!   In this
    our virgin cause
We of that sin must purify us — thus.

> [LISLE *bows to* MIRIAM, *who goes off
>   slowly and trembling.* LISLE
>   *starts to follow her, but controls
>   himself with effort. He goes
>   slowly to back, and as he stands
>   looking out, a low mutter of
>   thunder is heard.*

ACT II

ACT II

ACT II

TIME. — *Three weeks later: night.*

SCENE. — *The same as Act I.* MIRIAM AND MARTHA *discovered,* MIRIAM *touching mandolin absently.* MARTHA *at work on embroidery, a lamp beside her.*

MIRIAM. [*Sings.*]

I

Red skies above a level land
    And thoughts of thee;
Sinking sun on reedy strand,
    And alder tree.

47

II

Only the heron sailing home,

With heavy flight:

Ocean afar in silent foam,

And coming night.

III

Dwindling day and drowsing birds,

O my child!

Dimness and returning herds,

Memory wild.

MARTHA.　What sorrow of the gloaming

dost thou sing?

MIRIAM.　Of some bereaved woman in

the Fens.

[*Casting aside instrument and coming*

over to MARTHA.

O Martha!

MARTHA.   Well, child — will you help

    me here?

These eyes begin to fail in lamp-light now.

MIRIAM.   [*Kneeling by her.*] Dear

    Martha!

MARTHA.   Ah! just here I cannot — well,

Weary of music?

MIRIAM.   Let me lay my head

Here in thy lap as in the olden days

Then when I was a child.

MARTHA.   You'd have me idle

As you are, — there, then!

        [*Taking her face in her hands.*

MIRIAM.   Was I a bad child,

Martha?

  D

MARTHA. Ah, no! but headlong ever and
rash.

MIRIAM. Cruel?

MARTHA. Not with intention.

MIRIAM. Ah, but still
Of others too regardless?

MARTHA. As a child is.

MIRIAM. I am so happy; let me hide
my face
Here.

MARTHA. If so happy, child, why so
afraid?

MIRIAM. No! not afraid.

MARTHA. I am glad that you are happy,
That shows me you are humbler, that your
heart

Is tamed; thence only cometh happiness.

MIRIAM. [*Looking up.*] I am not tamed!

MARTHA.   Well — more at rest then.

MIRIAM.   Rest!

MARTHA. Now you are weeping.   Who

shall guess your soul,

Miriam?   So happy now, and now wild

tears.

MIRIAM. You know, you know, I would

not hurt you, no,

Nor — him, not willingly — never was cruel.

MARTHA. You say you would not hurt

me nor —

MIRIAM.   Your brother.

MARTHA. Your husband.

MIRIAM. No — not willingly — and yet —

MARTHA. What would you say?

MIRIAM. Nothing. I know not what.

[*She again takes up mandolin, then casts it down, coming to* MARTHA *again.*

Martha, dear Martha, why are you not kind?

MARTHA. Kind! you to say I am not kind.

MIRIAM. O, kind —

But — but you love me deeply, do you not?

MARTHA. What need to ask?

MIRIAM. Whate'er I *did*, me, me You love?

MARTHA. I fear so; but you will do nothing

I could not also love.

MIRIAM.   I cannot tell.

[*Then suddenly.*] Come, give me both your

    hands. I hold you fast —

You cannot fly — look not on me.   I fear,

I fear to be alone with him — the stranger,

Within our gates — cast me not from you

    yet!

MARTHA.   [*Rising.*] If this be true, it

    is a deadly sin!

The blackest — to your knees and seek

    your God.

But I'll not think it, cannot imagine, dream

    it.

'Tis folly, the fruit of too much idleness.

But hearken, Miriam! though it be but

    folly,

It must be plucked from out you, flung
  away,

Else I will seek my brother out, I am

His faithful friend — but 'tis unthinkable!

Enter MARDYKE, *hurriedly, with a letter in his hand, accompanied by* RATCLIFFE

MARDYKE. [To RATCLIFFE.] Summon
  the council hither, on the instant!

[*Exit* RATCLIFFE.

[*Turning to* MIRIAM.] Idle — still idle!
  and in time of war!

A night of peril! yet the strings are
  heard.

Mistress, bestir you! To your household
  tasks,

And make this dwelling ready for the
    night!

And then to bed! else will I lock you up:

Provide you bread to eat, water to drink.

I'll starve this fiend of indolence out of you.

MARTHA.   Brother, you speak not wisely.

MARDYKE.   Ah, do you
Sustain her?

MARTHA.   'Tis not wise to use her thus;

I tell you, 'tis not wise; such roughness
    makes

All women desperate.

MARDYKE.   Wisdom from women!

MARTHA.   You would not have your way
    with me thus — nor

Will you with her — your wife.

MARDYKE.   Leave us together.

[*Exit* MARTHA.

That which I spoke, I spoke it not in
jest.

I who have warred, and still do war for
God,

Will keep a diligent wife, a quiet house,

Still and severe as fits our sacred cause.

You hear me?

MIRIAM.   Sir, you hurt my wrist —
forbear.

MARDYKE.   Remember! To your duties
— then to bed!

[*Exit* MIRIAM.

Meanwhile the officers enter

How long, sirs, must we tarry idle here?

On all sides are we hemmed; where shall
    we strike?

IRON.   Where is Sir Hubert Lisle?

MARDYKE.   Shut in his room.

IRON.   The peril gathers, yet that vacant
    chair!

                    [*Murmurs from officers.*

Sirs, I will speak no treason, yet we marvel
Why thus we are hemmed in idle. I will
    voice
The general fear; he who should lead us,
    faints.

                    [*Murmurs of assent.*

Who captains us? One, dazed and dubi-
    ous.

Sir Hubert Lisle is fallen into a trance.

What purpose hath he, what direction,
    torn

This way and that, hither and thither
    blown ?

Now he commands, anon he counter-
    mands ;

Now is he hot for battle, now he cools,

This man, who fell amidst us like a brand.

And all the night he paces to and fro,

Murmuring and wrestling as with one
    unseen.

What curse lies heavy on him, or what
    spell ?

Now let him wake, or be some other
    chosen.

                                    [*Murmurs.*

MARDYKE.   Lift we a prayer that heaven

restore his mind.

IRON.   Yet, while we pray, is Rupert

thundering down.

Enter LISLE, *dreamily, with roses in his*

dress

LISLE.   Forgive, I pray you, sirs, this

tardiness.

Sirs, you all frown on me and stare distrust.

I have fallen into a lethargy of spirit

Which even now is passing from me.

Friends,

Let me not lose your faith.

MARDYKE.   Sir, we but ask

Some guiding from you, and some certain

light.

Darker our fortunes grow, on all sides pressed,

And threatened north and west.   Where shall we strike?

IRON.   I say, take water northward and relieve

Fairfax in Hull.

MARDYKE.   Or threaten suddenly

Newark, where now are horsemen swarming thick

Upon our flank.

CRABLOVE.   And, sir, still Willoughby

In vain beleaguers Castle Bolingbroke.

MARDYKE. Quick flies the night.   Shall we aid Willoughby?

Or hurl a force on Newark, or free Hull?

LISLE. [*Hesitatingly.*] To me it seems

  'twere wiser here to bide,

                        [*Murmurs.*

Holding the Whitton and the Welland line,

Breaking the foe with bog and with mo-

  rass;

Here let us lie, alert, but not o'er-hot.

We have much need of discipline severe,

Patience and quiet rule and still debate,

Till each man shall attain self-mastery.

Now leave me, sirs; for I must meditate,

And wrestle in spirit lest I be o'ercome.

  [*Exeunt officers, sullenly shaking their*

        heads.

MARDYKE. [*Rising.*] I will go up to

  the turret-room, and mark

If, in God's book, some chapter or some
   verse

May give us warning in our present need.

   [MARDYKE, *unlocking case, takes down*
      Bible, and ascends to tower with
      lighted candle. LISLE *sits plunged*
      in gloomy revery and studying a
      map distractedly. MIRIAM *passes*
      across the stage hurriedly, with
      keys at her girdle. LISLE, *seeing*
      her, comes forward.

LISLE. Lady, will you not touch the
   strings again?

With music lift from me this heaviness?

MIRIAM. I may not, sir. I am accused
   of sloth,

And must about the business of the house.

Here are my keys.

LISLE. [*Seeing her wrist.*] See, you

have hurt your wrist.

MIRIAM. 'Tis nothing.

LISLE. But 'tis bruised as by a blow!

Miriam! — my heart spoke then. This burn-

ing silence,

Secret eye lightnings, and deep mutual sighs,

And darting comprehensions of swift thought,

Must break in words at last.

MIRIAM. [*Trembling.*] I will not hear

them.

LISLE. Hear them! and then do with

me what you will.

When I spurred hither, all on fire for God,

Then did I gallop into human flame.

Cold I had lived, pure, narrow, temperate,

A girded swordsman pressing to the mark.

So rode I through that gate. Then sud-
    denly

Thy beauty like a tempest fell on me;

And in one moment was I rent and riven.

Stunned is my life; I wander, and I grope.

My voice in the council falters; in mid-act

This lifted arm falls at thy floating face.

They waver like to mist the ranks of war,

They waver and fade; he fades, the armèd
    man,

And spurring armies in a vision clash.

Or would I pray and upward fling my
    hands?

To thee I pray, thee, thee, with cries be-
  seeching.

I am lost, lost!

  MIRIAM.   O, I would be to thee

As gentle as the grass above the dead;

And have I been but darkness, and a
  sword?

  LISLE.   No! for a revelation breaks

  from thee.

Thou hast unlocked the loveliness of earth,

Leading me through thy beauty to all
  beauty.

Thou hast admitted me to mystery,

Taught me the different souls of all the
  stars;

Through thee have I inherited this air,

E

Discovered sudden riches at my feet,

And now on eyes long blinded flames the
world.

Thou shattering storm, thou eve of after
blue,

Thou deluge, and thou world from deluge
risen,

Thou sudden death, and thou life after
death!

[*A pause while she stands trembling.*

You speak not. Give me but a human
word.

MIRIAM. O, all my life has listened for
thy step!

LISLE. How have I walked in glory
unaware!

O, let your dear soul forth; stay it not

    now!

  MIRIAM. For thee alone came I into

    this world,

For thee this very hair grew glorious,

My eyes are of this colour for thy

    sake.

This moment is a deep inheriting,

And as the solemn coming to a kingdom.

  LISLE. Apart we two did wander in-

    land; now

Listen, the ocean of infinity!

Life hath no more in it.

  MIRIAM. [*Lying in his arms.*] My final

    peace!

  LISLE. Peace?

MIRIAM.   Doth the word seem cold?

A woman's peace,

It hath all fire in it, and burneth white.

LISLE.   Peace! Is there peace while

all —

MIRIAM. Wake me not yet,

Not for this moment!

LISLE.   While this dreaming love

Gives you the language of a child or a

bird,

Of a light and liquid rapture.

MIRIAM.   Speak not yet

Too human and too grave.

LISLE.   Yet every way

I look is darkness; for each moment

war

May call me off.

MIRIAM.   Peer not into the dark.

LISLE.   Else will it swallow us. O suddenly

We two must hew us out a path.

MIRIAM.   Disturb not

This hush and church of passion with the
    world!

LISLE.   How thy speech wantons, while
    I stare at life!

MIRIAM.   Hush! I am lifted even above
    hope!

LISLE.   He, he —

MIRIAM.   Thou hast my spirit,
    be content.

O, all that in me wanders and is wild

Gathers into one wave that breaks on

    thee!

LISLE. And I must bide, till this full

    beauty drop

Which even divinity did flush to dream.

Thou witherest like a virgin at his side.

       [*A sudden trumpet. They start apart.*

MIRIAM. Hark!

LISLE.   Tidings from the camp!

MIRIAM.   I'll leave you, then.

       [*Sound of hurried steps.*

LISLE. Some business easily despatched!

MIRIAM.   I'll walk

Here, on the terrace, till you shall decide

This petty business.

Enter soldier, with letter, accompanied by

FINCH

LISLE.　　A brief " Yes " or " No."

[*Exit* MIRIAM.　LISLE *takes letter and*

reads it silently.

Ah!

FINCH. You are stricken, sir; lean on

this arm.

LISLE. No! but stand by; this matter

presses. Go!

[*Exit soldier and* FINCH.

[*Reading aloud.*

" To SIR HUBERT LISLE, *Commander:*

" The Castle of Bolingbroke still bays all

attack. Those whom I have with me are

too few: the breach I have made too slight. Another day and relief bursts upon us from Newark.

"There is no way but by sudden onslaught, and that by daybreak. Who then shall lead this? Whom hast thou in the army of such desperate valour, that, in scorn of life, he will adventure? For he who shall lead such onslaught, may already count himself as dead. Yet, on this hazard, stand our fortunes in this region. Hast thou a man of such fiery zeal that others follow him? Then, send him quickly. Let him know what peril awaits him; but yet that on his peril hang our hopes.

" Knowing well thine own spirit, I entreat

that thou thyself shalt not so adventure ;

for thy life is of the worth of many cities.

Speed !   Speed !

"WILLOUGHBY."

[LISLE *sits down and spreads letter*
before him under lamp.

And why should I not send — him ?

He is ripe

With such experience as none other hath

In breaches and in onslaughts both in

France

And in the foreign fenland ; he, I say,

Of all the host is the one only man,

The apparent instrument.   I do but send

Him whom the peril asks, by man un-
blamed.

With God how stand I? Vain to palter
there.

I'd have the husband dead that I might
clasp

The wife secure. If then behind the
deed

The mind can murder, and the heart can
kill;

Then this mere silent wish, born of the
brain,

Might instantly start up a living thing

And able, without hands, to strike?

What were I better than the lurking thief,

Or hired assassin stealing from behind,

To stab him in the back? He shall
  not go.

Let him succumb to the slow hour, or
  drop

By sudden death-shot in mid-battle, or
  sink

In casual fever — I'll not do this thing.

Rather myself will go; leave pure this
  house,

And hurl this lurèd soul upon the breach.

   [*He starts to go when* MIRIAM *enters*
     softly, behind, from moonlit terrace.

MIRIAM. Hast thou despatched?

LISLE.   Ah, thou?

MIRIAM.   Hast thou not yet

Determined?

LISLE. [*Hesitating as he gazes at her.*]

No, not yet; there's more in this

Than I had looked for.

MIRIAM. [*Stretching out her arms for letter.*]

May I read it? Oft,

A woman's mind is lightning, where men

grope.

[LISLE *refuses to give letter to her.*

So weighty is it?

LISLE.   Even with life and death.

Nay, more: who knows? with all eternity.

MIRIAM. [*Quickly.*] Not perilous to thee?

LISLE.   Perhaps! Away!

Thy moonlight loveliness disturbs me.

MIRIAM.   Words

To make me stay; but, yet, I will not. I

Am heavy with the treasure thou hast

given me,

And I will steal within and spread it out.

I long to lock me in and be alone

With these new riches in the dimness.

LISLE. Ah!

Come back.

MIRIAM. [*Laughing softly.*] I shall disturb

thee.

LISLE. Yet stay on.

Can you not hear Time rushing past our

ears,

With audible, irreparable flight?

MIRIAM. [*Gazing outward and sighing.*]

How e'en the Fenland hath grown fairyland

And all these levels gleam as passionate

As the high gardens of Assyrian kings.

I shall not sleep — I cannot tell thee

why —

                              [Leaning toward him.

Oh, thou dost know! Good night!

LISLE.   Thou shalt not go.

Thy hair hath slipped, and showers round

thee. Now,

I hold thee all dishevelled in the moon;

I cannot clasp thy spirit; thee, I ask,

Thus in thy glorious body — thee!

MIRIAM.   I tremble.

LISLE. That smile hath made a mist of

all the world.

MIRIAM. [*Starting from him.*] Listen, one

cometh on us.

LISLE. Who?

MIRIAM. Alas!

[*Rushes from him.*

LISLE. [*Coming wildly down from terrace into the room, sees the letter and snatches it up. Steps are heard, and* MARDYKE *is seen slowly descending the stairs. Meanwhile the moon is clouded, and a light rain begins to fall.*] Old man, within this moment hast thou died.

Enter MARDYKE, *with Bible, which he lays on table.*

MARDYKE. It seemed, a while since, that a trumpet blew;
Still, by the book I sat; but have not found

Chapter or verse that lights our present
    need.

What tidings from the camp, what sud-
    den word?

  LISLE. Prepare to spur at once to
    Bolingbroke.

  MARDYKE. Now on the instant?

  LISLE.   On the instant. Thou
Art needed there. Grave conference is
    held.

Thy famed experience in foreign siege
The general asks. Thee only can I send.

  MARDYKE. The moon is quenched; yet
    lighten Thou this dark.

Thou great Taskmaster, if unto Thy service
Me Thou hast called, I go and murmur not.

LISLE. Arm thee and quickly, ere the
    blinded dawn

Peer on the drizzling levels. Fast!
    Away!

MARDYKE. With joy I go. I thank
    Thee, O my Lord,

That Thou hast not discarded me as old,

A cumberer of the ground, a loppèd
    branch,

But Thou hast service still for these grey
    hairs.

Light though the task, I'll kindle it with
    fire.

Restore to these old bones and crampèd
    limbs

Speed and the ancient strength of other days

F

Then when I battled and bled at La
   Rochelle.

Ratcliffe! at once my armour, and my
   horse.

   [*Exit* MARDYKE.

LISLE. [*Taking pen and writing.*] " I
send you the man fitted for our purpose;
of mighty zeal and valour, and one that
can enkindle others to a hazard. Let
him, then, lead this assault. He knoweth
his own peril and wherefore he is sent.
He himself beareth this letter. He
bringeth his life in his hand. Send me
swift news of the assault — and of him."

   [*Voices are heard, and the sound of
      running to and fro. Reënter*

MARDYKE, *half-armed, with* RAT-
CLIFFE, *who hastily helps him to
finish his arming.*

MARDYKE. [*To* RATCLIFFE.] Buckle
me closer there; and, here, more room.

RATCLIFFE. Thy back lies open here!

MARDYKE.   In such a cause
I fear no stab in the back; the front
is all.

LISLE. Here is a letter: into Willoughby's hand
Deliver it.

MARDYKE. Shall I be long from home?

LISLE. I think not — till to-morrow at
sunset.

Reënter MIRIAM *from the other side*

MIRIAM.   Whither so suddenly, in the
　　dead night?

LISLE.   Your husband summoned to the
　　camp, straightway.

MARDYKE.   Our officers hold conference;
no more,

My voice is needed; prattle not — to
bed!

Woman hath no concern in this.

MIRIAM.　　　　　　　But when
Shall you return?

MARDYKE.　　　　To-morrow, by sunset.

　[LISLE *goes out on terrace.* MIRIAM
　　　watches MARDYKE *finishing his*
　　　arming.

My sword, now!

Enter SERVANT, *hurriedly*

SERVANT.   Sir, the horse stands.

MIRIAM.   [*To* MARDYKE, *who goes to the
door.*] Sir, good-night!

MARDYKE.   There, then — [*Kisses her
on forehead.*] Such joy have I in
buckling me
Again in armour, all things I forget;
Suddenly wife and home are gone from
me.

          [MIRIAM *goes from him to the door.*
Good-night, Sir Hubert. Peace be on this
house!

LISLE.   [*Coming down.*] Sir, shall I go
in place of thee? 'Tis not
Too late!

MARDYKE. Have I not prayed? The
Lord hath chosen.

[*Exit* MARDYKE *with* RATCLIFFE.
  LISLE *goes out on terrace — sound
    of hoofs galloping away into the
    night. A cold glimmer of dawn
    appears far off.*

MIRIAM. When doth the conference
end?

LISLE.   To-morrow!

MIRIAM.   Then,
A little while is ours. So cold? But
now —

LISLE. A moment, Miriam! I must
think alone.

I am sore troubled.

MIRIAM.   Kiss me — I will go.

[LISLE *makes movement as though to*
embrace her, but cannot.

Am I despised, then, that I could not hide

What burned in me? I should have fenced
and fenced

And so had reverence — you despise me?

LISLE.   Ah!

The starkness of the dawn is at my heart.

MIRIAM. O, how I scorn myself — and

yet — [*Putting her hand on his shoul-*
der and looking in his face.] Good-
night!

[*Exit* MIRIAM.

LISLE. I ne'er did love thee so as at
this moment.

As he turns, enter RATCLIFFE

Who's there?

RATCLIFFE.   I, sir.

LISLE.   Well, well?

RATCLIFFE.   The holy Book!
I come to lock it safe.   Each night it is
My master's custom.   Or, I'll leave it thus;
If haply you would seek in it some verse
To light our present trouble.

LISLE.   Leave it, then!

[*Exit* RATCLIFFE.   *A sallow gleam of
    dawn falls on the Book, as* LISLE
    *opens and reads; and the sound
    of galloping hoofs is borne back
    once more on the wind.*

"And it came to pass in the morning,

that David wrote a letter to Joab, and sent it by the hand of Uriah. And he wrote in the letter, saying, Set ye Uriah in the forefront of the hottest battle, and retire ye from him, that he may be smitten, and die.

"And the men of the city went out and fought with Joab : and there fell some of the people of the servants of David ; and Uriah the Hittite died also."

[*A faint sound of galloping hoofs is again heard, and then ceases.*

that David wrote a letter to Joab, and sent it by the hand of Uriah. And he wrote in the letter, saying, Set ye Uriah in the forefront of the hottest battle, and retire ye from him, that he may be smitten, and die.

"And the men of the city went out and fought with Joab: and there fell some of the people of the servants of David; and Uriah the Hittite died also."

[*A faint sound of galloping hoofs is again heard, and then ceases.*

ACT III

ACT III

ACT III

TIME. — *Five years later.*

SCENE. — *A room in a house on the out-
skirts of the town of Wakefield. At
back a window looks out on the open
country. On its right a door communi-
cates with the outer courtyard; on the
left another opens into the sleeping rooms
of the house.* LISLE *discovered, seated,
with papers before him; on one side*
RATCLIFFE, *on the other two officers
in attendance.*

93

Lisle. Old Ratcliffe, ask my wife to
　　come to me.

Stay! She was hushing up the child to
　　sleep,

Low singing over him; say will she come

If he is sleeping now.

　　　　　　　　　　[*Exit* Ratcliffe.

　　　　　　　　　Sirs, we have seen

Three years of seeming peace; yet here I

　　hold

Letters in Fairfax' hand; he apprehends

In Kent and Essex disaffection; speaks

Of imminent trouble. What of Wakefield

　　then

And all this region; see you any cause

Here for disquiet?

OFFICER.   None, sir, save from bands

Roaming in indolent undiscipline,

Hither and thither, plundering purposeless.

LISLE.   No smouldering mischief then?

OFFICER.   None visible.

Enter MIRIAM *with child. Officers retire*

MIRIAM.   Hubert — he will not sleep,

   but must put on

His sword and strut with it. Ah! let

   him stay.

LISLE. Well — well! thy sword already

   girded on,

Yet, sir, they tell me that no peril

   threatens.

[*To* MIRIAM.] How straight he stands!

   His colour too not bright

Nor dull; but with a blander glow of
    blood.

I think that he hath more of me than
    thee.

MIRIAM. No, Hubert, no.

LISLE.   His eyes! Those are my eyes.

MIRIAM. Only in colour! but that way
    they ope

Wide at the world, that is all mine.

    LISLE.   Perhaps.

MIRIAM. Then, too, his mouth?

    LISLE.   Mine, mine in every curve.

MIRIAM. If you had watched him smile
    as close as I

You would not say that; all his smile is
    mine.

I grant that when he frets, his mouth will
    drop
Like to his father's.

LISLE.   So! from thee his joy,
From me his sadness.

MIRIAM.   Hubert, no! when he
Doth sadden, that same dimness o'er him
    comes
As upon me.

LISLE.   Will you claim all of him?
His eyes, his mouth, his sad hour and his
    bright?
His hair, now, see that curl behind the
    ear.
Come, you must yield me that.

MIRIAM.   O, that perhaps.

G

LISLE. Will you not leave me any part

in him?

MIRIAM. Oh, yes! his cry when he

would fight off sleep.

LISLE. [*Laughing.*] Well, well, sweet,

we will quarrel over him

No longer; he is fair and strong and

bright.

How his young face hath mellowed our

first passion,

What flamed then is a glow more beautiful.

Yet is thy love of me not less?

MIRIAM. How — less?

LISLE. The former fury hath gone out of it,

The pulsing life, the blinding dance of

blood.

MIRIAM.   The child hath brought a
  tremble into it.

I am grown fearful for the sake of him;

I dread the rustle of angels in his room.

  LISLE.   And now doth he divide what
    once was mine

Wholly.

  MIRIAM.   Ah, no! he hath enriched that
    love.

Once did it live upon thy look, thy
    voice,

Thy strength, thy courage, and thy con-
    queror soul,

This was enough, God knows.   But,
    Hubert, now

We two together to behold our boy,

That we have reared and planted sunward,

    grow,

While all our sighs like breezes come to

    him,

And all our tears fall down on him like

    rain.

I thought thou never couldst be more to

    me ;

But now is added to that rapturous fire

Much that perhaps of men is not esteemed,

But to a woman meaneth half her life.

To hold our sweet night council o'er his

    day,

To exchange bright understandings silently

At little words of his ; to bend, we two

Over him dreaming while thy hand on mine

Tightens a moment; then to watch together

Some little way of thee or me appear

Sudden in him; to feel our daily life

Grow solemn at his voice: to see our
  spirits,

Close though they met in kiss and
  breathèd word,

Visibly here commingled and made flesh.

LISLE. Now blows the future sweet into
  our eyes,

And even peril treadeth upon grass.

Enter RATCLIFFE

RATCLIFFE. A sudden messenger from
  Pomfret ridden!

Enter messenger, hurriedly

MESSENGER.　Sir, all the country around
　　Pomfret walls
Is risen up; the castle is cut off:
We foraging without, found no return.
They signal for relief; and one even now
Behind me rideth furiously, I fear
Bringing worse news.

LISLE.　[*To* RATCLIFFE.]　Bid Arlington
　　prepare
With all our horsemen instantly to spur
To Pomfret; then if he who rides behind
Bear us worse tidings, I myself will lead.

　　[*Exit* RATCLIFFE *with messenger.*

MIRIAM.　[*To child, who falls back on
　　her shoulder.*]　Ah, darling!

LISLE.　How, what ails the child?

Miriam.   There, there,

Is thy head heavy? On my bosom then.

Lisle.   Now, Hubert, little Hubert, draw

thy sword!

[*Child attempts, but fails to draw*

sword.

See thus! [*Drawing his own.*] Not even

a smile! Why he would laugh

And leap at this an hour since.

Miriam.   He is heavy.

Hush! do not speak to him.

Lisle.   [*Bending over him.*] What

dreams I have

For thee.

Miriam. What dost thou dream?

Lisle.   He shall be tall

MIRIAM. No taller than thyself.

LISLE.   I'd have him shoot
Beyond me both in inches and in deeds.

MIRIAM. A soldier?

LISLE.   No! when he shall grow a man
The land will cry for rest. I see him
    then
A healer and a closer up of wounds.

His task shall be to obliterate and soothe;

To bind, not break; to mingle, not to mar;

His counsel breathing on our England balm.

This labour more than battle asks a man.

MIRIAM. It is a noble dream.

LISLE.   And shall come true.
Or he shall build in new lands over sea
Some virgin commonwealth.

RATCLIFFE. [*Entering hastily.*] A horseman, sir,

Spurred sweating to the gate.

LISLE.   Summon him in!

Enter soldier, breathlessly

SOLDIER. From Pomfret, sir, where we
are hard beset.

The town may fall each moment, totters
now;

And only in the sight of thee is hope.

LISLE. [*To* MIRIAM.] Dear, I must go.

[*To soldier.*] Tell Colonel Arlington

That I myself will lead; let all stand by.

Ratcliffe, a breastplate and a helm enough!

[RATCLIFFE *hastily arms him.*

Old man, why do thy fingers fumble thus,

Or have thine eyes dimmed suddenly?

    Apace!

  RATCLIFFE. O, sir, this very night-time,

    five years flown,

Thus armed I my old master, when he fell

By Castle Bolingbroke.

  LISLE.   This very night?

  RATCLIFFE. This night; when I did

    leave the holy Book

Unlocked for you to search it.

  LISLE.   I remember.

  RATCLIFFE. Again the night is here!

    My fingers fumble

About the straps as then. Pray God this

    night

May not see dawn like that!

LISLE.   Leave me — enough.

                            [*Exit* RATCLIFFE.

[*Aside.*] I sent him then! Now I myself

  must go.

MIRIAM.   [*To child, with whom she is

  walking to and fro.*] Now thou art

  hot, now cold.

LISLE.   Art thou, dead man,

Urging me down that road where thee I sped?

MIRIAM.   [*Bringing child to* LISLE.]

  Hubert, his face!

LISLE.   [*Suddenly, gazing on child.*] Or,

  or — give me the child.

MIRIAM. What's this?

LISLE.   [*To child.*] Close, close, your

  arms about my neck.

No peril visible or invisible

Shall touch you so enfolded.

MIRIAM.   Why so fearful —

So on a sudden?

LISLE.   Is our son watch'd o'er?

Guarded each instant?

MIRIAM.   Hubert!

LISLE.   Wife, I speak not

Of common perils, but — of the approach

Of malice superhuman.   Ah! forgive me.

There came a little cloud upon my

brain.

Take him within; summon the doctor

straight.

He is ever within call.   Then send him

here

That I may speak with him.

   [*Kissing child and looking after them.*

     [*Exit* MIRIAM *with child.*

       Why on this night

Doth the child sicken suddenly? Ah, folly!

Childhood is quickly sick and quickly well.

        [*A pause.*

Or do the dead remember still? Perhaps

The spirit of the murdered fresh in wrath

Leaps out upon his murderer, but in vain,

Baffled by loss of corporal faculty.

May he not then a spirit vengeance seek,

A vengeance not of hands, and learn to blight

And cripple; and perhaps the matin chill

Can use, and all the fatal airs of night,

And can direct the wandering malady

Whither he will? If he then whom I slew

Is aiming in such vengeance at the child?

Wilt thou revenge thee on bright curls
and cheeks,

And wilt thou lunge, grey swordsman, at
a babe?

Enter doctor, from within

Now, doctor, now! How is't with him?

DOCTOR.   He lies

In some mysterious languor, and my art

Reaches him not.

    LISLE.   Is then the malady

To human healers new?

    DOCTOR.   To me at least.

LISLE. Is it not written in thy category?

DOCTOR. I cannot reach the seat and fount of it.

LISLE. Stands it not on the list, the cause, the cure?

DOCTOR. Show me the cause; then will I find the cure.

LISLE. What symptom hath he? Or what certain sign?

DOCTOR. No spot hath he, nor fever rash; yet fever.

LISLE. Doth he cry out? or lies he silent still?

DOCTOR. He makes no cry, yet struggles as he lies.

LISLE. With what doth the child struggle, how beset?

DOCTOR. He seems to fend a something from his throat.

LISLE. [*With a cry.*] Thou dead man, take thy fingers from his throat;

He is a young thing and a little — ah!

Back to him, doctor, linger not — yet stay;

Think you that heaven doth ever intervene

With special sickness, and for some rank fault

In us, doth strike us there where most we love?

DOCTOR. 'Tis our presumption to imagine it.

We fancy those regardless-rolling orbs,

Themselves inhabited, tremendous worlds,

Night-lights to reassure us in the dark.

We colour with our trespasses the eclipse,

And hear paternal anger in the storm;

Impute to sickness wrath, vengeance to
    death,

And memory to unrecording Nature.

LISLE.   Perhaps — back to his bed.

DOCTOR.   What man can do
I'll do.

[*Exit doctor.*

LISLE.   [*With uplifted hands.*]   O,

Thou that sittest in Thy heavens,

Mine was the sin; be mine the punish-
    ment,

But let him live.   End me with lightning, or

H

In fever let me burn down to the grave,

But let him live. Make ashes of my

life,

Take from me every hope — but let him

live!

Strike here, here, and not otherwhere!

Or if

I may not look for mercy, yet must she,

Who of that murder goeth innocent,

Walk with me hand in hand into this

fire?

By our two souls that anchor on his life.

O, wilt Thou smite where all is holiest,

Smite at the very fount of hope and faith,

And wring the spirit for the fault of

flesh?

Or if with mine her doom entangled be,

What hath he done that he must pay the

  price?

What crime committed save the being

  born?

Then must my sin cancel for him the

  light,

Put out the recent sunbeam, and make

  blank

The murmurs and the splendours of the

  world?

O Father, by that hour, when Thou wast

  dimmed

To human in the clouds on Calvary! —

  Enter soldier, suddenly

I come, but to a phantom conflict there;

I leave behind the real battle here.

[*Exit* LISLE.

[*After a pause*, RATCLIFFE *slowly
enters and puts out the lights
one by one, and goes out, leaving
the stage in complete darkness.
After a pause a female figure is
seen issuing from the door on the
left, who goes over to the window at
the back, and, withdrawing slowly
the curtain, the glimmer of dawn
is seen. She stands a moment
gazing outward; a single sigh of
wind is heard. Enter* RATCLIFFE,
*wearily, from the door on the
right. He is about to cross the*

*room when the woman stops him
with finger on her lip and points
to door of sleeping room.* RAT-
CLIFFE *retires, bowing his head.
As the woman crosses back to the
door on the left, she is met by a
nurse, who with whispers gives her
an empty phial. The woman goes
out with this by the door on the
right, the nurse remaining at the
other door, and listening. She then
starts and hurries inward. The
woman returns with the phial and
is met by the doctor, issuing from
door on left. He has a glass, and,
holding the phial to the light, pours*

some of it out carefully, drop by glimmering drop. Meanwhile the room is growing gradually lighter and more light. The nurse now quickly emerges, touching the doctor and motioning within. She and the doctor retire within, the woman standing beside the door motionless. Reënter RATCLIFFE *hastily and stealthily; he draws the woman into the middle of the room and points to window, while a noise of hoofs is heard approaching and ceases outside. A soldier now enters hurriedly, but, about to speak, is motioned to silence by* RATCLIFFE *and the woman.* RATCLIFFE *takes*

soldier down.

RATCLIFFE. Your news? But soft, in

whisper.

SOLDIER. Victory!

Pomfret relieved! — Sir Hubert from hot

fight

Returning — well-nigh home — already.

Listen.

[*Far off is heard the sound of the*

Puritan hymn of victory. It grows

louder and louder. There is a

sound of commotion without, and

enter LISLE, *casting aside his*

armour as he comes, followed by

certain captains.

LISLE.   How is it with the child?

[*The woman and* RATCLIFFE *motion
    him to silence.*

WOMAN.   Hush, sir, be still.
The moment is approaching and the
    struggle.

LISLE.   Let me go in to him. Hold
    me not back.

[*He rushes to door, but is met by
        nurse, with finger on lip. She
        stands before the door.*

NURSE.   Hist! do not now disturb him.
Now is come
The moment when he wakes or sleeps for
    ever.

[LISLE *signs to officers to withdraw, which they do in silence with bowed heads, and stealthily followed by* RATCLIFFE. *The nurse and woman retire within, silently.* LISLE, *left alone, goes to window at back, and, holding up his hands, causes the chanting of the soldiers, which has come nearer and nearer, to subside and cease. He comes down to the door and stands by it, breathing heavily.*

LISLE. God! God!

Reënter doctor, who stands with bowed head at door, unnoticed at first by LISLE, *who at length sees him*

The child is dead?

DOCTOR.　　　　　　The child is dead.

[Exit back into room.

LISLE.　The sin of David mine, and mine

the doom!

Would I had found the death I sought with

passion,

There in the storm of swords round Pomfret

keep!

Yet she—'tis she whom now I must re-

member;

She is alone with him and makes no cry.

No! she is very silent: most she needs

My arm supporting, and upholding words.

With her must I abide, lift, and sustain

her.

Enter MIRIAM.　*She stands alone by the door.*

MIRIAM. What have I done, that God hath taken my child?

LISLE. [*Hesitatingly and tenderly.*] How should thy deed bereave him of his breath?

MIRIAM. [*Slowly recognising* LISLE.] And thou! thou wast his father, wast thou not?

LISLE. And am thy husband upon whom to lean.

MIRIAM. How have I sinned? I do not understand.

LISLE. O, Miriam —

MIRIAM. Wherefore was he dangled bright Before my eyes a moment — then withdrawn?

He had just learned to run alone; and I

Had taught him a few words — and he is

    gone.

    LISLE.   How can I help you but a little,

    tell me?

    MIRIAM.   The causeless theft!   I say it

    were relief

To feel that here I paid for some far

    sin.

Sooner heaven's ire than heaven's indiffer-

    ence!

O, Hubert, yes — on me this doom has

    fallen.

    LISLE.   On thee!   Why thee?

    MIRIAM.   I rushed into thy arms

In headlong passion and in frenzied blood,

And recked not of my husband, nor of
    law.

This is my punishment!

LISLE.   Why charge thyself?

Shall we accuse us of the frozen bird,

Plead guilty to the fallen buds of spring?

MIRIAM. That bud was mine; and I
    have cankered it:

And though my boy came from me with-
    out spot,

And though his body from the scythe of
    Death

Lieth as sweet as mown grass in the even,

Yet on his soul were deep transmitted
    stains,

And tell tale scars, to spirits visible.

LISLE.   Peace !

MIRIAM.   I am held unworthy, as

who should say —

" She is unclean : ah, trust her not with

babes."

Sir, I was no fit mother for your child.

LISLE.   Miriam !

MIRIAM.   A mother ?   No ! not

even a nurse.

I had known too much to dare undress

thy babe.

Where lived I ere I came into your

service ?

Had you made close enquiry — you had

straight

Discharged me.

LISLE. Wife!

MIRIAM.   Yet there where he is gone,
There's none so pure could tend on him
  as I,
So brood above his opening eyes at dawn.
When was I wanting found? When, for
  one instant?
When was I caught a sentinel asleep?
What flash of absence, lightning of repose,
Is urged against me? Why, I did behold
And hear the coming hours approach like
  foes,
The night a thief, the stars with poised
  spears,
The sun like an incendiary rushed.

LISLE. Belovèd!

MIRIAM.   Yet that madness all outweighs;

In blind blood have I sinned, and he is

    struck.

And you! I have made you suffer!

    You'll not speak.

Yet the gripped hand, the soldier-silence

    tell.

Mercy, mercy, my lord!

                [She casts herself at his feet.

LISLE.   In mercy rise!

Cling not about my feet! Loose you my

    knees!

I will not see you suffer or abased!

Shudder away from me! Mine was the sin.

I, I alone have brought this vengeance

    down.

MIRIAM. Ah!

LISLE. He that *was* your husband —

MIRIAM. What of him?

LISLE. Fell in the wild assault of
Bolingbroke.

MIRIAM. Yes, yes!

LISLE. Yet died he by no accident.

MIRIAM. Hubert, this is all dark!

LISLE. Whoe'er should lead
That desperate onslaught, he must surely die.
I sent your husband.

MIRIAM. Knowing this?

LISLE. Because
I knew it. I'll not spare myself; I'll bare
This traitor heart unto your eyes at last.
I am no common murderer, Miriam.

I

I slew not in the open, nor in haste,

Nor wracked with jealousy: I trapped

    him to it,

Beguiled him with some common con-

    ference,

Then wrote a letter marking him for

    death,

And watched him ride, dying, into the

    night.

    MIRIAM. Therefore wast thou so cold,

    and could'st not kiss me.

Away!

    LISLE. He stood between us.

    MIRIAM.   Touch me not!

    LISLE. The path to you across his body

    lay.

MIRIAM.   Blood is upon you!

LISLE.   Yet — yet!

MIRIAM.   Not his blood,
O murderer!

LISLE.   And if murderer I be,
Then for thy sake am I a murderer.

MIRIAM.   No! not of him.

LISLE.   Of whom then?

MIRIAM.   Of my child.

LISLE.   That which I did, I did with
   reeling sense!
I see the moon still on thy tumbled hair,
That smile that made a mist of the great
   world.

MIRIAM.   O will you dare to make me
   your accomplice?

'Twas I that set you on, I beckoned
    you?

LISLE. No! but thy moonlit beauty mad-
    dened me.

MIRIAM. Ah! will you speak of beauty
    at this moment?

This beauty! and my boy so close and cold,

I sicken through all my body. Then these
    eyes

That still shine, and these lips that dare to
    speak,

This bosom, very snow from hills of Hell,

This flesh which still I wear, whispered
    you on?

This body was the bait then and the
    lure

That woo'd you to that murder — and, my
    God,

This — this conceived my darling! Dead
    is he?

When was he ever otherwise than dead?

As soon as quickened, sentenced, judged
    already,

Long, long ere he was born.

LISLE.   **I, I alone**

Am stained.

  MIRIAM. [*In frenzy.*] I'll mar this body
    — loose your hold.

Grasp not my wrists — this poison-tree I'll
    cleave.

  LISLE. On me thy fury! Me! Here is
    thy aim!

I only have sinned!

MIRIAM. [*With gradual calm.*] Yet this

did lure thee on.

Now on the wild night-festival of sense

The spirit morning dawneth — or is't per-

haps

Merely the drunkard's morning penitence —

A misery matutinal? All our marriage

Had from the first this taint on it. No

more

We'll meet, nor ever touch hands, nor for

a moment

Glance in each other's eyes, for here I see

God's finger fallen.

[*With a certain weary sweetness.*] Hubert

— it is past,

My wrath with thee — but let us fly each
other.

Between, an angel stands with flaming
sword,

And at his feet the body of our babe.

Quickly! Apart! Let water roll between us!

Away, like those first parents out of Eden!

Fiery behind us gates of Paradise!

LISLE. Yet was her hand in his for all
the wrath.

Still, still you love me? Tell me this at
least!

MIRIAM. Yes! but our love is as a thing
accursed.

LISLE. Woman, I grope to find you, but
I cannot.

O, is there no way to you, and no path,

No winding path?

MIRIAM.   No way for thee to me.

LISLE. Dear, have I lost you utterly?

MIRIAM.   For ever!

LISLE. God, can thy sea divide as does

    this sea,

O God, what is Thy severing grave to

    this?

[*A pause; then, approaching her wistfully.*]

The child did you resemble in his smile,

Yet me about the brow a little.

MIRIAM.   Hush!

LISLE. Leave me not utter darkness,

    give me some

Gleam of a far-off meeting ere we die,

Somewhere at last, at last in a strange land,

Or shingle at the ending of the world!

MIRIAM. I am utterly a-cold and without hope.

I would creep in beside the dead for warmth.

LISLE. Being so cold, love, whither will you wander?

MIRIAM. Away! to live with all dumb things that yearn.

I'll nest with thee, thou mother bird returned,

I feel thy dreadful circlings in my blood.

I'll be the friend of the robbed lioness;

Above me, lo! the unhindered desert moon!

O I am stone to human life henceforth!

Yet, if I feel, I feel we two must part.

LISLE. [*After a struggle.*] Come, then.

Good-by. Give me your hand once.

MIRIAM. [*Turning and seeing him.*] Ah!

Why did you turn *his* eyes upon me

then?

I cannot go for a moment.

LISLE. [*Coming close to her.*] Why at

all?

Miriam, it seems that now for the first

time

We two are joined together, man and

wife.

[*She makes to go.*] No, listen! Then go

from me if you will.

Our former marriage, though by holy bell

And melody of lifted voices blest,

Was yet in madness of the blood con-

    ceived,

And born of murder: therefore is the

    child

Withdrawn, that we might feel the sting

    of flesh

Corruptible; yet he in that withdrawal,

Folded upon the bosom of the Father,

Hath joined us in a marriage everlasting;

[*She raises her head.*] Marriage at last

    of spirit, not of sense,

Whose ritual is memory and repentance,

Whose sacrament this deep and mutual

    wound,

Whose covenant the all that might have
    been.

[*Solemnly.*]   And to this troth majestic
    shadows throng,

And stand about us in dumb sympathy.

In presence of these silent witnesses,

And one perchance that carrieth now a babe,

I take in mine thy hand and call thee
    wife —

Wife, wife, till the grave-shattering trumpet!

MIRIAM.   Yet
I want the little hands and feet of him.

   LISLE.   Dear, in a deeper union are we
    bound

Than by the earthly touch of him, or
    voice

Human, or little laughters in the sun.

We by bereavement henceforth are be-
trothed,

Folded by aspirations unfulfilled,

And clasped by irrecoverable dreams:

[*She falls with a cry on his heart,
where he holds her fast.*]

Last, by one hope more deep than certainty,

That though the child shall not return to
us,

Yet shall we two together go to him.

MIRIAM. [*Slowly taking his hand to lead
him.*] Will you come in with me and
look at him?

[*Exeunt slowly, with bowed heads.*

NERO

BY
STEPHEN PHILLIPS

CHARACTERS

NERO	. . . .	*Emperor of Rome.*
BRITANNICUS	. . .	*Nero's Half-Brother.*
OTHO	. . . .	*A Young Noble.*
SENECA	. . . .	
BURRUS	. . . .	*Ministers of State.*
TIGELLINUS	. . .	
ANICETUS	. . .	
A SEAMAN.		
PARTHIAN CHIEF.		
BRITISH CHIEF.		
XENOPHON	. . .	*A Physician.*
SLAVE TO NERO.		
AGRIPPINA	. . .	*Nero's Mother.*
OCTAVIA	. . .	*Sister to Britannicus.*
POPPAEA	. . .	*Wife to Otho, afterwards to Nero.*
ACTE	. . . .	*A Captive Princess.*
LOCUSTA	. . .	*A Poisoner.*
MYRRHA	. . .	*Maid to Poppaea.*
HANDMAIDENS, SPIES, ETC.		

Five years elapse between Acts I and II; two years
between Acts III and IV.

v

ACT I

ACT I

NERO

ACT I

SCENE. — *The scene is in the Great Hall in the
Palace of the Caesars. At the back are steps
leading to a platform with balustrade opening
on the air, and beyond, a view of the
city.*

[*On the right of the stage is a cedarn couch on
which* CLAUDIUS *is uneasily sleeping.
On the right is a door communicating with
the inner apartments. On the left a door
communicating with the outer halls.*

[XENOPHON *is standing by the couch of* CLAUDIUS. AGRIPPINA *is sitting with face turned to an* ASTROLOGER, *who stands at the top of the steps watching the stars.*

[LOCUSTA *is crouching beside a pillar, right. A meteor strikes across the sky. The* ASTROLOGER, *pointing upwards, comes down the steps slowly.*

ASTROLOGER. These meteors flame the dazzling doom of kings.

      [AGRIPPINA *rises apprehensively.*

XENOPHON. Caesar is dead!

AGRIPPINA. The drug hath found his heart.

      [*To* LOCUSTA, *who steals forward.*

Locusta, take your price and steal away!

Sound on the trumpet. Go! your part is done.

> [*Exit* LOCUSTA.

> [*Trumpet is sounded.*

That gives the sign to the Praetorians

Upon the instant of the Emperor's death.

> [*Answering Trumpets are heard.*

Hark! trumpets answering through all the

city.

Xenophon, you and I are in this death

Eternally bound. This husband have I slain

To lift unto the windy chair of the world

Nero, my son. Your silence I will buy

With endless riches: but a hint divulged ——

XENOPHON. O Agrippina, Empress, fear

not me!

AGRIPPINA. Meantime his child, his heir,

    Britannicus,

Must not be seen lest he be clamoured for.

So till the sad Chaldean give the sign

Of that so yearned for, favourable hour,

When with good omens may my son suc-

    ceed,

The sudden death·of Claudius must be hid!

Then on the instant Nero be proclaimed

And Rome awake on an accomplished deed.

    XENOPHON. Then summon Claudius' musi-

    cians in

To play unto the dead as though he breathed.

    AGRIPPINA. Call them! A lulling music

    let them bring.   [*Exit* XENOPHON.

          [*She turns to* ASTROLOGER.

O thou who readest all the scroll of the sky,

Stands it so sure Nero my son shall reign?

ASTROLOGER.   Nero shall reign.

AGRIPPINA.   What   lurks   behind   these
words?

There is a 'but' still hovering in the stars.

ASTROLOGER.   Nero shall reign.

AGRIPPINA.   The half!   I'll know the rest.

ASTROLOGER.   Peer not for peril!

AGRIPPINA.   Peril!   His or mine?

ASTROLOGER.   Thine then.

AGRIPPINA.   I will know all, however dark.

Finish what did so splendidly begin.

ASTROLOGER.   Nero shall reign, but he shall
kill his mother.

AGRIPPINA.   Kill me, but reign!

Enter SENECA

SENECA.   The trumpet summoned me,
And I am here.

AGRIPPINA.   Seneca! Speak it low!
Caesar is dead! Nero shall climb the throne.

SENECA.   I will not ask the manner of his
   death.

In studious ease I have protested much
Against the violent taking of a life.
But lost in action I perceive at last
That they who stand so high can falter not,
But live beyond the reaches of our blame;
That public good excuses private guile.

AGRIPPINA.   You, Xenophon and Burrus,
   stand with me.

Enter BURRUS, *right.   He salutes the corse*

of CLAUDIUS

BURRUS.   Obedient to the trumpet-call I

come.

AGRIPPINA.   Say, Burrus, quickly say, how

stands our cause

With the Praetorians who unmake and make

Emperors?

BURRUS.   The Praetorians are staunch,

And they are marching now upon the Palace.

AGRIPPINA.   Will they have Nero?

BURRUS.   Yes, and double pay.

There is a murmuring minority

Who toss about the name Britannicus.

These may be feared; let Nero scatter gold

There where dissension rises — it will cease.

Their signal when they shall surround the
    palace,

The gleam of my unsheathèd sword to the dawn.

AGRIPPINA. Stand there until I have from
    him the sign,

Then let thy sword gleam upward to the dawn.

[*Turning and pointing to body of* CLAUDIUS.

That is my work! Also, I must betroth

Nero unto the young Octavia,

And with the dead man's daughter mate my
    son.

This marriage sets him firmer on the throne,

And foils the party of Britannicus.

[*To* BURRUS.] You for the army answerable
    stand.

[*To* SENECA.] And, Seneca, I have entrusted

    Nero's mind

To you, to point an eaglet to the sun.

Nero? What does he?

    SENECA.   Nero knows not yet

That Claudius is dead. Rome hath not slept,

But to the torch-lit circus all have run

To see him victor in a chariot race,

Whence he is now returning. A night race

By burning torches is his newest whim.

    AGRIPPINA. A torch-lit race! And yet why

    not? My child

Should climb all virgin to the throne of the

    earth,

Not conscious of spilt blood: and I meantime

Will sway the deep heart of the mighty world.

The peril is Britannicus: for Nero,

Careless of empire, strings but verse to verse.

How shall this dove attain the eagle cry?

SENECA.   Be not so sure of Nero's harmless-

   ness.

AGRIPPINA.   What do you mean?

SENECA.   By me he has been taught,

And I have watched him.   True, the harp, the

   song,

The theatre, delight this dreamer: true,

He lives but in imaginations: yet

Suppose this aesthete made omnipotent,

Feeling there is no bar he cannot break,

Knowing there is no bound he cannot pass;

Might he not then despise the written page,

A petty music, and a puny scene?

Conceive a spectacle not witnessed yet,

When he, an artist in omnipotence,

Uses for colour this red blood of ours,

Composes music out of dreadful cries,

His orchestra our human agonies,

His rhythms lamentations of the ruined,

His poet's fire not circumscribed by words,

But now translated into burning cities,

His scenes the lives of men, their deaths a
    drama,

His dream the desolation of mankind,

And all this pulsing world his theatre.

> [*Steps heard without.*

The dead man's children startled from their
    sleep!

Britannicus, Octavia, wondering.

AGRIPPINA. Till the auspicious hour he is
not dead.

OCTAVIA *and* BRITANNICUS *enter*

OCTAVIA. We could not sleep: father is
very sick.

We fancied every moment that he called
us.

BRITANNICUS. And then these meteors full
of coming woe ——

OCTAVIA. So brilliant and so silent! O, I
fear them.

BRITANNICUS. Is father yet awake? We
want to ask him —

[THEY *approach the couch.* AGRIPPINA
interposes.

AGRIPPINA.   Do not disturb your father for

this night.

OCTAVIA.   We will not speak, nor make the

smallest sound

To wake him.   We must kiss him ere we sleep.

AGRIPPINA.   Children, he is in need of some

long rest.

Go back to bed: your father sleepeth sound.

BRITANNICUS.   I will go in to him, I will —

and you

Are not our mother.   By what privilege

Do you thus interpose yourself between

A father and his children?

AGRIPPINA.   Would you then

Trouble him, when to sleep is all he asks?

OCTAVIA.   Only a moment!   But to see him!

AGRIPPINA. No!

Come softly back to bed! no — no — this

way!

Britannicus, with the first peer of light

You shall behold your father; but not now.

So the physician, Xenophon, enjoined me.

Now take Octavia's hand — so, both of you.

[OCTAVIA *holds her face to be kissed.*

To-night I think I will not kiss you, child.

Good-night, good-night.

[*Exit* OCTAVIA *and* BRITANNICUS.

SENECA. How often have I taught

And written, 'Children shall not be beguiled

Even for good ends.' And yet, the single

lie

Must, for the general good, be spoken; yet ——

[MUSICIANS *meanwhile have entered, and are playing dreamy music.* AGRIPPINA *turns to* ASTROLOGER, *holding out her arms.*

AGRIPPINA.   How long till Rome shall greet her Emperor?

ASTROLOGER.   Behold the heavens! The moment!

       [*Exit* ASTROLOGER.

AGRIPPINA.   Give the sign!

[*Sounds of acclamation and cries of* '*Nero.*'   BURRUS *draws his sword.*

BURRUS.   See the Praetorians!

SENECA.   Nero returns.

Enter a HERALD *gorgeously dressed, bear-
    ing a silver wreath.*

MESSENGER. From Nero unto Agrippina
    greeting !

He comes a victor from the chariot race.

[*Sounds of acclamation grow louder, the
    crowd of* NERO'S *friends and satellites
    pours in: last comes* NERO *dressed as
    a charioteer.*

AGRIPPINA. [*Touching* CLAUDIUS' *body.*]
That music be a dirge: Caesar is dead.

                    [NERO *pauses wondering.*

Claudius is dead. Reign thou. Ave Caesar !

[BURRUS *leads* NERO *to back of platform,
    and addresses the soldiers at back.*

BURRUS.   Caesar is dead!   Behold Caesar!

[*A great shout of* 'NERO!'   'CAESAR!'
   Meanwhile AGRIPPINA *and* SENECA *are
   listening close together.   Discordant cries
   are heard of* ' BRITANNICUS!'   *A slave
   or attendant on* NERO *scatters gold in the
   direction of these discordant cries, which
   gradually subside, and are lost in one
   long shout of* 'Nero, Imperator.'   NERO
   motions for silence.

NERO.   [*Turning to Court.*]   Behold this
   forest of uprisen spears,
Symbol of might!   But I upon that might
Would not rely.   You hail me Emperor —
Then hail me as an Emperor of peace.
First, I declare divinest clemency.

No deaths have I to avenge, no wrath to

    bribe,

No desperate followers clamouring for spoil;

Pardon from me may beautifully fall.

Next, I bestow full liberty of speech;

I will not sway a dumb indignant earth —

Emperor over the unuttered curse.

Were I myself the mark, I will not flinch.

Yet citizens, if freedom of the tongue

I grant, I'd wish less freedom of the feast.

Then all informers who lie life away

I'll heavily chastise; let no man think

With hinted scandal to employ mine ear.

Last, over all my earth be perfect trust,

That every tribe and people, dusk or pale,

Legions extreme and farthest provinces,

May know that this my hand which striketh down

The oppressor and the tyrant from his seat

Shall raise the afflicted and exalt the meek.

And if this burden grow too vast at times,

Then, mother, teach thy son to bear the load.

[*Exit Court.*

AGRIPPINA.   [*Rushing to embrace him.   He is vested with the purple and laurel wreath.   The body of* CLAUDIUS *is borne off.   Exit* BURRUS.   NERO *comes down.*]   Nero, thou art my son !

NERO.   To rule the world. How heavy is the sceptre of the earth !

AGRIPPINA.   [*Coming down.*]   Nero, upon this arm behold I clasp

This amulet. One dawn two murderers

Despatched to kill thee, stealing to thy bed

Were frightened by a snake which from be-

    neath

Thy pillow glided. From that serpent's skin

I made this charm. Wear it, and thou shalt

    prosper;

But lose it, look thou for calamities.

    SENECA. [*Prepares to go also.*] You will

      need sleep, sir, for to-morrow's task.

    NERO. [*In terror.*] I am not pale? Not

      heavy-eyed?

    SENECA. No! No!

    NERO. An artist, whatsoever mood he rouse

In others, should himself be ever still.

Where is a mirror?

SENECA.   Sir, one graver word.

To-morrow when you first shall sit in judg-

  ment,

And set your name unto the scroll of death —

  NERO. [*Gazing at himself in mirror.*] Ah!

  Must I sign death-warrants? Then I

  wish

This hand had never learned to write.

  SENECA.   Dear pupil!

  AGRIPPINA. Your pupil now the awful

  purple wears.

You tremble but to grasp the pen! But they

Who dyed it thus, feared not to grip the brand.

  NERO. [*Again looking in mirror.*] It is an

  act to me unbeautiful.

To scatter joy, not sadness, was I born.

AGRIPPINA. It is an act to you most neces-

　　sary,

If you would sit secure where I have set you.

Now the light things of boyhood, toys of youth,

Unworthy that stern seat, you must discard.

Acte, the playmate of those careless hours,

Henceforth must be forgotten: you shall wed

A royal consort — young Octavia,

The child of Claudius, of the imperial line.

SENECA. My peaceful counsel you will not

　　forget.

NERO. [*Turning to* SENECA, *affectionately.*]

　　Old friend, I am not like to wade in blood,

Thee at my side! I think upon the dooms

Of Julius, Caius, and Tiberius,

All Emperors — all miserably slain.

SENECA. This dawn art thou the master of

    the world;

Then tremble at the task to thee assigned.

Meekly receive the purple and the wreath,

And on thy knees accept omnipotence.

Good-night, dear pupil! May my teaching

    lead

Thy solemn opportunity aright!

                       [*Exit* SENECA.

NERO. You powers sustain me to endure

    this weight!

Mother, I shall go mad!

AGRIPPINA.   Not while this hand

Is on thy brow, and this voice in thine ear.

NERO. To rule the world!

AGRIPPINA.   We two will rule the world.

NERO. We two?

AGRIPPINA. When you have need of me,
then call me.

NERO. I ever shall. I need you at this
moment
More even than when my toothless gums did
fumble
About thy breast in darkness of the night.

AGRIPPINA. My dear, dear son! And
Nero, well I know
That you could never hurt or injure me.
But you will not forget who set you here —
You will not, tell me?

NERO.   Never, mother, never!

AGRIPPINA. Mothers for children have
dared much, and more

Have suffered; but what mother hath so scarred

Her soul for the dear fruit of her body as I?

Thy birth-pang was the least of all the throes

That I for thee have suffered — a brief pain,

A little, little pain we share with creatures;

But what was this to torments of the mind,

The dark, imperial meditations,

Musing with eyes half-closed in moonless night;

The crimes — yes, crimes, the blood that has

    been spilt —

Why, I have made a way for thee through

    ghosts.

Nero, you'll not forget?

    NERO.   Ah! Never, never!

    AGRIPPINA. My son, this very night it was

    foretold

'Nero shall reign, but he shall kill his mother.'

Tell me the stars have lied.

NERO. [*Smiling.*]   The stars have lied.

Enter BURRUS

BURRUS.   The pass-word, sir, to-night?

NERO.   The best of mothers.

AGRIPPINA.   Kiss me; we both of us must

sleep awhile.

[*Exit* AGRIPPINA.   NERO *goes up, gazing*

out on the city as the dawn comes on

greyly.

NERO.   O all the earth to-night into these

hands

Committed!   I bow down beneath the load,

Empurpled in a lone omnipotence.

My softest whisper thunders in the sky,

And in my frown the temples sway and reel,

And the utmost isles are anguished. I but
 raise

An eyelid, and a continent shall cower;

My finger makes the city a solitude,

The murmuring metropolis a silence,

And kingdoms pine in my dispeopling nod.

I can dispearl the sea, a province wear

Upon my little finger; all the winds

Are busy blowing odours in mine eyes,

And I am wrapt in glory by the sun,

And I am lit by splendours of the moon,

And diadem'd by glittering midnight.

O wine of the world, the odour and gold of it!

There is no thirst which I may not assuage;

There is no hunger which I may not sate;

Naught is forbidden me under heaven!

[*With a cry.*] I shall go mad! I shall go

mad!

　　[ACTE *steals in noiselessly, and waits till*

　　　he turns, then comes down to him.

My Acte!

　ACTE.　[*Shrinking.*] O, I seem so far from

　you,

And so beneath you now; your care hence-

forth

The world and nothing less. Long have you

been

Nero to me, but Caesar must be now,

High throned, the nations crawling at your feet.

And yet be sure that if on some far day

The throne should pass from you; if you
    should stand

Lonely at last; your friends all fallen away

From you; the laurel upon other brows

Set; were you dyed in blood deep as the robe

That folds you; were you dead in rags reposing,

Yet would I find you, cover up your face,

Taking the last kiss from your lips, and I

Would gently bury you within the earth.

    NERO. Ah!

    ACTE. And though none came nigh you,
      being dead,

Who were in life so thronged about and pressed,

One hand at least would duly pluck you flowers,

One hand at least would strew them on your
      grave.

Sleep now, and I will charm these eyes to
'close.

[*She takes a harp, and as she plays* NERO
drops off to sleep. She, seeing him so,
softly kisses him and noiselessly disap-
pears. Meanwhile NERO *turns un-*
easily in his sleep, and a procession of
dead Emperors passes — JULIUS, *cover-*
ing his face, but withdrawing his cloak
to gaze a while on NERO; TIBERIUS;
CAIUS *wounded;* CLAUDIUS *holding a*
cup. NERO *rushes forward, uttering*
a cry. ACTE *again re-enters at the*
sound.

Nero, what ails you? Nero, how the drops
Stand on your brow!

NERO.   There, there, I seemed to see
As in procession the dead Emperors:
Julius, Tiberius, Caius, Claudius,
All bloody, and all pacing that same path.

ACTE. [*Trying to lead him on the opposite
way.*]   There is another path, will you but
take it.

[NERO *is led by her a little way, then hesitates, still gazing after the procession of
Emperors. Gradually he looses* ACTE'S
hand, and she leaves him, gazing.

D

ACT II

ACT II

SCENE.—*The same, but signs of excessive luxury and profusion. Rich carpets, gilded pillars, etc. As the scene opens, strange oriental music is heard, with singing.* GIRLS *enter slowly and place wreaths round the various statues of* NERO, *who is depicted now as Apollo singing, now as a charioteer.*

[ACTE *is reclining on a couch. The time is broad noon. A faint exotic odour pervades the palace.*

1ST MAIDEN.   O Lydia, I am drowsing, and my hands

Can scarcely wreathe the Emperor as Apollo.

37

2ND MAIDEN. Ah, crown this carefully!

 To-day he sings

In public; as Apollo will return

So crowned, so garbed.

 1ST MAIDEN. How is that wreath dis-

  posed?

 2ND MAIDEN. Excellent!

 3RD MAIDEN. O please tell me how to droop

These scarlet flowers.

 2ND MAIDEN. About the lyre then, thus.

 4TH MAIDEN. This bust now of the

  Emperor as a boy?

 1ST MAIDEN. O, covered with white flowers

  and birds of spring.

 5TH MAIDEN. This charioteer: with green

  I have dressed that.

3RD MAIDEN. Yes, for the Emperor's colour is the green.

1ST MAIDEN. Now all the busts are wreathed.

2ND MAIDEN. What more to do?

1ST MAIDEN. All is arranged. How heavy are my eyes.

3RD MAIDEN. And this low music on my spirit hangs.

4TH MAIDEN. And the faint odour steals upon my hair.

1ST MAIDEN. [*Moving up and leaning out.*] See, all the city is a solitude.

2ND MAIDEN. All Rome is gathered in the theatre

To hear the Emperor sing.

5TH MAIDEN.   O, I should sleep
On such a noon, in such a throng.

1ST MAIDEN.   That sleep
Would have no wakening, if your eyes but
    closed
While Caesar sang.

4TH MAIDEN.   To-night there is a feast.
Have you remembered?

3RD MAIDEN.   Yes, the dancing girls
From Egypt are arrived.

1ST MAIDEN.   We are to strew
Down from the ceiling flowers upon the
    guests.

   [*They recline in various attitudes about the
       seats and pillars.*

Enter SENECA *and* BURRUS

BURRUS. Ah, Seneca, five years since Nero climbed

The throne: and in this very chamber, now

So changed, this odour — pah! This was the place,

Grim, bare, for military virtues apt.

SENECA. And he how changed! The boy who dreamed so high

Of mightiest empire and unmeasured peace,

All I had taught him lost; by flattery sapped,

Jewelled and clothed as from the Orient,

He sings and struts with dancers and buffoons.

ACTE. [*Starting up.*] And you, when have you two dissuaded him?

Or when forbidden?   Do you teach him shun

Languor or luxury?   You lure him thither.

   SENECA.   'Tis true that we have not dissuaded

    him,

But out of high deliberate policy

Have suffered him to tread the path of folly

Rather than mischief.   We have ruled the world

With wisdom these five years while he has

    played.

   ACTE.   What of Poppaea, Otho's wife.

    Have you

Restrained that madness?   Rather have you

    not

Screened it and fed it?

   SENECA.   With the same design;

Better that he should vent his madness thus

In pastime to the State not perilous,

Amuse himself with her rather than Rome.

   ACTE. A woman without pity, beautiful.

She makes the earth we tread on false, the
     heaven

A merest mist, a vapour. Yet her face

Is as the face of a child uplifted, pure;

But plead with lightning rather than those
     eyes,

Or earthquake rather than that gentle bosom

Rising and falling near thy heart. Her voice

Comes running on the ear as a rivulet;

Yet if you hearken, you shall hear behind

The breaking of a sea whose waves are souls

That break upon a human-crying beach.

Ever she smileth, yet hath never smiled,

And in her lovely laughter is no joy.

Yet hath none fairer strayed into the world

Or wandered in more witchery through the air

Since she who drew the dreaming keels of
　　Greece

After her over the Ionian foam.

BURRUS.　Better an Emperor fooled than
　　Rome undone!

ACTE.　Though all unite to drive him to his
　　doom,

Yet I will not forsake him till he die.

　　　　　　　　　　　　　　[Exit ACTE.

[*Meanwhile there is an uneasy movement
　　among the* GIRLS, *as at the approach of
　　something sinister.* TIGELLINUS *enters,
　　gasping.*

TIGELLINUS. [*Looking after* ACTE.] She is

    a Christian!

BURRUS.   Tigellinus!

TIGELLINUS.   I

Come from the theatre. For three hours have

    sat

In the first bench, and feared to wink or cough.

The Emperor sang, and had for audience

The flower of Rome. In torment did we sit,

Nobles and consuls, captains, senators,

Bursting to laugh and aching but to smile.

Higher and higher rose the Emperor's voice,

But no man ventured to relax his lips.

And all around were those who peered or crept,

Inspecting each man's face, noting his look.

To sigh was treason and to laugh was death,

And yet none dared be absent: how were you

Excused?

   BURRUS.   I pleaded the old wound.

   SENECA.   And I

Reception of the Parthian and the Briton.

   TIGELLINUS.   I

Say not so much against his moody freaks,

But to be called from bed to hear him sing —

O, I must have my sleep at night — well, well —

To graver things.   Still the conspiracy

Of Agrippina swells: she aims to make

Her son a toy, a puppet, while she pulls

Unseen the secret strings of policy.

   SENECA.   Is't not enough to bear upon her

     back

Stripped continents?   To clasp about her throat

A civilisation in a sapphire, or

That kingdoms gleam and glow upon her
    brow.

Now doth she overstar us like the night

In splendour. Now she rises on our eyes

Dawning in gold; or like the blaze of noon

Taketh our breath on a sudden; or she glides

Silent, from head to foot a glimmering pearl.

But this is woman's business: 'tis not so

To listen screened to the ambassadors,

To ride abroad with Nero charioted,

Or wear her head upon the public coins.

   TIGELLINUS. And she intends this very day
    to hear

The Briton, seated by the Emperor's side.

Otho has joined her too.

SENECA.   But from what cause?

TIGELLINUS.   He is married.

BURRUS.   Ah, Poppaea!

TIGELLINUS.   Jealousy

Hath driven him into Agrippina's snare.

Fury at Nero's madness for his wife.

Now what if we could raise Poppaea up

As Agrippina's chief antagonist:

We match the mistress 'gainst the mother — pit

Passion 'gainst gratitude — a sudden lure

'Gainst old ascendency, the noon of beauty

Against the evening of authority,

The luring whisper 'gainst the pleading voice,

The hand that beckons 'gainst the arm that

    sways,

And set a woman to defeat a woman.

To Nero I have whispered that she dotes

Upon his poems, on his rhythm hangs

And cannot sleep for beauty of his verse.

SENECA. This day must Nero leave his
    mother's lap,

And stand up as an Emperor, and alone.

                              [*Trumpet.*

BURRUS. Hark! Caesar is returning.

> [*Sounds heard of* NERO *approaching amid
> cries of 'O thou Apollo!' 'Orpheus come
> again!' Then enter* NERO *with a group
> of satellites,* TIGELLINUS, OTHO, *and pro-
> fessional applauders and spies. His dress
> is of extreme oriental richness, and profuse
> in jewels: his hair elaborately curled. He
> carries an emerald eye-glass, and appears*

E

faint from the exertion of singing, from

which contest he has just come.

NERO.   This languor is the penalty the gods

Exact from those whom they have gifted high.

SENECA. [*Coming forward.*] Sir, late arrived

from Parthia and Britain —

NERO. [*Starting up.*] A draught!

[*Much hurry, zeal, and confusion among*

courtiers.

This kerchief closer round my throat!

[*They tie a kerchief round his throat.*

Was I in voice to-day?   The prize is won,

But I would be my own competitor

And my own rival.   Was I then in voice?

CHORUS.   O Memnon struck with morning,

nightingale,

Ghost-charming Orpheus, O Apollo — god!

SATELLITE. O Caesar, I am one who speaks

right out;

If it means death, yet must I speak the

truth.

Thy voice was harsh.

NERO. Was it so, friend?

SATELLITE. Harsh and uncertain. Had it

been another

Who sang, it would have ravished every ear,

But thee must I remember at thy best,

And what in others we count excellence

In thee we count a lapse, and falling off.

NERO. There's a good fellow!

SENECA. Caesar!

NERO. But a moment!

1ST SPY. [*Stealing forward.*] Licinius smiled,

   sir, at thy final note.

NERO. Nothing! an artist must bear ridicule.

Were I incensed, I were ridiculous

Myself.

   1ST SPY. Shall nothing then be done?

NERO.   Nothing!

2ND SPY. [*Stealing forward.*] Sir, Labienus,

   in thy second song

Coughed twice.

ANOTHER SPY. [*Cringing.*] Nay, Caesar,

   thrice.

2ND SPY. What punishment?

NERO. None! Interruption must I learn

   to bear.

What patience must we own who would excel!

Anger I never must permit myself,

Or ruffling littleness to this great soul.

   3RD SPY. [*Creeping forward.*] Sir, Titus

     Cassius yawned while thou didst sing.

   4TH SPY. Nay, Caesar, worse, he slept, and

     must he live?

   NERO. [*Gently.*] No! he must die: there

     is no hope in sleep.

Witness, you gods, who sent me on the earth

To be a joy to men: and witness you

Who stand around: if ever a small malice

Hath governed me: what critic have I feared?

What rival? Have I used this mighty throne

To baulk opinion or suppress dissent?

Have I not toiled for art, forsworn food, sleep,

And laboured day and night to win the crown,

Lying with weight of lead upon my chest?

Ye gods, there is no rancour in this soul.

                          [*Thunder.*

Silence while I am speaking. He must die,

Because he is unmindful of your gifts

And of the golden voice on me bestowed,

To me no credit; and he shall not die

Hopeless, for ere he die I'll sing to him

This night, that he may pass away in music.

How foolish will he peer amid the shades

When Orpheus asks, 'Hast thou heard Nero

    sing?'

If he must answer ' No !' I would not have him

Arrive ridiculous amid the dead.

    SENECA. Caesar, the Parthian and the

        British chiefs.

NERO. I cannot, sirs, so suddenly return

Unto life's dreary business, or descend

Out of the real to the unreal: from that

Which is to that which is not. Leave me still.

From art to empire is too swift a drop.

OTHO. Now what to do? Still drags the

o'erlong day.

We have driven, we have eaten, we have drunk.

But all the brilliance is a burden still.

ANICETUS. No cloud upon the noon of this

despair.

O for some edge, some thrill unknown!

LUCAN.   Remorse?

[NERO *shakes his head.*

SENECA. Jealousy then?

NERO.   No, no — we have outlived

All passions: terror now alone is left us.

I have within me great capacities

For terror: fear, the last, the greatest passion!

OTHO.   Can one rely on death for something

new?

Some other life perhaps.

SENECA.   The gods forbid!

The Power that sent us here would lead us there.

One sample is enough.

LUCAN.   Death's a dull business,

Of that one may be sure.   What says the poet?

'When I am dead, let fire devour the world.'

[NERO *starts at these words and comes among*

them.

NERO.   Nay, while I live!   The sight!   A

burning world!

And to be dead and miss it! There's an end

Of all satiety: such fire imagine!

Born in some obscure alley of the poor

Then leaping to embrace a splendid street,

Palaces, temples, morsels that but whet

Her appetite: the eating of huge forests:

Then with redoubled fury rushing high,

Smacking her lips over a continent,

And licking old civilisations up!

Then in tremendous battle fire and sea

Joined: and the ending of the mighty sea:

Then heaven in conflagration, stars like cinders

Falling in tempest: then the reeling poles

Crash: and the smouldering firmament subsides,

And last, this universe a single flame!

[OTHO, *seeing the steward and musician,*
who have entered, speaks.

OTHO. Nothing is left us but to eat and drink.

[*Takes bill of fare which the steward passes*
to him.

NERO.   The feast!

                    [*Takes bill of fare from* OTHO.

You understand that in the perfect feast

To please the palate only is not art,

But we should minister to the eye and the ear

With colour and with music.   Introduce

The embattled oysters with a melody

Of waves that wash a reef — whence do they
     come?

STEWARD.   From Britain, sir.

NERO.   Perhaps an angrier chord

Of island surf might be permitted then.

From Britain? Now I see thy uses, Britain.

Britain is justified: she gives us oysters,

And therefore Claudius invaded her.

Sausages upon silver gridirons?

   STEWARD.   Yes.

   NERO. Dormice with poppies and milk

      honey? There

A slumberous music, heavy lingering chords.

Ah! slices of pomegranate underneath.

Snow — purest snow of course.

   STEWARD.   'Twas not forgot.

   NERO. Then glorying peacocks: here a

      sounding march,

Something triumphal — even a trifle loud.

And, ah! the mullets! You remembered them?

STEWARD.   O Caesar, yes.

NERO.   Let these be introduced

By some low dirge.   And let us see them die —

Slow dying mullets within crystal bowls,

Dying from colour unto colour: now

Vermilion death-pangs fading into blue —

A scarlet agony in azure ending.

There we have colour! And at last the tongues

Of nightingales — the tongues of nightin-

      gales?

O, silence with the tongues of nightingales.

     [*He dismisses* STEWARD.]

TIGELLINUS.   Sir, grant us three a moment's

audience.

     [NERO *dismisses friends and satellites with*

      gesture.

SENECA. Your mother, sir, this very day

 intends

To hear the British chiefs in audience,

Sitting beside you. Know then that the

 world

Will not endure to have a woman's rule.

 BURRUS. No, nor the army.

 TIGELLINUS. And thy mother laughs

In public at thy verse.

 NERO. She has no ear.

I pity her — remember what she loses.

 TIGELLINUS. Ah, be not laughed at, sir, be

 it not said

Nero is tied unto his mother's robe.

Be brilliant, cruel, lustful, what you will,

But not a naughty child, rated and slapped.

Poppaea too, she will not suffer you

With her to indulge your fancy.

    SENECA.   Caesar, rise!

    BURRUS.   Rise — rise, and reign!

    TIGELLINUS.   And be no more a doll

That dances while she pulls the string be-

    hind.

Then young Britannicus!

    NERO.   O nothing!

    TIGELLINUS.   Yet

He is winning on the people: he hath charm,

His voice is sweet.

                        [NERO *starts.*

                Caesar, I judge it not,

But speak the common drift; and his re-

    cital,

So I am told, has for accompaniment

Gesture most eloquent.

[NERO *is more and more roused.*

His poems, too!

NERO.   [*Breaking the silence.*]   His poems!

Why, why, not a line will scan

To the true ear; and what variety,

I   ask   you   all — what   flow,   or   what   re-

source

Is shown?   A safe monotony of rhythm!

[*He paces to and fro angrily.*

TIGELLINUS.   Caesar, I cannot speak to such

a theme.

Merely Rome's mouthpiece.

NERO.   And his gesture, why,

'Tis of the Orient, and gesticulation

More happily were called; never a stillness,

Never repose, but one wild whirl of arms.

TIGELLINUS.   I spoke not of fulfilment, but

of promise,

The artist's dazzling future.

NERO.   A sweet voice!

Rome hath no critics! I would write a play

Lived there a single critic fit to judge it.

Whether a dancing girl kick high enough —

On this they can pronounce: this is their trade.

With verse upon the stage they cannot cope.

Too well they dine, too heavily, and bear

The undigested peacock to the stalls.

TIGELLINUS.   Should Agrippina on a sudden

change

Her front, and clasp hands with Britannicus?

NERO. Your words awaken in me a new
thirst.

SENECA. Sir, hear the Parthian and the
British chiefs.

NERO. [*Going to the throne.*] Summon them!

[*Exit* SENECA.

Think not, though my aim is art,
I cannot toy with empire easily.
The great in me does not preclude the less.

[*Re-enter* SENECA *with* PARTHIAN *and*
BRITISH AMBASSADORS, *followed by the*
Court. SENECA *brings forward the*
PARTHIAN CHIEFS, *when* AGRIPPINA
enters magnificently dressed and begins
to mount steps of throne. NERO *with*
courteous decision brings her down.

F

Mother, this is man's business, not for thee.

You jar the scheme of colour — mar the effect.

PARTHIAN. Caesar, we starve: all Parthia
    parches: all

Our crops sun-smitten bleach upon the plains.

We ask thy aid.

NERO.   And ye shall have my aid

Even to the fullest: further, I will open

The imperial granaries for your people's
    wants.

PARTHIAN. Caesar, we thank thee: and if
    ever thou

Shouldst need the Parthian aid, whate'er the
    cost

That aid thou shalt find ready at thy side.

                              [*Exit.*

BRITISH CHIEF. Caesar, the tax that thou
   hast laid on us
Remit, we pray thee, else we rise in arms
And will abide thy battle.

NERO.   So! You dream
That Caesar being merciful is weak.
I who can succour, I can strike; I'll
   launch
The legions over sea, and I myself
Will lead them, and the eagles will unloose
Through Britain — I who sit on the world's
   throne
Will have no threatening from Briton, Gaul,
People or tribe inland or ocean-washed.
The terror of this purple I maintain.
You are dismissed.

[NERO, *spreading his hands, dismisses the Court, and comes down to his mother.*

NERO.   Now, mother!

AGRIPPINA.   I will speak

With you alone, not compassed by these men.

[*To* SENECA *and* BURRUS.] To me you owe the height where now you stand.

Who took you, schoolmaster, from exile? Who

Unstewarded you, Burrus? If I have made,

I can unmake — Now leave me with my son.

[*To* TIGELLINUS.] You are self-made. Gods!

I'd no hand in that!

[*Exeunt* SENECA, BURRUS, *and* TIGELLINUS.]

Nero, have you forgot who set you there?

NERO. Not while I hear it twenty times a
day.

AGRIPPINA. You should not need that I
remind you of it.

NERO. A kindness harped on grows an
injury.

AGRIPPINA. Are you the babe that lay upon
my breast?

NERO. I was: but I would not lie there for
ever.

AGRIPPINA. Have I not reared you, tended
you, and loved you?

NERO. Yes, but to be your puppet and your
toy.

AGRIPPINA. Boy, never since I first looked
on the sun

From man or woman had I insolence,

Who have sistered, wived, and mothered
Emperors.

NERO. I speak no insolence — you weary
me!

AGRIPPINA. Gods! you have hit on a new
thing to tell me.

[*Coming to him.*] Does your heart beat? Are
you all ice and pose?

Has nothing gripped you — is there aught to
grip

In you, pert shadow. Have you e'er shed
tears?

NERO. For legendary sorrows I can weep:
With those of old time I have suffered much,
And I, for dreams, am capable of tears;

But not for woe too near me — and too

loud.

AGRIPPINA.   O wall of stone 'gainst which I

beat in vain!

Nero, I will do much to win you back

For your own sake: and though it hurts me

sore,

Your passion for Poppaea I will aid.

When did a mother yield herself to this?

NERO.   When had a mother such a lust for

rule

That she could even yield herself to this?

AGRIPPINA.   [*Clasping his knees.*]   Child, I

have done with scorn, with bitter words,

With taunt, with gibe. Now I ask only

pity —

A little pity from flesh that I conceived,

A little mercy from the body I bore,

And touches from the baby hands I kissed.

Nothing I ask of you, only to love me,

And if not that, to bear with me a while,

Who have borne much for you: no, Nero, child,

I will not weary you, I yearn for you.

Forgive me all the deeds that I have done for you,

Forget the great love I have spent on you,

Pardon the long, long, life for you endured.

[NERO *is moved and kisses her, then speaks*
with effort.

NERO. Mother, if I have seemed to be forgetful,

Or cruel even, impute it not to me

But to the State.

                              [AGRIPPINA *starts.*

                    'Tis thought that neither Rome,

The provinces, nor armies, will endure

To see a woman in such eminence.

Therefore, it is advised that you retire

To Antium a while, and leave Rome free.

    AGRIPPINA. [*Starting up.*] Leave Rome!

    Why, I would die as I did step

Outside her gates, and glide henceforth a

    shadow.

The blood would cease to run in my veins, my

    heart

Stop, and my breath subside without her

    walls.

All without Rome is darkness: you will not

Despatch my shadow down to Antium?

   NERO. We were remembering your toils,

     your age.

   AGRIPPINA. My age! Am I old then?

     Look on this face,

Where am I scarred, who have steered the bark

     of State

As it plunged, as it rose over the waves of

     change?

I was renewed with salt of such a sea.

Empires and Emperors I have outlived;

A thousand loves and lusts have left no line;

Tremendous fortunes have not touched my hair,

Murder hath left my cheek as the cheek of a

     babe.

[*At this moment* BURRUS, SENECA, *and*
    TIGELLINUS *return, hearing the scene;*
    and as AGRIPPINA *continues her impre-*
    cations, the COURT *return and stand in*
    groups listening.

AGRIPPINA.   My age! Who then accuses
    me of age?
Was this a flash from budding Seneca,
Or the boy Burrus' inspiration? Say?
Do I owe it to the shrivelled or the maimed?

SENECA. Empress, it is determined you retire.
And you will better your own dignity
And his assert, if you will make this going
To seem a free inclining from yourself.

AGRIPPINA.   Bookman, shall I learn policy
    from you?

Be patient with me.   Nero, you I ask,

Not schoolmasters or stewards I promoted.

Is it your will I go to Antium?

Speak, speak.   Be not the mouthpiece of these

    men:

Domitius!

  NERO.   Mother, 'tis my will you go.

  AGRIPPINA.   Then, sir, discharge me not

    from your employ

Without some written commendation

That I can tire the hair or pare the nails,

That those who were my friends may take me

    in!

  NERO.   Lady!

  AGRIPPINA.   O, lady now?   Mother, no

    more!

NERO. [*Pacing fiercely to and fro.*] Beware

the son you bore: look lest I turn!

Chafe not too far the master of this world.

AGRIPPINA. See the new tiger in the dancer's

eye:

'Ware of him, keepers — then, you bid me go?

[*A pause.*

Then I will go. But think not, though I

go,

My spirit shall not pace the palace still.

I am too bound by guilt unto these walls.

Still shall you hear a step in dead of night;

In stillness the long rustle of my robe.

So long as stand these walls I cannot leave them.

Yet will I go: behold you, that stand by,

A mother by her own son thrust away,

Cast out — ha, ha ! — in my old age, infirm,

To totter and mumble in oblivion !

NERO. [*To* SENECA *and* BURRUS.]   A little

violent that — did you not think so?

And yet the gesture excellent and strong !

AGRIPPINA.   Romans, behold this son: the

man of men ;

This harp-player, this actor, this buffoon —

NERO.   Peace !

AGRIPPINA.   — sitting where great Jul-

ius but aspired

To sit, and died in the aspiring: see,

This mime — my son is he ?   And did I then

Have one mad moment with a street musi-

cian ?

SENECA.   Have you no shame ?

AGRIPPINA.   This son

now sends me forth,

Yet it was I, his mother, set him there.

                              [*Murmur.*

And, ah! if it were known at what a price,

Witness, you shades of the Silani!

SENECA.   Peace!

AGRIPPINA.   And witness Messalina on vain

knees!

                              [*Murmur.*

And witness Claudius with the envenomed cup.

NERO.   Silence, or ——

AGRIPPINA.   Not the seas shall stop me

now,

Raging on all the shores of all the world.

Witness if easily my son did reign,

I am bloody from head to foot for sake of him,

And for my cub am I incarnadined.

[*Murmur.*

I'll go, but if I fall, Rome too shall fall:

I'll shake this empire till it reel and crash

On that ungrateful head; and if I fall,

The builded world shall tumble down in thun-

der.

[*Murmur.*

Ah!

[*Seeing* BRITANNICUS.] To my arms, boy!

[*Snatches him to her side.*] Tremble now and

shake!

Here is the true heir to the imperial throne,

Deposed by me, but now by me restored.

[*Uproar.*

I'll to the Praetorians!

[*Clamour.*

To the camp!

And there upon the one side they shall see

Britannicus the child of Claudius,

And me the daughter of Germanicus;

And on the other side a harp-player,

A withered pedant, and a maimèd sergeant,

Disputing for the diadem of the earth.

Come, Caesar, away to the Praetorians!

[*Exit* AGRIPPINA *leading* BRITANNICUS,

followed by COURT *in great excitement,*

all but BURRUS *and* SENECA, TIGELLI-

NUS *and* NERO — *a blank pause.*

SENECA.   How what to do?

TIGELLINUS.   Already can I hear

The roar of the Praetorians and their march,
This time to crown another. Burrus, you
Command them.

BURRUS.   They would tear me into pieces,
As hounds a master entering in on them
Unrecognised, if Agrippina once
Halloed to them the name 'Germanicus.'

TIGELLINUS. Surely Britannicus must be
    our aim:
He gone, what threat, what counter-move hath
    she?
Removing him, we take the sting from her;
Then let her buzz at will.

BURRUS.   But he is gone.

SENECA. Even as an eagle snatches up a babe,
So Agrippina caught him up and flew.

TIGELLINUS.   For once my wits are lost.

SENECA.   Still, what to do?

[NERO *has been sitting with his back to them, suddenly rises.*

NERO.   Leave this to me!

TIGELLINUS.   O Caesar!

NERO.   [*To* ANICETUS.]   Go thou fast
And intercept my mother on her way,
And say thou thus: 'Nero thy son repents
His former ire and cancels the decree
For Antium; and prays thou may'st return
To supper, as a sign of amity,
And bring with thee the prince Britannicus.'

[ANICETUS *is going, but* NERO *stops him.*
And as you go, send in to me Locusta.

[*Exit* ANICETUS.

I have conceived — not fully — but conceived

The death-scene of the boy Britannicus.

Leave this to me.

TIGELLINUS.　　　O Caesar!

NERO.　　　　　　　　　　　It shall be

Performed to-night at supper: get you seats;

It shall be something new and wonderful,

Done after wine, and under falling roses;

And there shall be suspense in it, and thrill:

It shall be very sudden, very silent,

And terrible in silence — I the while,

Creator and arranger of the scene,

Reclining with a jewel in my eye;

And Agrippina shall be close to me,

Aware, yet motionless: Octavia,

Though but a child, yet too discreet for tears.

This you may deem as yet a little crude,

But other details I will add ere supper.

> [SENECA *withdraws in horror, as do the*
> *others, slowly.*

SENECA.   Here's what I feared!

TIGELLINUS.   His eyes now!   Yet how calm!

So steals the panther, stirring not a leaf!

> [*Exeunt slowly* SENECA, TIGELLINUS, *and*
> BURRUS.   NERO *walks to and fro, con-*
> *structing the scene in pantomime to him-*
> *self.*   LOCUSTA *enters down, right.*

NERO.   You are Locusta, and your trade is
poison.

> [*She makes obeisance.*

[*Uneasily.*]   Is poison but a trade with you, or
art?

Surely to slay is the supreme of arts;

And with no ugly wound or hideous blow,

But beautifully to extinguish life.

Have you some rare drug that kills suddenly?

As I have planned it, I can have no pause —

Death must be sudden — silent. And my
    guests

Must not be wearied with a pang prolonged,

And there must be no cry. That understand.

       [LOCUSTA, *grovelling at his feet.*

LOCUSTA.   O Caesar, such a drug is known
    to me, —

But I will not reveal it.

NERO.   Die then.

LOCUSTA.   Die?

O, I love life, but this I'll not reveal.

NERO. Ah, you must live — you are an
artist too.

LOCUSTA. I have a poison that is slipped in
wine —

Not nauseous to the taste.

NERO.   An artist still!

Let me have that, and suddenly. And listen —

The cup presented to Britannicus

Must be too hot: so that he calls for snow

To cool it. In that snow the poison lurks.

                  [*Exit* LOCUSTA.

                  [ANICETUS *hastily returns.*

ANICETUS. O Caesar, the Augusta had not
left

The palace; and now, o'erjoyous at thy
words,

She will be present at the supper-board,

Bringing with her the prince Britannicus.

> [*Servants enter with various dishes and arrange the tables and couches for the guests, and supper begins.*
>
> [*They all recline amid a low hum of conversation. Dreamy music is heard, which might be a continuation of the music played before.* NERO *reclines at the head of the central table between* AGRIPPINA *and* OCTAVIA. POPPAEA *is a prominent figure.* BRITANNICUS, *with other youths, lies at a side table.* SENECA, BURRUS, *and* TIGELLINUS *present with other members of the Court. At a sign from* NERO *dancing girls enter and per-*

form a strange, wild measure, after

which the hum of conversation is re-

sumed.   Again, at a sign from NERO,

odours are spurted over the guests amid

cries of delight.

[*At a sign from* NERO, *flowers descend*

from the ceiling.   At first lilies, then

of deeper and deeper colour.   At last

a tempest of roses which gradually

slackens.

NERO.   Britannicus, I voice a general wish.

Sweet is it, early and thus easily

To have garnered fame: the crown is for the

    few,

And these are tasked to reach it ere they

    die.

Oftener the laurel on grey hairs is laid,

Or on the combèd tresses of the dead.

> [BRITANNICUS *goes to the top of the stairs*
>
> *to recite, and at a sign from* NERO *wine*
>
> *is handed to him.*

BRITANNICUS. This is too hot: some snow

to cool it: so —

> [*Cold snow is put in and he drinks. He*
>
> *then recites.*

Beside the melancholy surge I roam —

A sad exile, a stranger, sick for home:

A prince I was in my far native land

Who wander to and fro this alien sand:

Riches I had, and steeds, a glimmering crown;

Never had known a harshness or a frown.

Now must I limp and beg from door to door,

Wet with the storm, or in the sun footsore:

I, by a brother's cunning dispossessed,

Crave for these languid limbs a place of rest.

Pity me, robbed of all!

> [*He gives a cry and falls headlong. His
> limbs quiver a moment and then are still.
> Meanwhile the shower of roses has
> slackened. There is a dead silence, and
> in the silence slowly all the guests turn
> and look at* NERO, *who rises, with the
> emerald in his eye.*

NERO.   Lift up the prince and bear him to
his room.

I do entreat that none of you will stir

Or rise perturbed: my brother, since his
birth,

Was ever thus: the fit will pass from him.

Refill the cups: proceed we with the feast!

> [*There is an attempt to renew the feasting,
> but soon a scene of uproar and confusion
> arises, and the guests leave the tables in
> alarm.*

> [AGRIPPINA *alone remains unmoved, and
> then, as the guests have departed in dis-
> order, she confronts* NERO *alone.*

AGRIPPINA. Thou hast done this.

NERO. Mother, I am thy son!

ACT III

SCENE I

SCENE. - - NERO'S *private chamber.* *Enter* NERO *hastily and perturbed, followed by* SENECA, BURRUS, *and* TIGELLINUS, *his privy-councillors.*

BURRUS.   Caesar, still glides the dead Britannicus

About the palace, and his memory

Your mother, Agrippina, uses: makes

Out of his ghost a faction for herself.

She grows a public peril; much you owe

To her, but more to Rome; from Antium

She rages disappointed to and fro.

Me for your army you hold answerable,

But can no longer if you suffer her

To lure the legions from their loyalty.

Her creatures whisper to your sentinels,

Corrupt your officers, inflame your guards.

A sullen silence on the camp has fallen,

A word, and it will roar in mutiny.

TIGELLINUS.   Everywhere steal her agents

    and her spies,

Gliding through temples, baths, and theatres;

Possess all angles, corners, noonday halts,

And darknesses; they flit with casual poison

Softly; the city secretly is filled

With murmurs, lifted eyebrows, and with sighs.

The mischief's in the very blood of Rome

Unless the sore that feeds it is cut out.

NERO. Why, I myself have visited the
　　fleet

With Anicetus: sullen droop the sails

Or flap in mutiny against the mast.

Burdened with barnacles the untarred keels,

Drowse on the tide with parching decks un-
　　swabbed,

And anchors rusting on inglorious ooze.

All indolent the vast armada tilts,

A leafless resurrection of dead trees.

The sailors in a dream do go about

Or at the fo'c'sle ominously meet.

Should any foe upon the sea-line loom

They'll light with ease upon an idle prey.

And yet I felt the grandeur of stagnation

And the magnificence of idleness.

H

BURRUS. She hath seduced the breast-plates
and the sails.

NERO. [*Distracted.*] Here I pronounce her
exile.

TIGELLINUS.   Whither then?

ANICETUS. To Britain send her. There for
Claudius
I fought; a melancholy isle, alone,
Sundered from all the world; and banned by
God
With separating, cold, religious wave,
And haunted with the ghost of a dead sun
Rising as from a grave, or all in blood
Returning wounded heavily through mist.
Her rotting peoples amid forests cower,
Or mad for colour paint their bodies blue.

There in eternal drippings of the leaf

Or that dead summer of the living fly,

And by the eternal sadness of the surf,

Ambition cannot live, hope cannot breathe.

Even the fieriest spirit there will rust

Or gutter like a candle in the rain.

To Britain send her.

   TIGELLINUS.   Never isle remote

On the sad water, never desert sand

In trembling flame, nor rock-built prison-house

Shall tame her: there's the danger, that she

   lives.

While she hath life, it is no matter where,

While she hath breath, no other dares to

   breathe,

Not Caesar, even!

NERO. This breath to her I owe.

TIGELLINUS. [*Cautiously and slowly watching* NERO, *as do the others.*] Caesar, there
is a region of exile

Whence none hath yet returned — your pardon, sir —

NERO. [*Starts and turns away.*] No, no,
no! I remember very clear

How gently she would wake me long ago.

BURRUS. Then be thy mother's son still and
surrender

This toy of Rome to her: she bought it you:

Now, wearied, give it back!

NERO. Ah, patience, sir!

I cannot in one moment gird myself

To murder all these kisses, and she hath

A vastness in this narrow world so rare,

A sweep majestical about the earth —

True, that she hath no ear for verse ——

TIGELLINUS. For thine.

NERO. Yet passion, fury, and ambition, these

Are primal things in our elaborate age.

Ill can we spare them.

BURRUS. Now, 'tis you or she.

NERO. A little time in which to fix my
mind.

I go to Baiae; for I am not housed

Here as I should be: all the palace seems

To me a hovel; scarcely can I breathe.

I should be roofed with gold, and walled with
gold,

Should tread on gold; and if I cast mine eyes

Over the city, they should view a scene

Of spacious avenues and breathing trees,

And buildings plunged in odorous foliage.

This is a petty city: I have thought

It might be well to raze it to the ground

And build another and an ampler Rome,

More worthy site for this imperial soul.

I'll go to Baiae, there to dream this dream.

   TIGELLINUS.   Might I propose you go not all

    alone?

At times the answering flash from other

    eyes

Can aid the mightiest; and a woman's

    thought ——

   NERO.   Yes — Yes — Poppaea!

   BURRUS.   Otho will be jealous.

TIGELLINUS. And is already dangerous; he

  has joined

The Agrippina faction.

NERO.   He must be

Promoted then to — Lusitania.

TIGELLINUS. Thule were safer — still.

NERO.   Here I appoint him

Sole governor of Lusitania.

To Baiae now — Poppaea — a new Rome!

       [*Exit* NERO.

TIGELLINUS. He hesitates — but I will see

  Poppaea:

She can find means we cannot, and we thus

Can use her beauty for our policy.

  [*Exeunt* TIGELLINUS, BURRUS, SENECA, *and*

    ANICETUS.

SCENE II

Scene. — The tiring chamber of POPPAEA *— signs of luxury, implements of a Roman lady's toilet of the period.* POPPAEA *reclining, with a single maid.*

POPPAEA. Myrrha, more gold upon these builded curls.

How often, child?

MYRRHA.   Mistress, forgive me.

[*A slave has entered.*

POPPAEA.   Well?

SLAVE. Mistress, the Emperor's minister, Tigellinus.

[POPPAEA *signs* MYRRHA *to go.*

Enter TIGELLINUS

TIGELLINUS. Lady, I am loth to interrupt this toil,

But come on a secret errand.

POPPAEA. Well, what is it?

TIGELLINUS. Long have I watched you, and to me it seemed

You had some mighty wish within your soul

As yet unspoken? Ah, I know it well.

You would climb high, even to the very height?

POPPAEA. [*Rising.*] I would.

TIGELLINUS. You would be — mistress of the world?

POPPAEA. Ah!

TIGELLINUS.   And shall be: we aim at the
same goal.

You from ambition, I from policy.

POPPAEA.   Speak clearer.

TIGELLINUS.   'Tis our wish to free young
Nero

From Agrippina's dangerous dominance —

To free him of her quite.   Now she too stands

In your own path.   Your loveliness may
work

Upon him: and we with policy the while —

Will you make cause with us?

POPPAEA.   I understand.

You need this beauty as an added bait

To lure when policy can drive him not.

What do I gain at last?

TIGELLINUS.   The throne itself.

Octavia is a shadow: cannot stand

Between you and the world: but Agrippina,

Never will suffer you while she has breath.

POPPAEA.   I will not tempt him to a mother's

murder.

TIGELLINUS.   Nor do we ask it: only that

you draw

His wandering fancy from her with a sweet

Interposition of this loveliness,

Free him of her, then bind him to yourself.

POPPAEA.   I will attempt it.   I will fly at it.

I go to him to Baiae this same day.

TIGELLINUS.   Remember all the earth is in

thy reach.

[*Exit* TIGELLINUS.]

POPPAEA *claps her hands — enter various maids*

POPPAEA.   Lorilla, see, this henna is o'erdone.

LORILLA.   O pardon, mistress.

POPPAEA.   And you, Lalage,
My lips more brilliant.

LALAGE.   Yet ——

POPPAEA.   Remember, child,
That I walk ever veiled: what in the sun
Glares, being veiled a finer richness takes
And more provokes: how many struggling flies
This veil, the web of mine, hath struggling held
Which else were freed!

                    [*Gazing at her face in mirror.*
                    Ah! this left eyebrow — who?
Who painted this?

MAID. [*Trembling.*] I, madam.

POPPAEA.   You are young:

Else I would have you stripped and lashed till
  blood

Flew from you.

MAID.   Mercy!

POPPAEA.   Call old Lydia.

Lydia, this eyebrow — the old touch.

LYDIA   My hands

Tremble, but I'll essay.

POPPAEA. [*Gazing in mirror.*] So—that is well.

Children, when there shall come, and come
  there must,

The smallest marring wrinkle on this face,

And come there must — our bodies fall like
  flowers,

This face shall feel the ruin of the rose —

When time, howe'er light, shall touch this
    cheek,

Then quick farewell! Listen, I will not live

Less lovely, nor this cruel beauty lose,

And I perforce grow kind: I'll not survive

The deep delicious poison of a smile

Nor mortal music of the sighing bosom

That slowly overcomes the fainting brain.

It shall not dawdle downward to the grave;

I'll pass upon the instant of perfection.

No woman shall behold Poppaea fade:

And now to Baiae!

    Myrrha.   Thence the Emperor

Hath sent three messengers already.

    Poppaea.   Ah!

Blue Baiae, warm beside a sparkling sea

Where I will win young Nero — and the world!

Enter OTHO *hastily*

OTHO. The Emperor hath sent three mes-

sengers

Demanding you for Baiae: yet am I

Not asked: what means this lonely summons,

wife?

POPPAEA. Can you not trust me?

OTHO.   When I gaze on you,

Yes — when your voice is murmuring at my

ear,

Yes — but at times when I am pressed by

crowds

Or yearn alone beside the breaking wave ——

POPPAEA. Will you not trust me? Why
then do I go?

Is't for myself? You know well — 'tis for
you;

To praise the Emperor's verses — but for you;

To applaud his feeblest gesture — but for you;

To coax from him a kingdom — but for you!

Yet are you angered.

OTHO.   'Tis a perilous game.

Nero may ask more of your loveliness.

POPPAEA.   A woman may surrender inch by
inch

Even to the edge of shame: then sudden rise

Unmelting ice.

OTHO.   Poppaea, I like it not.

POPPAEA.   All is for you.

Enter an OFFICER *with* ATTENDANTS

OFFICER.   Sir, from the Emperor.

Thus Caesar saith: 'Hereby do we decree

Otho, our bosom's friend, sole governor

Of Lusitania: with imperial leave

Whom to appoint, dismiss: all revenues

In his control: thither let him proceed

To-morrow ere sunset.'

    OTHO. [*Looking at* POPPAEA, *then turning*

    to OFFICER.] I shall obey

             [*Exit* OFFICER *and* OTHERS.

Dismiss the slaves.

    POPPAEA.   Otho, I swear ——

    OTHO.   Dismiss them.

    POPPAEA. Myrrha, stay by me! On my

    knees I swear ——

I

OTHO. Stand up! You knew this?

POPPAEA. Dear, I never could ——

OTHO. [*Taking her by the arm.*] You go to

    Baiae into Caesar's arms.

I am — promoted — to the ends of the

    earth,

Anywhere, anywhere, so I be not there

To interrupt.

    [*He throws her from him — snatches his*

      dagger.

POPPAEA. Kill me then if you will.

Here — here! I will not flinch, so I die true.

You'll not suspect my corpse.

    OTHO. It has been planned,

Thought out, and timed — for in his deepest

    plot

Our Nero has an eye for drama still.

He hath imagined that which now we act.

POPPAEA. Kill me — I love you! Ere you

strike, one kiss.

OTHO. Ah! [*Recoiling.*]

POPPAEA. But one kiss — a kiss of olden

days,

When we two were most happy: Caesar was

not,

And you had laughed at him! A harp-player,

But not my man, my Otho! Think you I

Who have had these arms about me, and these

lips

Burn up my own, could languish for a mime?

I am a child — I have done wrong — forgive

it —

I sighed for thy advancement — speak to me!

Now slap my hands or send me to my bed,

I am a baby in these deep affairs.

    OTHO. Go not to Baiae then: depart with
      me

To Lusitania; words I'll count no more,

But deeds — to Lusitania, come with me.

    POPPAEA. Is it wise to disobey — is it wise,
      I ask?

Set me aside, be mindful of yourself.

    OTHO. So you'll not come?

    POPPAEA.   For you alone I linger.

I'll tarry but a little while behind you,

And when I come, I'll greet you full of riches.

    OTHO. I dread to leave you in your love-
      liness.

POPPAEA. Then I'll not go with you.

OTHO. You will not — Why?

POPPAEA. Because you will not trust me.

Show to me

That you can trust me, Otho; and what joy,

What satisfaction can you have to drag

Your wife behind you, from dull jealousy

Because you do not dare leave her behind

For fear — I'll not be such a wife.

OTHO. Poppaea,

No more I'll ask you to depart with me,

I'll go alone: but this remember still —

Gay have I been, a spendthrift and an idler,

A brilliant fly that buzzed about the bloom.

But I had that in me deep down, and still,

Of which you, you alone, possess the key,

A sullen nobleness to you disclosed

E'en then with shame: and by no other
  guessed.

This you well know: betray not that at least;

For even the lightest woman here is scared,

And dreads to dabble deeper in the soul.

We have no children.

  POPPAEA. [*Coming to him and putting up
  her face.*]   Am I not child enough

Who should be woman?   You shall kiss these
  lips

Once ere you go — so close they are to you.

  OTHO.   The gods laugh out at me — but I
  must kiss you.

  POPPAEA.   Can I not help your preparation?

OTHO.   No.

I shall not go with pomp; but as a soldier.

POPPAEA.   I think you are still angry?

OTHO.   No! Farewell,

I have brief time.

POPPAEA.   Ah! take me with you, then.

OTHO.   What! You will come?

POPPAEA.   I wish — I wish 'twere wise.

My love shall bear your litter all the way.

> [*Exit* OTHO *hastily*.

Re-enter MAID

MAID.   Has he gone, lady? Had I such a
man

I could not let him part thus, not for
Caesar.

POPPAEA.   For Caesar!   No: but Caesar
means the world!

For Baiae!   The new gold-dust!

MAID.   Here, I have it.

POPPAEA.   Bear it yourself — entrust it to no
other.

[*Exeunt.*

SCENE III

NERO'S PRIVATE CHAMBER *in the villa at Baiae,
looking directly upon the bay. Left, doors
leading into the apartments. The water laps
close up to the marble quay or terrace on which
the action takes place. Right are seen prows
of galleys at their moorings. Beyond is the
curving shore of the bay, crowded with
villas and temples. The scene is of extreme
southern richness and serenity. Time
noon.*

⌐NERO *is pacing restlessly to and fro. Enter a
servant.*

NERO. The lady Poppaea! Is she yet
arrived?

SERVANT. Sir, an hour since.

NERO. [*Impatiently.*] Then why is she not
here? [*Exit* SERVANT.

An hour since: yet she lingers while I ache

With passion. She comes not, still she delays.

To fly to her? No, 'twere unworthy of me —

And yet, and yet — Ah! I must go to her.

Enter slaves bearing POPPAEA *on litter*

POPPAEA. [*Standing aloof and veiled.*]
Caesar, by thee thrice summoned, I am
here.

What is your will?

NERO. To have you at my side.

POPPAEA. Caesar, I am thy subject, and
   obeyed
Unwillingly.

NERO.   Unwillingly?

POPPAEA.   I come
In loyalty: what service can I render?
If none, then suffer me now to depart.
I tremble to be seen with thee alone;
No whisper yet has touched me.

NERO.   So you come,
But out of loyalty.

POPPAEA.   As fits thy subject.

NERO. No, I am thine!

POPPAEA.   Caesar, I will not hear,
I must not if I would — that you know well.

NERO. You come in cold obedience?

POPPAEA.   I have said so.
Yet ——

NERO. [*Eagerly.*] Well — well ——

POPPAEA.   Nero — nay, Caesar — my
lord.

NERO. Nero, I'd have you say.

POPPAEA.   That slipped from me —
Is't treason? I know nothing of the laws.

NERO. You come because thrice summoned?

POPPAEA.   In my mind
There lurked another reason for my coming.

NERO. What then?

POPPAEA.   A thought that like a
captive bird

I have kept warm about my heart so long

I am loth to let it fly forth to the cold.

NERO. [*Approaching her.*] Tell me this

thought.

POPPAEA.   Then, Caesar, I have long

Brooded upon the music of thy verse.

It doth beset me — and, O pardon me,

If, little fool that I am, I longed to speak

But once alone with him who made it. Now,

What have I said? I will return forth-

with.

NERO. O not thy beauty moves me but thy

mind!

POPPAEA. I think I have some little ear for

verse.

There is one line ——

NERO.　　　Yes — yes ——

POPPAEA.　　　　　Of burning Troy —

'O city amorous red, thou flagrant rose' ——

NERO. A regal verse! But the arm extended thus

Toward doomed Ilium. Say on.

POPPAEA.　　　　　My eyes
Are filled with tears.

NERO.　　　Remove thy veil and weep.

POPPAEA. [*Starting back.*] For no man —
save my husband — O my lord!

He is despatched to Lusitania.

NERO. Know you not why?

POPPAEA.　　　I know not — cannot guess.

NERO. That he might stand no more between us two.

POPPAEA. O sir, he is my husband, and
   my way
Is with him wheresoe'er he go. My duty ——
   NERO. But your inclining?
   POPPAEA.   That I will not say.
But Lusitania is henceforth my home.
Nero, I will speak truth: I'll not deny
There is some strange communion of the soul
'Twixt you and me: but I'll not yield to
   this,
No, nor shall you compel me, Caesar: I
Will follow Otho even to banishment.
There are more sacred things in my regard
Than mutual pleasure from melodious verse.
   NERO. Nothing, when soul meets soul
   without alloy.

POPPAEA. I fear you do forget I am a
woman.

Dear to us before all are household cares.

NERO. O to the average, not to thee.

POPPAEA.   Farewell!

NERO. You shall not go thus.

POPPAEA.   Caesar, chain me here,
But in neglected duty I shall pine.

NERO. [*Angrily striding to and fro.*] Ah!

POPPAEA. And imagine that he did not
live —

That I were free to indulge this panting soul —

Still there are bars between us none can break.

NERO. You mean my wife Octavia?

POPPAEA.   Well — and yet
Not she, perhaps.

NERO.   Who then?   What other bars?

POPPAEA.   Your mother Agrippina.

NERO.   Still my mother!

POPPAEA.   She would not bear it: would

command her son

To leave me: a younger woman has no hope

Against her.

NERO.   I am not her lackey.

POPPAEA.   No?

Ah, but her child, and born but to obey.

And yet though wiser, mightier, than my-

self,

You shall not find in her a listener

So still, so answerable to your mood.

And, I will say it, you'll not find in her

One who has dived so deep into your soul,

K

Who sees — I cannot flatter — sees that great-
    ness

Which she too long keeps under: were I you

I would be Caesar, spite of twenty mothers,

And seem the mighty poet that I am.

I'll go.

   NERO.   You madden me ——

   POPPAEA.   Farewell again.

   NERO.   Poppaea, go not, go not.   All the
    east

Burns in me, and the desert fires my blood.

I parch, I pine for you.   My body is sand

That thirsts.   I die, I perish of this thirst,

To slake it at your lips!   You madden me.

     [*He seizes her cloak and she stands re-
       vealed.*

Goddess! What shall I give thee great
    enough?

I'll give thee Rome — I'll give thee this great
    world,

And all the builded empire as a toy.

The Mediterranean shall thy mirror be,

Thy jewels all sparkling stars of heaven.

The orb of the earth — throw it on thy lap

But for a kiss — one kiss!

POPPAEA.   But Agrippina?

NERO.   Agrippina?

POPPAEA.   No — I'll not think of it!

I'll have no violence for my sake com-
    mitted.

If by some chance unlooked for she should
    die,

If in some far, far time she should succumb

To creeping age — then ——

NERO.　　　　　　　　　　Then?

Enter MESSENGER *hurriedly*

MESSENGER.　　　　Sir, urgent business —
The State demands you.

NERO.　[*Furiously.*]　　　Pah! — the State!

POPPAEA.　　　　　　　　O Nero!
Remember first the State — me afterward!

NERO.　Empress!

　　　　　　　　　　　　[*He leads her out.*

　　[*He returns and stands as in a dream while
　　　the* COUNCILLORS *enter.*

BURRUS.　　　How long?　How long, sir?

Agrippina

Is drawing to her net the dregs of Rome,

Makes mutinous the rabble and the scum.

[NERO *makes weary gesture.*

SENECA. And, sir, she has not scrupled to

enroll

The ragged, shrieking Christians, who wash not,

The refuse of the empire, all that flows

To this main sewer of Rome she counts upon.

TIGELLINUS. [*Stealing forward.*] And, sir,

if these things move you not — a letter.

NERO. [*Reading.*] ' I, Agrippina, daugh-

ter of Germanicus, of Claudius widow, of

Nero mother, hereby do declare that though

I have sat tame under private injuries, I will

not forgo my public privileges, nor consent

to be banished from high festival or ceremony. I purpose then to be present at Baiae

at Minerva's feast, together with the Emperor,

and will hold no second place. This is my

ancient right and to that right I cleave.

'The Augusta.'

Seneca. This is her ultimate audacity.

Tigellinus. And this our utmost oppor-

tunity.

Nero. Sirs, seeing that the State demands

this life,

Seeing that I must choose 'twixt her and Rome,

I do consent to Agrippina's death.

The State like Nature must be pitiless,

And I must ruthless be as Nature's Lord.

But I'll be no Orestes, I'll not lift

This hand against her: see you then to that!

It is enough to have conceived this deed.

The how, the when, the where, I leave to you.

TIGELLINUS.   She is delivered now into our

hands,

And runs into the toils we had not set.

In Baiae no Praetorians are camped,

No populace inflamèd in her cause;

A solitary woman doth she come.

Caesar, receive her graciously and well.

Smile all distrust away and speak her soft,

While we devise for her a noiseless doom.

ANICETUS.   Caesar, a sudden thought hath

come to me.

A pleasure pinnace lies in Baiae Bay

Built for thyself: on this let her return

In the deep night after Minerva's feast,

Or supper given in sign of amity.

I will contrive a roof weighted with lead

Over the couch whereon she will recline.

Once in deep water at a signal given

The roof shall fall: and with a leak prepared

The ship shall sink and plunge her in the waves.

In that uncertain water what may chance?

What may not? To the elements this deed

Will be imputed, to a casual gust

Or striking squall upon the moody deep.

NERO. Wonderful! This gives beauty to

an act

Which else were ugly and of me unworthy.

So mighty is she that her proper doom

Could come but by some elemental aid.

Her splendid trouble asketh but the sea

For sepulchre: her spirit limitless

A multitudinous and roaring grave.

Here's nothing sordid, nothing vulgar. I

Consign her to the uproar whence she came.

Be the crime vast enough it seems not crime.

I, as befits me, call on great allies.

I make a compact with the elements.

And here my agents are the very winds,

The waves my servants, and the night my

    friend.

  BURRUS. Suppose the night be clear, with

    a bright moon,

A calm sea.

  NERO.   On the moon I can rely.

Last night I wrote to her a glimmering verse;

She is white with a wan passion for my lips.

The moon will succour me.   Depart from me —

Trouble me not with human faces now.

[*Exeunt* COUNCILLORS.

[*Meanwhile* POPPAEA *appears behind in a*
gorgeous dress with white arms extended
against the curtains.

SCENE IV

SCENE. — *The same — glittering starlight.*

Enter various servants bearing wine-jars and dishes from the inner supper-room, in procession. Then BURRUS, SENECA, ANICETUS, *and* TIGELLINUS.

BURRUS.   'Tis not man's work to witness
    this.   I have fought
Neck-deep in blood and spared not when the
    fit
Was on me, but I cannot gaze on this.
Have you a heart, old man?

TIGELLINUS. No, not in hours

Like these: the brain is all. I fear, I fear
him

The last farewell — he will not bear it out!

SENECA. How to excuse my soul, yet I am
here.

Was this mere acting, or a true emotion?

ANICETUS. A little of both, but most, I fear
it, true.

TIGELLINUS. Is all prepared and timed?
No hazard left?

ANICETUS. Yonder the barge with lights
and fluttering flags.

The canopy whereunder Agrippina

Will sit is heavily weighted: at a sign

A bolt withdrawn will launch it on her head.

Enter NERO

NERO. I cannot do it: if she goes, she
goes.

I cannot say farewell, and kiss her lips,

Ere I commit her body to the deep.

TIGELLINUS. All hangs upon the fervour of
farewell,

The kiss, the soft word, and the hand de-
tained,

All hangs on it; go back.

NERO.   'Tis difficult.

[NERO *turns. Enter* AGRIPPINA.

Come out into the cool a moment, mother.

AGRIPPINA. This seemeth like to old days
come again,

Evenings of Antium with a rising moon.

> [*Stroking his hair.*

My boy, my boy, again! Look in my eyes.

So as a babe would you look up at me

After a night of tossing, half-awake,

Blinking against the dawn, and pull my head

Down to you, till I lost you in my hair.

. Do you remember many a night so thick

With stars as this — you would not go to bed,

But still would paddle in the warm ocean

Spraying it with small hands into the skies.

NERO.   Yes, I remember.

AGRIPPINA.   Or when you would sail

In a slight skiff under a moon like this,

Though chidden oft and oft.

NERO.   Ah! I recall it.

AGRIPPINA.   A wilful child — the sea — ever

the sea —

Your mother could not hold you from the sea.

Will you be sore if I confess a thought?

NERO.   Ah! no, mother!

AGRIPPINA.   So foolish it seems now.

Awhile I doubted whether I should come.

NERO.   Why, then?

AGRIPPINA.   Now, do not laugh at

me — I say

You will not laugh at me?

NERO.   No!

AGRIPPINA.   Why — I thought

That you perhaps would kill me if I came!

Truly I did!

NERO.   I kill you!

AGRIPPINA.   'O,' I said,

'I have wearied him: he is weary of his

    mother.'

NERO. Oh!

AGRIPPINA. In my ears there buzzed that

    prophecy —

'Nero shall reign but he shall kill his mother.'

                [NERO *starts*.

AGRIPPINA. Now — now — I had not told

    you had I not

Been above measure happy. Now no more

Wild words, no more mad words between us two,

Who all the while are aching to be friends.

O how your hands come waxen once again

Within my own: again behind your voice

The hesitating tardy bird-like word

And the sweet slur of 'r's.'   O but to-night

Even grandeur palls, the splendid goal: to-night

I am a woman and am with my child.

　　　　[*A pause and she strains him to her.*

Beautiful night that gently bringest back

Mother to son, and callest all thy stars

To watch it.   Quiet sea that bringest peace

Between us two.   Hast thou not thought how

　　still

The air is as with silent pleasure?   Child,

Is not the night then more than common calm?

　NERO.   A sparkling starlight and a windless

　　deep.

　AGRIPPINA.   Never until to-night did I so

　　feel

The lure of the sea that lures me to lie down

　　　L

At last after such heat. Ah, but the stars

Are falling and I feel the unseen dawn.

Son, I must go at once. Where is my maid

To wrap me? Sweet and warm now is the
    night

And I am glad I had prepared to go

By water, not by land.

Enter SERVANT, *hurriedly*

SERVANT.   O Caesar!

NERO.   Well?

SERVANT.   Thy mother's galley by a random
    barge

Was struck, and now is sinking fast.

AGRIPPINA.   Alas!

Now must I go by land.

NERO. Yes, go by land.

[TIGELLINUS *signals to* ANICETUS.

ANICETUS. Yonder there lies a barge with

fluttering flags,

A gilded pinnace, a light pleasure-boat

Built for you with much art and well designed.

Will you return in her? Easily she

Can swing round to the landing-stage.

AGRIPPINA. Yes — yes —

I'll go in her — Why not?

NERO. It was foretold ——

Enter ACCERONIA, *who elaborately wraps*

AGRIPPINA

AGRIPPINA. Nero, my maid a moment to

enwrap me.

[*As the wrapping is finished.*

I have slept ill of late: but I shall have

A soft and steady breeze across the bay.

I shall sleep sound.   Now, Nero, now good-bye.

For ever we are friends?

NERO.   Good-bye: yet stay!

[*During this dialogue he is continually de-*

taining her.

Have I been kind, this last hour? Say.

AGRIPPINA.   Most kind.

NERO. You have no need to go this moment

— one

More moment of thee, mother.

AGRIPPINA.   You shall see me

To-morrow. Will you cross the bay to me,

Or shall I come to you?

NERO.   I'll come to you

To-morrow! Ah! to-morrow! But to-night.

Now let me have you once more in my arms.

                              [*Detaining her.*

Is old Cynisca with you still?

AGRIPPINA. [*Going.*]   She is.

NERO. Stay, stay, give her this ring: she

   nursed me.

AGRIPPINA.   Yes.

I see you have my amulet.

NERO.   O yes.

AGRIPPINA. So bright the night you'll see

   me all the way

Across the shining water.

NERO. [*Clinging to her.*] O farewell!

AGRIPPINA. [*Descends to water.*] Good-night, child! I shall see you then to-morrow.

Already it hath dawned.

NERO.   Mother, good-night.

                              [*Exit* AGRIPPINA.

TIGELLINUS. [*To crew in barge.*] Strike up the music there, a joyous strain!

And sing, you boatmen; the Augusta comes.

    [*Sounds of joyful music are heard, and
        singing, as the pinnace puts off with
        measured beat of oars.*

NERO. It hath put off: she hath gone: she sitteth happy.

See, the dead woman waves her hand to me.

Now the bark turns the headland.

ANICETUS.   But will soon

Steal into sight, well out upon the bay.

TIGELLINUS.   Caesar, let none deny thou art

an actor.

NERO. [*Passionately.*] Was I all actor then?

That which I feigned

I felt, and when it was my cue to kiss her,

The whole of childhood rushed into the kiss.

When it was in my part to cling about her,

I clung about her mad with memories.

The water in my eyes rose from my soul,

And flooding from the heart ran down my cheek.

Did my voice tremble?   Then it trembled true

With human agony behind the art.

Gods!   What a scene!

TIGELLINUS.   Listen!

ANICETUS.　　　　　　　She is well out,

Glassed in the bay with all her lights and flags.

Soon will a crash and cry come in our ears.

NERO. [*Going out.*]　How calm the night

　　when I would have it wild!

Aloof and bright which should have rushed to me

Hither with aid of thunder, screen of lightning!

I looked for reinforcement from the sky.

Arise, you veiling clouds; awake, you winds,

And stifle with your roaring human cries.

Not a breath upon my cheek! I gasp for air.

[*To* OTHERS.]　Do you suppose the very

　　elements

Are conscious of the workings of this mind?

So careful not to seem to share my guilt?

Yet dark is the record of wind and wave,

This ocean that creeps fawning to our feet

Comes purring o'er a million wrecks and bones.

If the cold moon hath sinned not, she hath been

    privy.

She aids me not, but watches quietly.

A placid sea, still air, and bright starlight.

  ANICETUS.   But Caesar, see, a gradual cloud

  hath spread

Over the moon; the ship's light disappears.

She is vanished.

  NERO.   She is veiled from sight.

  TIGELLINUS.   My eyes

Can find her not; she is enwrapped in mist.

  SENECA. A dimness and no more.

  BURRUS.   And silence.

  NERO.   Hush!

How wonderful this waiting and this pause.

Could one convey this in the theatre?

This deep suspense, this breathlessness? Per-

haps.

The air weighs on the brain — what sound was

that?

TIGELLINUS.   Nothing, sir.

NERO.   In this thrill a leaf would thunder.

[*A pause.*

I never noted so exactly how

The shadow of that cypress falls aslant

Upon the dark bank yonder.

BURRUS.   Would it were over!

NERO.   Feel you no shuddering pleasure

in this pause?

But me this fraught expectancy allures;

The tingling stillness, for each moment now

The crash, a cry, may come, but it comes not.

TIGELLINUS. Anicetus, have you bungled?

[*A cry is heard far off, and a crash, then*

    silence.

NERO.   It is done.

I cannot look: peer seaward, one of you —

What do you see?

SENECA.   Darkness, and veilèd stars.

NERO. Is there no shimmer of a floating

    robe?

Pierce through the darkness!

BURRUS.   Nothing visible.

NERO. I seem to see her lying amid shells,

And strange sea-things come round her wonder-

    ing,

Inspecting her with cold and rheumy eyes.

The water sways her helpless up and down.

BURRUS. Caesar, you have no further need

of me?

NERO. [*Dreamily.*] No, sir.

BURRUS. Good-night, and pleasant be thy

dreams.

SENECA. Or me?

NERO. No, no!

SENECA. At least bear witness, sir,

I had no hand in this: but was compelled,

A loth spectator, to behold thy deed!

ANICETUS. Caesar, you'll not forget the

service done?

NERO. Never shall I forget thee, Anicetus.

Leave me alone.

[*Exeunt all but* TIGELLINUS, *who creeps
    back again.*

TIGELLINUS.   Sole master of the world!
Caesar at last: the Emperor of the earth,
Now thou art free — to write immortal verse,
To give thy genius wing, to strike the stars.
And thou hast made this tragic sacrifice,
Slaying what is most dear, most close to thee,
To give thy being vent and utterance.
Apollo shall reward thee for this deed.

  NERO. Go to thy room, old man, and —
    wilt thou sleep?

  TIGELLINUS. Already I am drowsing; early
    then
To-morrow I will come to you.

  NERO.   Good-night.

TIGELLINUS.   Caesar, good-night.

                                [*Exit* TIGELLINUS.

                                [*Thunder heard.*

NERO.   Ah! thunder! thou art come

At last, too late!   What catches at my heart?

I — I — her boy, her baby that was, even I

Have killed her: where I sucked there have I

    struck.

Mother!   Mother!   [*He drinks.*

The anguish of it hath taken hold of me,

And I am gripped by Nature. O, it comes

Upon me, this too natural remorse.

I faint! I flinch from the raw agony!

I cannot face this common human throe!

Ah!   Ah! the crude stab of reality!

I am a son, and I have killed my mother!

Why! I am now no more than him who tills

Or reaps: and I am seized by primal pangs.

Mother!   [*He drinks.*

     The thunder crieth motherless.

Ah! how this sword of lightning thrusts at me!

O, all the artist in my soul is shattered,

And I am hurled into humanity,

Back to the sweat and heart-break of mankind.

I am broken upon the jagged spurs of the earth.

I can no more endure it.   Mother!

   [*He drinks again, walking distractedly to
      and fro, not looking seaward. But as he
      at last turns, slowly out from the sea
      appears the figure of* AGRIPPINA *with
      dripping hair, who comes slowly towards
      him in silence.*

[*He cries aloud and falls in a swoon. She comes and looks at him.*

AGRIPPINA.   Child!

[*She stoops, removes the amulet from his arm, flings it into the sea, and passes out in silence.*

SCENE V

SCENE. — *The same. Dawn breaking;* NERO
discovered lying in a swoon.

NERO. [*Slowly.*] Dawn! In the night o'er-
past a lightning flash!

Ah! I remember — here my mother's ghost

Stood — on this very ground — I feel the air

Still cold from her — and here the lightning

burned.

So I awake my mother's murderer.

That was her ghost that stole on me sea-
marred,

Silent — the ocean falling from her hair.

Enter Tigellinus

Tigellinus.   Caesar at last!   Sole master

of the world!

Nero.   O Tigellinus, in the mid of night,

The spirit of my whelmèd mother stole

Hither upon me, dumb out of the deep.

Heaven gave a flash: I saw her face and fell.

Tigellinus.   Her spirit!   Better that than

she herself.

Dismiss dark fancies now — this day thou art

free.

Nero.   No, but enthralled by her for ever-

more.

She is my air, my ocean, and my sky.

Tigellinus.   The night has wrought this

sickly mood on you —

Natural — it will pass.

NERO.   Never, O never!

You flatter, you console, you would assuage,

But you are human, can forget and change.

But yonder rocky coast remembers yet.

That countenance changes not: that conscious

    bay

Maintains its everlasting memory.

This privy region saw, and it shall see

For ever what was done. The amulet!

Filched from me! Was it then a ghost I saw?

Enter SEAMAN *hurriedly, followed by* BURRUS

SEAMAN.   Caesar, my news must plead for

    this intrusion.

I was aboard the ship whereon the Augusta

Set sail: when the roof fell, thy mother's maid

Cried 'Save me! I am the Emperor's mother!'

　　Straight

Crushed under many a blow, she dropped and

　　died.

But silently thy mother Agrippina

Slid from the ship into the water and swam

Shoreward. With white and jewelled arms she

　　thrust

Out through the waves and lay upon the

　　foam.

We heard her through the ripple breathing

　　deep,

And when we heard no more, we watched her

　　still —

Her hair behind her blowing into gold

As she did glimmer o'er the gloomy deep;

And all the stars swam with her through the
   heavens,

The hurrying moon lighted her with a torch,

The sea was loth to lose her, and the shore

Yearned for her; till we lost her in the
   dark,

Save now and then some splendid leap of the
   head.

NERO.   You know not if she be alive or
   dead?

SEAMAN.   Caesar, rejoice — thy mother
   lives.

NERO.   She lives?

SEAMAN.   When I at last touched shore, I
   spoke with two

Night-wandering fishermen. These two, it
   seems,
Had borne her in their boat across the bay
To her own villa.

   NERO. [*Falling hysterically on neck of* SEA-
   MAN.] I am no murderer then!

   TIGELLINUS. Have you considered, sir,
   what now may urge
Thy mother, Agrippina, knowing all,
Seeing that by no chance or accident
Or sudden flurry of the ocean floor
The ship collapsed. Safe is she, but how
   long?
Will she not burst upon us suddenly?
Sir, she must die to-night.

   NERO.   I'll not attempt

A second time that life the sea restored;

She is too vast a spirit to surprise.

Even Nature stood aloof ——

My mother shall be gloriously caged,

Imprisoned in purple and immured in gold.

In some magnificent captivity

Worthy the captive let her day decline.

[*Shouts without: enter* BURRUS.

BURRUS.   Caesar, great news I bring: the
          Armenian

Lies helpless on Tigranocerta's plain

O'erwhelmed by Corbulo, and the huge host

Dissolved.   Armenia lies beneath your feet:

Rome yearns to welcome you.

NERO.   To Rome I go

Free-souled and guiltless of a mother's blood,

Resume the accustomed feast, the race, the
    song,
And I shall be received with public joy
And clamour of congratulating Rome.

            [Great cheering without: exit NERO.

                     [A pause.

TIGELLINUS. Burrus, she'll strike at us
    whate'er the cost :
She'll slay the ministers if not the master.

BURRUS. We are both dead unless some
    sudden scheme —

          Enter ANICETUS *at back*

[Turning.]   Here is another doomed as we our-
    selves.

TIGELLINUS. Ah, Anicetus ! Agrippina lives,

And she will launch her vengeance on us

    three,

But first on you: you first set Nero on —

You first proposed the scheme.   You on the sea

Bungled — Now on the land retrieve the error.

To you we look.

Enter POPPAEA *from behind and stands listening.*

  ANICETUS.   My error is repaired

Already. I first heard the Augusta lived,

And instantly despatched a faithful troop

To slay her at her villa o'er the bay.

  TIGELLINUS. How shall we know if they

    have found and slain her?

  ANICETUS. All this I have arranged and

    clearly planned.

If they shall find that she hath fled to Rome,

Hark for one trumpet-call across the bay:

If they have found her at the villa, then

Hark for two trumpet-calls across the bay:

If they have found her and have slain her,
    then

Hark for three trumpet-calls across the bay!

> [*A burst of music without, and sounds of
>   advancing procession.*

> [*Enter soldiers and satellites, with attend-
>   ants bearing a litter. Lastly* NERO.

TIGELLINUS. Now as a conqueror in tri-
    umphant vein

Ride through the thundering ways of risen
    Rome,

Anticipating the Armenian car.

NERO. [*Ascending litter.*] Set out for

  Rome! And you, accusing coasts,

Accuse no more. Guiltless I say farewell,

And with a light heart journey toward Rome.

Joyous I go, for Agrippina lives.

> [*A great triumphal shout swells up again,
> and to the sound of military music,* NERO
> *and the procession pass off. Meanwhile*
> TIGELLINUS *is left in a listening attitude.*
> POPPAEA *stands breathless at back.
> There is a pause. Then a trumpet-call
> is heard far off; a second; and a third.*
> POPPAEA *rushes to* TIGELLINUS *and
> clasps his hand.*

ACT IV

ACT IV

SCENE I

SCENE. — *A tower overlooking Rome.*

Enter SENECA, BURRUS, *and* PHYSICIAN

SENECA.   How dark the future of the Empire

glooms!

BURRUS.   Now the Gaul mutters: the Prae-

torians

Sullenly snarl.

SENECA.   The Christians privily

Conspire.

BURRUS.   The legions waver and whisper

too.

SENECA.   [*To* PHYSICIAN.] What of the

Emperor?

175

PHYSICIAN.   Through Campania

He rushes: and distracted to and fro

Would fly now here, now there; behind each woe

He sees the angered shade of Agrippina.

Now hearing that Poppaea sinks toward death,

Hither is he fast hurrying.

SENECA.   Ah, Poppaea,

No sooner Empress made than she must die ——

BURRUS.   See: she is carried hither.

SENECA.   Here to look

Her last upon the glory of the earth.

   [*Exeunt* SENECA, BURRUS, *and* PHYSICIAN.

   [POPPAEA *enters, supported by handmaids.*

She takes a long look at Rome, then is

assisted down to couch.

POPPAEA.   Give me the glass again: beauti-

ful yet!

This face can still endure the sunset glow,

No need is there for me to sue the shadow,

Perfect out of the glory I am going.

MYRRHA.   Lady, the mood will pass: still

you are young.

POPPAEA.   Why comes not Nero near me?

O he loathes

Sickness or sadness or the touch of trouble

MYRRHA.   Nay, lady; hither he is riding fast,

In fury spurring from Campania,

And trouble upon trouble falls on him —

Misfortune follows him like a faithful hound.

N

POPPAEA.   I snared him, Myrrha, once; let

him flutter away!

But to relinquish the wide earth at last,

And flit a faint thing by a shadowy river,

Or yearning without blood upon the bank —

The loneliness of death!   To go to strangers —

Into a world of whispers ——

[*Looking at and lifting her hair.*

And this hair

Rolling about me like a lighted sea

Which was my glory and the theme of the earth,

Look!   Must this go?   The grave shall have

these eyes

Which were the bliss of burning Emperors.

After what time, what labour the high gods

Builded the body of this beauty up!

Now at a whim they shatter it! More light!

I'll catch the last of the sun.

Enter SLAVE

SLAVE.   Mistress, below

The lady Acte stands and asks to see you.

POPPAEA. Come to inspect me fading: I

fear not.

Even a woman's eyes I need not shun.

Bring her.   [*Exit* SLAVE.

Now, Myrrha, watch her hungering eyes.

Enter ACTE, *ushered by* SLAVE

POPPAEA. [*Vehemently.*] Take Nero! I

am dying.

ACTE.   Ah, not yet!

POPPAEA. I am dying. But you shall not

    hold him long —

O, do not think it. Can you queen his heart?

Can you be storm a moment, sun the next?

A month, a long day under open skies,

Would find your art exhausted, ended. I !

I was a hundred women in an hour,

And sweeter at each moment than them all.

Why, I have struck him in the face and laughed.

  ACTE. I love him: that concerns not him,

    nor you.

A different goal I would have sought for

    him,

A garment not of purple, but of peace.

  POPPAEA. Of peace ! Ha, ha !

  ACTE.   Vain now — I know it, vain.

But if your words are true, and death is on

   you,

Let us two at the least be friends at last.

   POPPAEA.   I bear no rancour — and yet if I

   dreamed

That I was leaving you upon his bosom —

But no: let there be peace between us two.

                    [ACTE *comes and kisses her.*

Your kiss falls kind upon my loneliness.

But, Acte, to let go of glory thus —

For I have drunk of empire, and what cup

Afterward can you offer to these lips?

   ACTE.   Of late there has been stealing on

   my mind

A strange hope — a new vision.

   POPPAEA.   What is this?

ACTE.   Do not laugh out at me: a sect

despised —

The Christians, tell us of an after life,

A glory on the other side the grave.

If there should be a kingdom not of this world,

A spirit throne, a city of the soul!

POPPAEA.   I want no spirit kingdom after

death.

The splendid sun, the purple, and the crown,

These I have known, and I am losing them.

ACTE.   Yet if the sun, the purple, and the

crown

Were but the shadows of another sun,

Splendider — a more dazzling diadem?

POPPAEA.   These can I see at least, and feel,

and hear.

ACTE. Yes, with a mortal touch that falters

now.

POPPAEA. [*Sobbing.*] O Acte, to be dumb,

and deaf, and blind!

ACTE. Or live again with more transcendent

sense,

Hearing unchecked, and unimpeded sight.

If we who walk now, then should wing the air,

Who stammer now, then should discard the

voice,

Who grope now, then should see with other

sight,

And send new eyes about the universe.

POPPAEA. O, this is madness!

ACTE.   Is it? Is it? Well —

Yet have I heard this ragged people speak,

And they have stirred me strangely: life they
    scorn,
And yearn for death's tremendous liberty,
But I — I cannot speak; yet I believe
There is a new air blowing on the world,
And a new budding underneath the earth.

    POPPAEA. Ah, ah! the sun! The sun! It
    goeth down,
How cold it grows: the night comes down on me.
I'll have no lamp: but hold my hand in thine.

    ACTE. Sister, forget the world, it passeth.

    POPPAEA. [*Falling back.*] Rome!

SCENE II

SCENE. — *The same.* SENECA, BURRUS,
ACTE, *and* PHYSICIAN.

PHYSICIAN.   The   Emperor   comes   from
gazing on Poppaea.

What woe may that dead face not work on
him,

After such rain of dark calamities!

SENECA.   Why hath he summoned me?

PHYSICIAN.   He knows not why.

The infatuate orgies in Campania,

Defeat, revolt, have wrought upon his mind,

Till it begins to reel — behind each woe

He sees the angered shade of Aggrippina.

185

> [*Enter* NERO *with tablets, murmuring to*
>> *himself.   He comes to the* COUNCIL-
>> LORS, *gazes at them, and retires to*
>> *parapet.*

'Beautiful on her bed Poppaea lay' —

I have begun to write her epitaph.

> [*He again gazes over parapet, murmuring*
>> *to himself.   Then turning.*

Ah, blow supreme!   Ah, ultimate injury!

I can no longer write: my brain is barren.

My gift, my gift, thou hast left me.   Let me

die!

Ah! what an artist perishes in me.

> [*He again returns to parapet, gazing and*
>> *murmuring, and throws his tablets from*
>> *him.*

Dead Agrippina rages unappeased.

At night I hear the trailing of a robe,

And the slain woman pauses at my door.

O! she is mightier having drunk of death;

Now hath she haled Poppaea from my arms;

Last doth she quench the holy fire within

    me ——

Enter MESSENGER

MESSENGER. Caesar, I bring dark news:
Boadicea the British Queen is risen,

And like a fire is hissing through the isle,

Londinium and Camulodunum

In ashes lie: the loosed barbarians

In madness rage and ravish, murder and burn.

BURRUS. Caesar, despatch.

                [Brings NERO *paper.*

NERO.　　　　　　Ah, this is still the deed
Of Agrippina.　Listen!　Did ye not hear
The rustle of a robe?　　　　　　*[Starting up.*

Ah! thou art come!
I — I no order gave!　Then did the brine
Drop from thy hair: but now blood falls from
　　thee;
There, where they struck thee, once did I sleep
　　sound.
What shall I do to appease thee?　Let me die
Rather than see that wonder on thy face,
And stare on me of terrible surprise.
Thou com'st upon me!

　ACTE.　　　　　Ah! what ails your mind?

　NERO.　She is gone!　The red drops those
　　that fell from her!

ACTE. Lo! I am with thee!

NERO. Thou! And who art thou?

Enter in great haste an OFFICER, *followed by*

OTHERS

OFFICER. Caesar, Rome burns! We can-

not fight the fire

Which blazes and consumes. How it arose

None knows and none can tell. What shall we

do?

ANOTHER. It sprung in the Suburra:

whether lit

By accident, dropped torch, or smouldering

brand ——

ANOTHER. Or by design ——

ANOTHER. Caesar, the Christians,

Who hate the human race, have done this
thing:
They loathe thy rule and would abolish thee,
And with thee, Rome.

ANOTHER. They have a prophecy
That now the world is ending, and in fire
The globe shall shrivel, and this empire fall
In cinders.

ANOTHER. And the moon be turned to
blood.

NERO. The moon be turned to blood! But
that is fine!
These Christians have imaginations then!
The moon in blood, and burning universe!
Why, I myself might have conceived that
scene!

Enter OTHERS *from the opposite side*

OFFICER.   Caesar, what shall be done?   Still

   spreads the fire!

A quarter of Rome in ashes lies already,

And like a blackened corpse: and screaming

   mothers,

Hugging their babes, dash through the fearful

   flames,

And old men totter gasping through the blaze

Or fall scorched to the ground.   Stifled with

   smoke

The population from their houses reel.

Meantime the Christians, prophesying woe

And final doom upon a wicked world,

Hither and thither run, and with their dark

Forebodings madden all the minds of men.

To thee they point! To thee, the source of
    fire,

Who has drawn down on them celestial flame.

NERO.   Magnificent! The aim of heavenly
    fire!

ANOTHER.   They say the world shall crumble,
    and the skies

Fall, and their God come in the clouds of heaven

To judge the earth!

ANOTHER.   But we are wasting breath

Over the Christians: what now shall be done?

To thee, Caesar, to thee, we come: for thou

Alone mayst with this conflagration cope.

NERO.   Listen! Did ye not hear a wailing
    then?

The wailing of a woman in her grave?

Again! A wailing, and I know the voice!

Enter OTHERS *hastily*

MESSENGER. Caesar, the fire has reached
  the Palatine!

Rome will be ashes soon.

ANOTHER.   We have fought fire

With water: matched the elements in vain,

For the fire triumphs: Caesar, what aid from
  thee?

Enter ANOTHER

MESSENGER. Caesar, the temple of Jupiter
  is aflame.

The shrine of Vesta next will crash to the
  earth.

          O

ANOTHER.   Open the sluices of the Campus

   Martius.

ANOTHER.   Issue some sudden edict: give

   command.

NERO.   No edict will I issue, or command.

Let the fire rage.

CHORUS.   O Caesar!

NERO.   Let it rage!

ANOTHER.   Caesar, 'tis said this fire was lit

   by thee.

That thou wouldst burn old Rome to build a

   new,

A Rome more glorious issuing from the flames:

This tale hath maddened all the common folk

Who, from their smouldering homes, curse thee

   aloud.

NERO. This fire is not the act of mortal mind,

But is the huge conception of a spirit

Dreaming beyond the tomb a mighty thought.

She would express herself in burning fire:

This is the awful vengeance of the dead;

This is my mother Agrippina's deed.

I will not baulk the fury of her spirit.

No! Let her glut her anger on the city,

For only Rome in ashes can appease her,

Let the fire rage and purge me of her blood!

[The flame flashes upward.

Rage!

Rage on!

See, see!

How beautiful!

Like a rose magnificently burning!

                   [The flame flashes up.

        Rage on!

Thou art that which poets use,

        Or which consumes them.

        Thou art in me!

Thou dreadful womb of mighty spirits,

        And crimson sepulchre of them!

                [The flame flashes up.

        Blaze! Blaze!

How it eats and eats!

        How it drinks!

What hunger is like unto the hunger of fire?

    What thirst is like unto the thirst of

flame?

                [The flame flashes up.

O fury superb!

O incurable lust of ruin!

O panting perdition!

O splendid devastation!

I, I, too, have felt it!

To destroy — to destroy!

To leave behind me ashes, ashes.

> *[The flame flashes up.*

Rage! Rage on!

Or art thou passion, art thou desire?

Ah! terrible kiss!

> *[The flame flashes up.*

Now hear it, hear it!

A hiss as from mighty serpents,

The dry, licking, wicked tongues!

Wouldst thou sting the earth to death?

What a career!

To clasp and devour and kill!

To dance over the world as a frenzied
dancer

With whirling skirts of world-wide flame!

            [The flame flashes up.

        Blaze! Blaze!

Or art thou madness visible,

Insanity seizing the rolling heavens.

              [He points up.

Thou, Thou, didst create the world

   In the stars innumerably smiling.

Thou art life, thou art God, thou art I!

            [The flame flashes up.

      Mother! Mother!

    This is thy deed.

Hist! Hist! can you not see her

Stealing with lighted torch?

She makes no sound, she hath a spirit's tread.

Hast thou sated thy vengeance yet?

Art thou appeased?

[The flame flashes up.

Be satisfied with nothing but the world,

The world alone is fuel for thee.

Mother!

[The flame flashes up.

And I! See what a fire I have given thee,

Rome for a funeral couch!

Had Achilles a pyre like to this

Or had Patroclus?

Had they mourners such as I give to thee,

Bereaved mothers and babes?

Now let the wailing cease from thy tomb,

 Here is a mightier wail!

Now let the haunting trumpet be dumb!

 ACTE. Nero!

 NERO. Blaze! Rage! Blaze!

  [The flame flashes up more fervently.

For now am I free of thy blood,

 I have appeased and atoned,

Have atoned with cries, with crashings, and

 with flaming.

 Thy blood is no more on my head;

  I am purged, I am cleansed;

I have given thee flaming Rome for the bed of

 thy death!

  O Agrippina!

[He falls in a swoon — ACTE *runs towards him.*

FAUST

FREELY ADAPTED FROM GOETHE'S DRAMATIC POEM

BY

STEPHEN PHILLIPS AND J. COMYNS CARR

CHARACTERS

Faust	Burgomaster
Mephistopheles	Frosch
Margaret	Siebel
Martha	Lisbeth
Valentine	Elsa
Brander	Lisa
Altmayer	Laine

THE WITCH

APES, WITCHES, STUDENTS, SOLDIERS, ETC. ETC.

PROLOGUE

PROLOGUE

SCENE. — *A range of mountains between Heaven
and Earth.*

[*The Archangels* RAPHAEL, GABRIEL, *and*
MICHAEL *discovered. A faint* CHORUS *of
invisible* ANGELS *from above.*

RAPHAEL. The sun his ancient music makes,

Rolling amid the rival spheres;

Still his predestined course he takes

In thunder speed throughout the years.

By angels, though uncomprehended,

Strength from his aspect still is drawn;

The universe abideth splendid,

And fresh as at Creation's dawn.

GABRIEL. Swift, beyond understanding quite,

 Circles the earth in glorious guise,

Now plunged into profoundest night,

 Now sparkling into paradise.

The ocean foams up from the deep,

 And over ricks and crags is hurled,

And crags and ocean onward sweep —

 On with the rapid spheres are whirled.

MICHAEL. Contending tempests rage and rain

 From land to land, from sea to sea;

Weaving a girdle and a chain

 Out of their hissing enmity.

A flashing desolation thence

 Ushers the awful thunder-way;

But, Lord, Thy servants reverence

 The gentle order of the day.

ALL THREE. By angels, though uncompre-
    hended,
Strength from Thy aspect still is drawn;
The universe abideth splendid,
    And fresh as at Creation's dawn.

[MEPHISTOPHELES *appears suddenly on the*
    peak. He is dressed in a glimmering robe
    suggestive of a glory obscured.

[NOTE ON APPEARANCE OF MEPHISTOPH-
    ELES: — *Both in the Prologue and in the*
    Epilogue of this drama MEPHISTOPHELES
    appears as the Fallen Angel or Satan of
    tradition. His speech is suited to this
    character. But when, in pursuit of his
    wager and the soul of FAUST, *he appears*
    on earth, he has put on the form he judges

most serviceable to his ends — that of a

cavalier-troubadour of the Middle Ages; and

his speech is light, cynical, and of the world.

MEPHISTOPHELES.   Hail to mine ancient friends,

my present foes!

This neutral mountain between Hell and Heaven

Is still permitted to these exiled feet;

Here may my Darkness mingle with your Light.

RAPHAEL.   Whence com'st thou now?

MEPHISTOPHELES.   From

yonder speck, the earth;

From wandering up and down upon the place,

And pacing to and fro in hate unresting.

And yet man so torments himself, my toil

Seems idle: and heedless my unceasing task.

I would he were more difficult to damn!

He is a grasshopper that flies and springs,

And from the grass the same old ditty sends.

Better he always lay among the grass.

Had I a free rein given me to seduce,

There is no soul on earth I could not win

Were it permitted me.

                  [Stretching his hand upwards.

   [An ANGEL *descends from above, and stands*

       on a superior peak at back.

ANGEL.   It is permitted!

Man writhes to glory but through pain of error.

MEPHISTOPHELES. Angel   sent   down   from

bliss! Have I permission

Whence all permission flows, to lure and snare

A human soul, and draw it my own way?

However rich or rare, I will seduce it.

ANGEL. Whence all permission flows, thou

hast permission.

MEPHISTOPHELES. A wager vast! Look

down upon the earth! [*He points downward.*

Whom shall I choose? That theologian

That sits and blinks at Truth, and toys with

words?

Too easy! Or yonder mighty emperor,

Who sitteth, dark against the Orient,

Throned above prostrate millions? No, not

him!

My victory shall be deep and not of show.

Or yonder lady in the convent garden

Pure from the world, and pacing lawns of

peace?

Not her! No spirit starved will I select!

xiv

See! I will choose for test a rarer soul!

Yonder he sits, the famous Doctor Faust.

Has Heaven a better servant on the earth?

ANGEL. None!

MEPHISTOPHELES. Yonder soul I choose then

    for my wager;

Nothing the tumult of his heart assuages,

For all of earth and all of heaven he asks.

The ferment drives him to the far-away.

And yet is he half-conscious of his madness.

To grasp the far the near he hath neglected,

And still has nothing grasped, and now regrets

The once despiséd pleasures of the world.

I will so draw him onward to lost pleasures,

So plunge him deep in sensuality,

His heavy soul no more shall upward strive.

ANGEL. So long as he is breathing on the
　earth,

So long is nothing unto thee forbidden.

Thou art permitted to ensnare the spirit

Of Faust, and turn it from the fountain-head;

Till thou shalt stand abashed at last, and
　learn

That a good man, though in the dark he
　strives,

Hath still an instinct for the truer way.

RAPHAEL. And thou shalt batter thee, and
　all in vain,

Against an influence appearing slight,

And frail as the resistance of a flower;

And yet a power thou canst not comprehend.

He through the woman-soul at last shall win.

ANGEL. Man is too prone to slumber, and
    he needs
As a companion one who goads and works,
And who, being devil, must be up and doing.

ALL THREE. But we to Eternal Beauty turn
    again,
Lord, and in bliss Thy splendours contemplate;
Though we Thy angels may not fathom them,
Thy works are fresh as at Creation's day.

RAPHAEL.   [*Turning towards* MEPHISTOPHE-
    LES.] And thou! Wilt thou not cease vain
    war with Heaven?
To will the evil, and achieve the good?

MEPHISTOPHELES. Never! Until that hour
    when the Usurper,
Who wrested from my mother Night her reign,

And fevered Chaos with his blistering stars,

Shall be himself deposed, consent, and cease.

For this same light but lives by what it breeds,

A carrion offspring suckled by the sun.

And never will I cease this war with Heaven

Till the bound elements shall mutiny,

And the imprisoned thunder shall be freed,

And old tremendous blasts shall fly abroad,

And all His millions of rash fires be quenched;

And space shall be again as once it was

Ere He disturbed us with his fiery brain,

Timeless and tideless, limitless and dark!

Mother! Still crouching on the bounds of light,

With face of sea and hair of tempest, still

Huddled in huge and immemorial hate,

Behold thy son, and some dark aid extend!

So, Faust, to win this wager and thy soul

Pass we from heaven across the earth to hell.

[*Thunder and darkness as* MEPHISTOPHELES,
   with wings outspread, swoops suddenly
   like lightning downwards to the earth.

ACT I

ACT I

SCENE. — *A gloomy, narrow Gothic chamber.*

[FAUST *at his desk, restless. Midnight.*

FAUST. Alas! What boots it to have mastered

    now

Philosophy, medicine, even theology,

With unremitting zeal and toil unceasing?

Lo! here I sit no wiser than before.

True! I can lead my scholars by the nose;

They hail me master, doctor, fawn on me,

But I, I know how deep is my defeat,

I only know that nothing can be known.

                            [*A pause.*

And urged by this insane and desert thirst,

What have I missed! All honour, rank, and
  wealth,

Even the thrill of kisses and of wine.

Science, farewell! To Magic now I turn,

From Magic I may wring some secret yet

And learn what forces bind and guide the world.

·   [*Moonlight floods the room.*

O thou full moon, whom I so many a night

Have watched ascending! Would that thou
  didst gaze

For the last time upon my trouble! Ah,

If now no longer stifling amid books,

I in thine argent twilight floated free!

But no, this dungeon-lumber I behold,

A self-created prison of mould and dust,

Where God His pulsing human creature set.

I dwell but with the dead — in what a world!

                    [*He turns to the Magic book.*

Here is my way of freedom: here the sign

Of the Earth-Spirit. How dost thou invade me!

How like new wine thou runnest in my veins!

The woe of Earth, the bliss of Earth invite me.

The lamp goes out — a horror from the roof

Descends on me. Spirit, reveal thyself!

I feel thee suck my soul, absorb my heart,

I'll look on thee, although my life it cost me.

    [*He seizes the book and pronounces the sign of*

       the Earth-Spirit.

                    [*The* SPIRIT *appears in a flame.*

SPIRIT. Who calls me?

FAUST.   Terrible to look on!

SPIRIT.　　　　　　　　　　　　　　　　Me
Hast thou with might attracted from my sphere.

FAUST.　Woe!　I endure not thee!

SPIRIT.　　　　　　　　　　　　Yet didst thou long
To gaze on me: thy yearning drew me down.

Where art thou, Faust? whose strong voice pierced

　　to me?

Is't thee I see — this terror-stricken worm?

　FAUST.　I fear no more — I am Faust — I am

　　thy peer!

SPIRIT.　Thou art like the Spirit which thou

　comprehendest,

Not me!

　　　　　　　　　　　　　　　　[SPIRIT *disappears*.

FAUST.　Not thee! I, image of the God-head!

　　　　　　　　　　　　　　　　　　　[*A knock*.

Death! At this moment this poor witless wretch

Disturbs me, teasing me from the full vision!

[*Enter* WAGNER *with a lamp.*

WAGNER.   Surely, you read some old Greek

   tragedy:

I heard the declamation — and a preacher

They say might learn from a comedian.

   FAUST.   [*Irritably.*]   Yes, when the preacher —

as the case is often,

Is in himself a born comedian.

WAGNER.   I've studied long to be an orator.

FAUST.   Studied!   What use! unless heart

   speaks to heart?

If children's monkey's gaze be to your taste,

Then be content!   'Tis all that study gives you.

Read, read! and stand a tinkling fool at last.

WAGNER. Ah, God! but art is long, and life
is short,

And then to die, so many books unscanned!

FAUST. Is parchment thy sole fount of
inspiration?

Is this the draught that slakes th' eternal thirst?

WAGNER. And yet to apprehend the mighty
world!

FAUST. Those few who apprehended it at all

And dared to bare their breasts unto the brand,

Have evermore been burned or crucified.

And now, good night!

WAGNER.   Much have I learnt already;

To know all I aspire.

FAUST.   Aspire — and go!

[*Exit* WAGNER.

He never need despair who clings to trash.

There goes myself — as great a fool am I,

And when I flung those bitter words at him

'Twas at myself I railed. It seemed indeed

As if my past life mocked me in his words!

Dust, dust, and ashes!

> *[He sinks dejectedly on a chair.*

                       Ah, that Spirit splendid!

He with a thunder word swept me away.

I am no god. Deep in my heart I feel it,

I am a worm beneath the wanderer's feet.

Grin on, thou skull! thy brain was once as mine.

> *[Gazing around, his eye is caught by a gleaming*
>
>   *flask.*

Why dost thou lure me so, thou gleaming goblet,

Drawing me like a magnet? Seeing thee

The stings of pain diminish, struggle ends.

The air glows now like moonlight in a forest,

I see a dreaming ocean and new shores.

Shall I unlock the one door left to me

And, draining this deep draught of slumber

    juices,

Venture on death, although I sleep for ever?

Come down, then, from thy shelf, thou flask of

    crystal.

How often at old banquets didst thou pass

From hand to hand, gladding the solemn guests!

Now to a neighbour never shall I pass thee.

Here is the deadly juice: I chose, prepared it.

Hail to the morn! I drink my final cup.

    [*He sets the cup to his lips, when there is heard*

        a chime of Easter Bells and a Choral Song.

Christ is arisen!

Hail the joyful morn!

The tomb He hath broken,

Our bonds He hath shattered,

Death is defeated.

FAUST. [*Setting down the cup.*] I cannot

drink: the ancient music holds me.

And the remembered bells of Easter morn.

CHORUS

Christ is ascended:

Bliss hath invested Him,

Our woe He hath ended.

FAUST. Once on my childish brow the Sab-

bath stillness

Fell like the kiss of heaven: mystical bells

And prayer dissolved my yearning soul in bliss.

Sound on, ye hymns of heaven! ye sacred bells!

The old tear starts! Earth has her child

again.

[*A pause.*

But I shall ne'er regain the ancient rapture,

When as a child I watched the sun recede

Firing the peaceful vales and mountain peaks,

And some eternal longing came on me

To flee away and up! as over crag

And piney headland slow the eagle soared,

And past me sailed the crane to other shores.

But now not only childhood shattered lies,

But manhood, too, is sold for a barren dream.

Ah! now those fleeting songs I would recall

Which I despised; the feast, the lips of women,

The brief yet luring hours all lost to me.

Only the cup is left.

      [*He again takes the cup and again pauses.*

        And yet, and yet,

One power I ne'er invoked I might invoke.

Seeking the light I called not upon darkness.

Spirit of Chaos, now to thee I turn.

The choice before me lies of Death or Hell, —

Death that leads on to sleep, or Hell that yields

That riot of the blood my soul hath spurned.

I cry to God: the vacant Heavens are dumb;

He answers not. On Evil then I call.

I will not die; I'll risk the eternal woe

So I be rapt into the whirl of sense.

    Ye elemental spirits four,

      Fire and Water, Earth and Air,

From riven skies, from Ocean's floor,

    I bid ye hither! Beware! Beware!

        [He raises the sign of the Hexagon.

Salamander! by thy name

I call thee from thy haunt of flame,

Fair Undine, whose sea-worn home

Lies beneath the circling foam,

Sylph whose feet have found their way

Through the viewless fields of day,

And thou poor gnome who evermore

Art tied and tethered at Earth's core,

I here command ye! Yield unto my sight

From out the dusky cohorts of the night

The Spirit of the Dark who dreads the Light.

      [A flame leaps in the hollow of the chimney,

        and from the risen vapour that follows

the flame the form of MEPHISTOPHELES

gradually emerges.

FAUST.   What art thou?   Speak!

MEPHISTOPHELES.   A part of that fell power

Which ever seeking ill, yet makes for good.

FAUST.   Some riddle doth lurk here!   Yield up

thy name.

MEPHISTOPHELES.   My name?   I am the spirit

that denies.

And wherefore not?   For all created things

That are, are naught or should be turned to

naught.

This whirling planet issuing from the void,

Teeming with empty life, I would consign

Unto the void once more.   There where I ruled

A part of Primal night that knew no dawn —

Prince of the darkness that brought forth the

　　light!

Now, all-conceiving, all-consuming night

Hath lost her ancient place. The upstart day

Disputes her throne. Yet not for ever so!

For Dawn and Day have but their place in Time,

And shall as surely yield that place again

When earth's poor spawn have spent their little

　　hour

And timeless Night resumes her larger sway.

Meanwhile for lighter sport I tread the earth,

Tormenting those I may not yet destroy.

　　FAUST. Strange son of Chaos, now I know

　　　　thee well.

　　MEPHISTOPHELES. Yet when all's said there's

　　　　little left to boast of!

This poor blind mole o' the world, howe'er I

    shake it,

With flood or earthquake, storm and fire and

    plague,

Hath a dull way of settling down again

Most heart-breaking to one who loves his trade.

And even mankind, my latest perquisite,

Proves a poor plaything. Though I kill 'em off

Like flies in jelly, myriads at a stroke,

They breed again before my back is turned.

Then all's to do once more, a weary toil!

Look where I may there's naught but birth and

    life

From Water, Earth, and Air for ever teeming;

And were it not for a poor modest crib

Lit by a flick of flame that still is mine —

      c

That last red rod in pickle down below —

I'd quit the business straight.   But there, enough!

An egotist makes but a sorry devil,

So now for your commands!

FAUST.   Nay, I have none;

My prayer half-uttered dies upon my lips.

MEPHISTOPHELES.   Good Doctor, not so fast,

  ere night shall fall

We'll tread a merrier measure, you and I,

For see you here, I cast aside that garb,

Stitched in the nether world for working hours,

And stand revealed a gallant gentleman —

A part the devil's very apt to play!

  [*The dusky cloak falls from him and he stands*
        under a lightning flame in his dress of scarlet.

Go swiftly, Doctor, find a worthy garb

To match this gay attire. Then, arm in arm

We'll sally forth from out this mouldy den

And look on life.

FAUST.   Nay, that were all in vain;

No outward change can change this outworn world

Where every passing hour croaks but one cry; —

"Abstain, renounce, refrain, and for reward

Take the dried parchment of Life's withering law."

Such is the strain that echoes in men's ears

From waking dawn to phantom-haunted night,

Whose every dream is shattered by the day.

There is no cure but Death. I'll fight no more!

MEPHISTOPHELES. Yet death, too, has its

    drawbacks, so I've heard!

FAUST. Happy the warrior whose blood-

    stained brows

Death's marble fingers crown.　Thrice happy he

Who, drunk with passion, on his lover's lips

Prints the last kiss and finds death waiting there.

MEPHISTOPHELES.　　And yet I know a Doctor

hereabouts

Who grasped the cup but let the liquor go.

FAUST.　You spied and saw me fail.

MEPHISTOPHELES.　　　　　　Ah, Doctor, no!

FAUST.　Where all is known 'twere vain to hide

the truth.

MEPHISTOPHELES.　I know a thing or two, yet

not quite all!

FAUST.　Cursed be the coward hand that

held me back,

And cursed those winning strains of childhood

born,

That snared my soul upon the edge of all!

A curse on life, honour, and wealth and fame,

Ambition's toils, the cheating gleam of gold,

And pomp and power — the empty spoils of war,

A curse on all; aye, even the best of all,

The vine's ripe juice that brings the trance of

    love

And love's brief ecstasy that turns to hate.

And last of all on man, that patient drudge

Who still endures what Death may fitly end.

    MEPHISTOPHELES. Doctor, let me prescribe!

    For such a case

I know a sovereign cure! You wrong yourself

In tearing at a wound my arts may heal!

For think not I would thrust you midst the herd

Of common folk whose lot you rightly spurn.

No! While I'm here I move among the best,

Naught else would suit my quality. Trust to me

To guide you through life's maze, and you shall

    learn

This Earth can furnish unimagined joys

Of sense unfettered by the illiberal bonds

The haunting spirit forges for the flesh.

Now and henceforth through Time's unmeasured

    span

I'll be your comrade, servant, and your slave.

Shall that content you?

    FAUST.   What is thy reward

When this long service hath run out its course?

    MEPHISTOPHELES. We'll call the reckoning

    when the feast is done.

    FAUST. Nay, I would know the cost!

MEPHISTOPHELES.   Then hearken, Doctor.

Till Time's unfathomed waters cease to flow

I'll stand beside thee at thy beck and call.

The Earth and all its countless joys are thine

And I thy willing slave to serve the feast!

FAUST.   And then?

MEPHISTOPHELES.   Why, then I'll ask as

much of thee.

What's here is thine, the all hereafter mine.

FAUST.   That doth not fright me! When

this shattered world

Thou hast cast into the abyss, what else may

come

To fill the vacant void may count for naught.

Our hooded vision vainly seeks to pierce

What lies beyond the ruin of this earth, —

Cradle and grave of every joy and pain

The soul hath sense to capture. — 'Tis not that

Which bids my spirit halt.

MEPHISTOPHELES. Why then, good Doctor.

There's nothing left but just to close the bargain;

That done, I'll get to work, and with swift arts

Will yield thee such a harvest of sweet sense

As none have dreamed of yet.

FAUST. What canst *thou* know

Of joys the uplifted soul would seek to win?

The sordid sweets of sated appetite

Whose savour dies, untasted, on men's lips,

Like fruit that rots within the hand that grasps it,

Dead leaves that scatter ere the buds have
burst:

I know them all!

MEPHISTOPHELES. Nay, be assured, good Doctor;

I would not traffic in such damaged wares.

That were to lose all custom! From this hour

With pleasures new for newly-born desire

Your cup of life shall bubble to the brim.

FAUST. If in thy boasted store of rich delights

Thou hast but one that is not linked with pain,

If from all time one moment thou canst pluck

So rich in beauty that my soul shall cry

Tarry! thou art so fair! —

Then shalt thou claim the immortal part in me!

Then let Time's beating pulses cease to stir:

The shattered hands upon the dial's face

Fling down into the dust: their use is gone,

And Hell itself shall toll the final hour.

So stands my challenge!

MEPHISTOPHELES. Count the bargain closed!
Yet ponder well! The Devil hath a trick
Of not forgetting!

FAUST.　　　　　Nor shall I forget!

MEPHISTOPHELES. But one thing more remains: we're formal folk!
One line of writing just to seal the bond!

FAUST. My soul is pledged, yet wouldst thou
still exact
The feebler witness of this faltering hand!

MEPHISTOPHELES. An idle whim of mine
which sometimes serves
To save dispute hereafter.

FAUST.　　　　　Have thy way!

[MEPHISTOPHELES *produces a document.*

MEPHISTOPHELES. And for our present purpose we will choose

One drop of blood. See here! I prick the vein.

FAUST. Be it so. I am content!

MEPHISTOPHELES.   And I content!

[MEPHISTOPHELES *punctures* FAUST'S *arm
and hands him the pen.* FAUST *signs the
parchment.*

MEPHISTOPHELES. I love that crimson stream:
what's current here

Is of a different colour!

FAUST.   Have no fear!

Lest I should break the bond! My rightful place

Is henceforth by thy side. To plumb the depths

Of every earthly pleasure born of sense,

To win from life a world of new desire,

And quench desire in unimagined joys, —

Is all that's left to one who vainly sought

To win the secrets of the Universe.

MEPHISTOPHELES.   Fall to, then, with a will;

the table's spread

With every dish most cunningly devised!

But first we'll make an end of all this lumber

Of empty knowledge stored for empty heads!

No longer wield the flail on barren straw

That yields no wheat; nor seek to teach to

youth

What age has failed to learn.   There are fools

enough

Wearing a Doctor's gown, whose addled brains

May well suffice to fill the addled brains

Of fools who seek to learn.   Your freer soul

Deserves a richer diet.

[*Knock at door.*

Some one knocks.

One of your faithful students waits without!

FAUST.   I have no heart to see him.   Bid

him go!

MEPHISTOPHELES.   Nay, he hath journeyed

far; 'twere scarcely fair

To leave his famished brain without a meal!

Lend me your hood and gown, my wit may

serve.

Meanwhile make ready for our wayfaring.

FAUST.   Across the world!

[*Exit* FAUST.

MEPHISTOPHELES.   Across the world to Hell!

I hold him fast and sure. That bolder spirit

That drove him upwards, onwards past those
    joys

Man may inherit here, shall prove at last

The rock to wreck his soul.

> [*The knocking is repeated.*

Come in! Come in!

A STUDENT *enters.*

STUDENT. Great Doctor, I have journeyed
    from afar

To set mine eyes upon the face of one

Whose fame spreads through the world.

MEPHISTOPHELES.   You flatter me.

I'm but a simple man, or something more,

Or haply something less. It's hard to tell.

STUDENT. I'm all athirst for knowledge.

MEPHISTOPHELES.   Happy youth!

You couldn't have done better than come here.

STUDENT. Yet, to confess a fault, these

    haunts of learning

Sometimes oppress me. Something in the air

Falls on my brain like lead.

MEPHISTOPHELES.   Nay; that will pass!

The new-born child turns from its mother's

    breast,

Then turns again to take what it refused.

The paps of learning do not lure at first,

The rapture grows in feeding.

STUDENT.   Thank you, Doctor!

I would in all be led by thy advice.

MEPHISTOPHELES. What is the special faculty

    you seek?

STUDENT. All fields of knowledge either in

Earth or Heaven,

All secrets Science wrings from Nature's breast, —

These I would call my own!

MEPHISTOPHELES. 'Tis fortunate

You have made no larger choice! A prudent

lad!

Yet even for this narrow course of study

Attention will be needed.

STUDENT. Body and soul

And all my life I freely consecrate

To this great task! Although in summer time

I own my spirit longs for summer joys.

Is that a fault?

MEPHISTOPHELES. No! that can be arranged.

Yet with this tendency, which think you not

I would condemn — that never was my plan, —

Perhaps 'twere wiser in the first, at least,

To take some special province.

STUDENT.   Once I thought

To choose the Law, but now, I know not

    why,

My spirit turns from it.

MEPHISTOPHELES.   And mine, sweet youth.

I own I have no liking for the Law, —

A rebel prejudice that haunts me still.

STUDENT. Your wiser words confirm me.

    If I may

I'll start my studies with Theology.

MEPHISTOPHELES. Ah! that's my special sub-

    ject! hold to that!

Its laws are simple, and its facts are sure.

    D

Unlike those merely human fields of thought

Where men dispute, and rage in angry strife,

This study makes for peace — and when all's

    learned, —

Your spiritual belly crammed with creeds, —

And you shall come to teach the heavenly law,

See that you spice your list of punishments

That wait on evil-doers! Cite them all

As though the Devil stood beside your chair.

        [*He hisses this in the* STUDENT'S *ear.*

STUDENT. Doctor, you frighten me.

MEPHISTOPHELES.   Why so, my lad?

There's warrant for such teaching.

STUDENT.   True; there is.

MEPHISTOPHELES. But come, a three years'

    course may well suffice

To sift the lumber of the centuries

Men call Theology — and after that?

STUDENT. I thought of Medicine.

MEPHISTOPHELES.   A pretty thought,

Yet deem not that this ancient science dwells

In mouldy parchment. There's a shorter way

To reach to eminence. For true disease,

Death is your sole and sovereign remedy!

Leave all such cases to those meddling fools

Who seek to hinder Nature in her task.

But there's a world of women's maladies

That have one source, and only need one cure.

There you may win distinction. Tend them

    well!

In consultation always feel their pulse;

Look long into their eyes, for there it is

The symptoms show themselves. And now and
then

It may be needful in the cause of science

To test the heart beneath a loosened bodice,

Or even to pass an arm about the waist

Just to discover if the corset strings

Are over-tightly drawn. These simple hints

Should serve to set a student on his way.

The rest is easy if you love your work.

STUDENT. Oh, thank you, Doctor; never
until now

Has science seemed so plain; I almost wish

This very hour my studies might begin.

MEPHISTOPHELES. The fruit of knowledge
hangs upon the tree

And only needs the plucking.

STUDENT. Ere I go

Here in my album pray you write one word.

MEPHISTOPHELES. Most willingly.

[*He writes and hands back the book, from*
which the STUDENT *reads:*

STUDENT. "Be self-possessed and thou
Shalt own the world."

[*Exit* STUDENT.

MEPHISTOPHELES. Young hopeful should go far,
And maybe at the goal we'll meet again.

[*Enter* FAUST.

Ah, Doctor, so thou art ready! All the world
Lies spread beneath our feet.

FAUST. Yet in that world
The years that bow me down must keep me still
An exile from all joy.

Mephistopheles. That's swiftly cured!

There lies a cavern in the cloven earth

Where dwells a witch served by an apish brood

That are her slaves and mine.   There, as she sits

Beside a cauldron that is ever seething,

She weaves a spell that yields to outworn age

The prize of youth.   Straightway we'll journey

    there.

[A roll of thunder.

See, as I cast this garment round about thee

We are speeding on our way!   The hills divide

As down the vacant highways of the dark

We sink in sudden flight.   Above our heads

The circling eagle dwarfed to a dusky star

Soars o'er the moonlit world.   Dost thou not feel

The rush of midnight air upon thy brows

As upward from the deep in chorus chanting

My subject spirits signal our approach?

Chorus

Through shaken rocks that are rent and riven,

    Across the fallow fields of night,

He drives his steeds as a flame is driven

    From Deep to Deep in measureless flight.

Mephistopheles. Time cannot count the

    lightning lapse of time

Till we are there! Hark! we are nearing now.

Chorus of Apes

Beside a cauldron ever brewing,

    We weave a garment of earth and air,

The withered hide of age renewing

    With wondrous tissues shining fair.

[*During the preceding speech of* MEPHIS-
TOPHELES *and the accompanying* CHORUSES
*the Scene fades and darkens, with only a
glint of light upon the* TWO FIGURES *who
stand at the side of the stage. At first the
change is to a world of cloud and vapour,
the effect at the back so contrived by the
rushing upward course of the clouds as
to make it seem as though* FAUST *and*
MEPHISTOPHELES *were swiftly descending.
When the clouds finally disappear and
reveal the Witches' Cavern, they are seen
standing on a ledge of rock slightly raised
from the stage.*

[*The Scene should be designed to represent a
hollowed cavern at the base of a deep, torn*

fissure in the earth. The APISH FORMS

are grouped round a cauldron.

FAUST. Why hast thou brought me to this

filthy den?

The antics of this foul mis-shapen crew

Offend my spirit.

MEPHISTOPHELES. That's strange! they please

me well!

Look where they frolic with that glowing ball

That sinks and rises o'er the savoury stew.

What's that, my winsome puppet? Tell your story.

APE

The world's a ball

Shall rise and fall,

It soars like a star

Afar and afar!

Then falls and falls

As its master calls.

'Tis fashioned of clay

And shall last a day.

Hark! the word is spoken,

'Tis shivered and broken.

Away! Away!

[He flings the orb to the ground, and it breaks

into fragments upon which the APE *and*

his COMRADES *dance in revelry.*

MEPHISTOPHELES. Where is thy mistress?

APE

Up and away

To the fields of day,

Gathering mice

And bats and lice,

With simples new

To feed our stew.

FAUST.   What need to call on her?

MEPHISTOPHELES.   What need to ask?

'Tis in thy service she is summoned here.

FAUST.   If thou wouldst give me back my

vanished youth

This hag's foul witchery is naught to thee.

Canst not thy larger power weave the spell?

MEPHISTOPHELES.   That power is naught

which uses but itself.

The mightier spirit that conceives all ill,

Still needs all service to complete its task.

Since time began a myriad whirring looms

In varied hues of texture, ever changing,

Have wrought the constant pattern of man's fate.

Ape

Hark, hark, and hark!

On the winds of the dark

As a plummet plumbs

To the water's floor

She comes, she comes,

She is here once more!

[*The cauldron suddenly boils over; a great flame leaps up, and the* WITCH *shoots down as though through a chimney in the rock.*

[*She seizes the ladle and threatens the* APES, *who scatter at her approach.*

WITCH. Ye damned crew, so this is how ye work!

Letting our precious potage boil and spoil.

[*Turning to* Faust *and* Mephistopheles.

And ye, what do ye here, accursed pair?

Let burning fire lick all your flesh away,

Consuming heart and brain.

[*She fills the ladle from the cauldron and*

flings the fire towards them.

Mephistopheles.   Vile, filthy witch!

Dost thou not know thy master? At a word

I'll scatter thee and all thy antic brood

In countless fragments to the hissing flames.

So there! and there!

[*He seizes the ladle and smashes the goblets and*

pitchers that are piled around the cauldron.

Witch. [*Grovelling   at   his   feet.*]   Good

master, pardon me.

In truth I did not see the cloven foot.

MEPHISTOPHELES.   Umph!   Well,   of   late

    I've chosen a neater shoe

That better suits the tripping courtly measure

I tread up there on Earth.

WITCH.   Most noble master,

Would I had leave to call thee by thy name.

MEPHISTOPHELES.   Nay, not just now.   I have

    some work on hand

That claims another title.

WITCH.   Tell me then

How I can serve thee best?

MEPHISTOPHELES.   My comrade here

Would like to taste that ancient brew of thine.

WITCH.   You'll pay me for it?

MEPHISTOPHELES.   On Walpurgis night

Ask of me what thou wilt, it shall be thine.

But mark you, of the best with age in bottle!

We want no third-rate vintage.

WITCH. [*Pointing.*]   That was brewed

A thousand years ere yonder ape was born.

[*Whispering.*

Yet have a care, it either kills or cures,

There's no half measure.

MEPHISTOPHELES.   I'll look after that!

I know his malady: he needs the drug.

So quickly to your craft, and when all's done

Fill up the glittering goblet to the brim.

WITCH. Come, then, make ready.

[*The* APES *gather round her in a circle, making
their backs a reading desk for the great book
she opens; then she turns to* FAUST.

FAUST.   This poor jugglery

Was made for fools. I loathe its apish tricks
And would no more.

    MEPHISTOPHELES. Nay, patience! patience,
    Doctor!
The end is near, and while she weaves her spell
Look well in yonder hollow of the rock —
'Tis said that once ere Eden's lawns had flowered
The Mother of the Mother of the World
Lay hidden there.

    [*The* WITCH *continues her incantations and
    as she does so a* VISION *appears, — a*
    VISION *of a* FIGURE *nearly nude and
    draped by the growth of leaves about her
    form, in which she seems partly incorporate.*

    FAUST.   Wonderful form divine,
Pure primal mould of every separate charm

Created nature owns. Oh, lend me, Love,

The swiftest of thy wings that I may speed

To that enchanted bower wherein she lies!

Can this be mortal, or may mortal mate

With that celestial beauty?

MEPHISTOPHELES.   Nay, turn thine eyes,

The cup is ready, brimming to the full.

What's imaged there the world that waits thee holds

In myriad changing shapes, yet ever one.

See, now 'tis gone.

               [*The* VISION *fades.*

FAUST.   Ah, yield it back again.

MEPHISTOPHELES.   The drink will yield thee

   all, for all lies there.

   [*He holds the cup to* FAUST *as the* WITCH

     pronounces the spell.

E

Witch

Here the shrunken skin of age

   In the cauldron sinks and dies,

All the learning of the sage,

   All the wisdom of the wise,

   Count for naught beside what lies

Hidden in that magic brew.

   Drink! and thou shalt feel the fire

Of youth renewed with pulses new,

   Longings that shall never tire

Freshly born of fresh desire, —

   All are there and all are thine,

Hidden in that magic wine.

[Faust *sets the cup to his lips and then starts*

back as a flame leaps from it.

MEPHISTOPHELES. A mate of mine and
wouldst thou shrink at fire?
Drink deep and have no fear.

 [FAUST *drains the cup. The Scene suddenly
darkens. There is a crash of thunder, and
then in a lightning flash* FAUST *appears
richly clad, with youthful face and form.*

WITCH.   'Tis done! 'Tis done!

 [*With a wild shriek she leaps away, pointing
towards* FAUST, *who stands in shining light.*
MEPHISTOPHELES *with a red glow upon
his face, and the* WITCH *surrounded by
her* ATTENDANT APES, *circle in a wild
dance as the Curtain falls.*

CURTAIN

ACT II

ACT II

ACT II

SCENE I

SCENE. — *An open square in a mediæval German city. On one side is a tavern with table set beside the door, round which a group of* STUDENTS *are seated, and with them one or two* SOLDIERS *in armour. On the other side are the steps of the Cathedral.*

[*The Scene opens with* STUDENTS' SONG.

SONG

Up, nightingale, and wake my dear,

Hi! Bird — Ho! Bird!

The lattice opens, thy love is near,

Hi! Bird — Ho! Bird!

Nay, who is that who clambers down?

'Tis the veriest knave in all the town,

But thy kiss hath cost him a broken crown

With a Hi! Bird, Ho!

[*A roll of the drum is heard off L.*

BRANDER.   Enough of thy cracked tuning!
Dost not hear the drum which summons our
comrades?

1ST SOLDIER. Truly 'tis time to join our
troop.

FROSCH. Well, here's to all men of valour
who go forth to war.

ALTMAYER. And to all valorous men who
sit at home and sing of victory.

SIEBEL. Nay, in war-time your student counts
for little, drink as deep as he may. I can boast
it that I have as pretty a way with women as any

man in all the city, yet have I been vilely deceived.

BRANDER. And look you where she goes with yon bearded warrior by her side!

ALTMAYER. Alack! 'tis true. Would I had been a soldier: it should have fitted me well.

BRANDER. Dost hear him? Why, old buttertub, there is not enough steel in all Augsburg to make a case for thy belly.

ALTMAYER. Yet had I the wit to fall in battle, 'tis like I should win a maid's kiss at the last.

SIEBEL. Ay, when there was naught left of thee but a blown carcase beneath the moon.

ALTMAYER. Truly that must be thought of! When all's said, the wine-cup makes the safest kissing, and drink, not love, is your wiser beverage.

[*A* TROOP OF SOLDIERS *enter, followed by a*
CROWD OF TOWN FOLK. *The* SOLDIERS
*who had been drinking join them, and all
move off to the sound of the drum.*

FROSCH. Is Valentine not among them?

SIEBEL. No, he's for the next troop — and,
look you, here he comes!

ALTMAYER. Then here's a flagon for him,
and for all, and at my account! We shall drink
deep to serve him.

BRANDER. [*Looking off.*] Have a care, old
waggle-tongue. He hath his sister Margaret with
him, who loves not ribaldry.

ALTMAYER. Nay, then we'll drink deep but
dumb.

[*There is a sort of hush upon the revellers as*

VALENTINE *and* MARGARET *enter from
R. above the revellers. The music is heard
from the Church and* CITIZENS *pass behind
them, ascending the steps of the Cathedral.*

MARGARET.   Must you go now?

VALENTINE.   I must, dear Margaret;
That beating drum forewarns me.

MARGARET.   Then good-bye!
There'll be no hour I shall not think of thee,
No day at dawn I shall not pray for thee.

VALENTINE.   And I, dear sister, shall for ever

keep

Thine image next my heart.   Once as I trudged
Across our snows in winter, all my thought
Sped backward to a little lonely flower
That decked the spring.   So it shall be again!

Beneath War's thunder skies where'er I go

I'll think of thee the whitest flower of all.

> > > > *[The drum draws nearer.*

My troop draws near.

MARGARET.   I cannot see thee go,

But there within, before the Virgin's shrine,

I'll pray that Heaven may yield thee safe once

more.

Good-bye!

VALENTINE.   Good-bye!

> *[The music within swells as* MARGARET *enters
> the door, and at the same time the beating
> drum draws nearer.* VALENTINE *pauses
> on the steps of the Cathedral, looking after
> her.   The revellers break out again in
> laughter.*

ALTMAYER. Come, Valentine, there's time and place for just one draught !

SIEBEL. And just one toast!

VALENTINE. Most willingly! Here's to you all !

ALTMAYER. And to thee, good Valentine; and a speedy return from the war with just wounds enough to win a tear from thy sweetheart.

FROSCH. Ay, name her to us! Thou hast kept her hidden till now. That shall be our toast.

VALENTINE. When I find her 'twill be time enough to name her. Sweetheart have I none. Such sport is for idle dogs who lag at home. A soldier's sweetheart is his sword.

ALTMAYER. Yet a toast there must be, else there's no cause for drinking.

BRANDER. [*To* VALENTINE.] Pray you take pity on him, poor soul, for he would fain drink.

VALENTINE. Well, then, here's to my sister Margaret; and he who has the worth to win her shall then toast the purest maid in our city.

[*As they drink the* TROOP *comes on to the stage, and* VALENTINE *rises to join them.*

VALENTINE. Farewell, comrades! Have a care to leave just one bottle for my return.

BRANDER. 'Twill surely be no more than one, if Old Altmayer lives so long!

[*Amid general laughter and shouting of farewell, the* TROOP *marches off,* VALENTINE *with them, to the sound of the drum.*

[*As the* SOLDIERS *go off and the* CROWD *disperses,* FAUST *and* MEPHISTOPHELES *have entered and stand at the foot of the Cathedral*

steps.

FAUST.   There goes a gallant soldier to the war!

MEPHISTOPHELES.   Ay, to be spitted on a

friendly pike

And so win death or glory, haply both.

In truth, good Doctor, 'tis most fortunate

That our first upward flight should land us here,

For in this little life is mirrored all.

Those weeping maids who whisper fond farewells

Shall, laughing, yield their lips unto another

Ere the day dies.   So here in brief you see

Both love and glory, Life's twin fading dreams.

[*Pointing to Cathedral.*

And here are those who pray, then quit the shrine

To sin again that they may pray again,

Body and soul still chasing one another

Like kittens who would seek to catch their tails.

FAUST. [*Pointing to revellers.*] And there,

   what life is there?

MEPHISTOPHELES.   The best of all.

Such wine-butts are your true philosophers,

Who neither pray, nor dream, nor fight, nor love,

But pass from cup to cup to life's last goal.

FAUST. Poor sodden fools! Is this in truth

   life's goal?

MEPHISTOPHELES. Nay, not for thee. I do

   but show thee here

How mortals fare who lack the Devil's aid.

Our feast is better ordered. But meanwhile

We'll board these roisterers. Good morrow, sir!

                    [*To* FROSCH.]

SIEBEL.   [*To* ALTMAYER.]   Who are these

gallants?

ALTMAYER. Nobly born, be sure,

For so their garments speak them.

BRANDER.   Nobly born!

More like poor mountebanks who ply their trade

In borrowed plumes.

MEPHISTOPHELES. [*To* FAUST.] There are

some folk, you'll find,

Who never know the Devil when they see

him.

FAUST. Fair greeting, gentlemen!

SIEBEL.   You come from far?

MEPHISTOPHELES. Lately from Spain, that

land of wine and song.

ALTMAYER. Said I not so?

F

FROSCH.   I'll board them, you shall see!

Didst chance to meet my noble cousin there?

MEPHISTOPHELES. Ay, the Court fool! He

had the same pork face,

And slobbered at the lips as thou dost now.

ALTMAYER. A shrewd stroke that! He had

thee there, sweet Frosch!

Wouldst join us in a drink?

MEPHISTOPHELES.   Your pardon, sir,

I only drink the best.

BRANDER.   That's one for thee!

Our friend is set on drinking: if naught else,

The drippings from the counter will content him;

So that it burns his throat, he hath no care

To name the vintage.

MEPHISTOPHELES. Time may come, perhaps,

When he shall find a liquor to his liking ;

I know the cellar where it waits for him.

Meanwhile, if so you please, we'll broach a

    cask

Of something worth the tasting.

    ALTMAYER.   Willingly !

Go, call the landlord.

    MEPHISTOPHELES.   Nay, sir, let him be.

I own a richer store than he can boast of.

Give me a gimlet.

    ALTMAYER.   Yonder one there lies

Within that basket. Look you, noble sir,

We want no scanty sample just to taste,

But full and brimming measure.

    MEPHISTOPHELES.   [*Boring hole in table.*] Give

    it a name.

ALTMAYER.   I'm local in my cups and patriotic —

Rhenish for me!

FROSCH.   Have you so many kinds?

MEPHISTOPHELES.   Call what you will.   I'm

here to serve all tastes.

BRANDER.   This is some juggler's trick.

MEPHISTOPHELES.   A little wax

To serve as stoppers.   Quick, old pot-belly,

That none be wasted.   Now, good sir, your choice.

BRANDER.   Champagne, if you can yield it.

MEPHISTOPHELES. [*To* FAUST.]   Mark you

that,

Your cultured patriot calls an alien brand

And fills his Prussian paunch with Gallic wine.

SIEBEL.   I crave for something luscious!

MEPHISTOPHELES.   Then for you

We'll broach this old Tokay. And you, good sir?

STUDENT. I'll name the vintage when I see

it flow.

This knave doth fool us all!

MEPHISTOPHELES. Say you so?

Then draw the stoppers forth and drink your fill.

[*They hold their glasses and the wine flows.*

SIEBEL. Most wonderful!

ALTMAYER. This is a happy day.

MEPHISTOPHELES. Yet have a care no drop-

pings from your glass ——

[ALTMAYER *lets his glass fall and the wine*

turns to flame.

ALTMAYER. Help! Help! The flames of Hell!

MEPHISTOPHELES. No, no!

A touch of purgatory — nothing more.

[SIEBEL *has drawn another stopper and fire*

flies in his face.

SIEBEL. He uses some vile magic. Out on him!

BRANDER. 'Tis witchcraft! Strike him down!

We'll none of it!

[*They draw their knives on* MEPHISTOPHELES.

MEPHISTOPHELES

Snare their senses, close their eyes,

Bear them hence to Southern skies.

[*They draw back in a trance.*

SIEBEL. What land is this?

BRANDER.   A land of milk and honey.

ALTMAYER. With luscious purple grapes on

every bough.

BRANDER. [*Seizing* ALTMAYER'S *nose.*] Here

hangs a glorious bunch that needs but cutting!

[He puts his knife to ALTMAYER'S *nose.*

FROSCH.   And here another!

STUDENT.   This is best of all!

MEPHISTOPHELES.   Now see them change again,

while 'neath this cloak

We stand invisible.

End their dream and ope their eyes,

Lead them back from Southern skies!

FROSCH.   Why, what is this?

Where are those vines?

SIEBEL.   In truth we've been bewitched.

BRANDER.   *[To* ALTMAYER.]   I took thy nose

to be a purple grape.

MEPHISTOPHELES.   *[Aside.]*   No wonder, for

the vine hath painted it!

ALTMAYER.   And so I deemed was thine.

SIEBEL. [*To* FROSCH.]   And thine.

FROSCH. [*To* SIEBEL.]   And thine.

MEPHISTOPHELES. [*Aside.*] Poor fools! Begone! the Devil's jest is ended.

SIEBEL. Whither hath he fled?

ALTMAYER.   Methought I saw him ride

Over yon steeple on a butt of wine.

BRANDER. Were the knave here, I'd cleave his
head in twain!

MEPHISTOPHELES. [*Aside.*] Go, braggart, ere
I spit thee on a skewer.

FROSCH. Let's go within. There's something
in the air

That freezes all my marrow.

ALTMAYER.   Ay, within!

There's hiding in the cellar. Drink's the cure!

For witchcraft drink's your sovereign remedy.

[*They go into the house like men dazed. A*

laugh from MEPHISTOPHELES.

FAUST.   Let's quit the place; these drunkards

sicken me.

[*Music from Church.*

MEPHISTOPHELES.   Nay, hark! the mass is

ended.   Wait awhile.

Prayer's a provocative and ofttimes sets

The senses newly itching.

[*They begin to stream out of Church.*

See you there

That buxom housewife on her husband's arm?

Last night she kissed the butcher 'neath the elm

That shades their garden patch.   Yon 'prentice

youth

With sheeplike eyes that ever seek the ground,

Can boast of more than his indentures warrant.

Ask of his master's daughter, she can tell thee!

And that pale priest who but an hour ago

Confessed a maiden who will ne'er confess

The thing she learnt of him, — see how his gaze

Would seem to mount toward Heaven!

> [MARGARET *has come from the Church and
> stands at the head of the steps as she gives
> a flower to a child.* FAUST'S *gaze has been
> riveted upon her during the* DEVIL'S *speech.*

FAUST. Enough, enough!

> [*He advances towards* MARGARET.

Fair lady, let me see you to your door?

MARGARET. I am no lady, sir, nor am I fair,

And have no need of escort on my way.

[She passes across and off.

FAUST. By Heaven, how beautiful! In all

the world

Dwells not her equal. Fresh and sweet and

pure

As the first flower of spring that greets the snow,

Yet with red lips that ripen for a kiss

Those downcast eyelids still refuse to yield.

Ah! could I would win that maid!

MEPHISTOPHELES.   What maid is that?

FAUST. She who but now passed by. Look

where she goes.

Didst thou not see her shrink at my approach?

MEPHISTOPHELES.   Oh, that young thing! She's

lately from confession.

I stood beside her whilst the greasy priest

Absolved her of her sins, for she has none.

I would you had looked higher: these fledgling
  buds

Take far more plucking than a full-blown rose.

  FAUST.   There is no higher, nay, nor none so
  high.

  MEPHISTOPHELES.   [*Aside.*]   The scentless per-
  fume of pure innocence

Works like a poison in the air I breathe,

Its very frailty saps all my powers.

  [*To* FAUST.]   I could have set the fairest at
  thy feet,

Disrobed an Empress but to serve thy sport,

Or sacked the centuries to yield thee back

Dead Queens whose beauty wrecked an elder
  world.

Yet with this feast outspread thou needs must
    choose

A wind-flower from the hedgerow. Think again!

FAUST. My choice lies there; naught else I
    care to win.

Yield to my arms this image of delight

Or count our bargain ended.

MEPHISTOPHELES.   Not so fast!

The thing needs time, that's all! — and strategy.

FAUST. Time! that's a mortal's plea: it fits
    thee not.

It needs thy will — no more. Be swift and sure.

Bear me some token that shall speak of her —

A kerchief from her breast — I care not what!

Then lead me where she dwells —

MEPHISTOPHELES.   Nay, sir, not yet!

The day is still a-dying.   When the moon

Peeps through her lattice — that's love's fitting

   hour.

   FAUST.   Meanwhile I need some gift to bear

      to her.

   MEPHISTOPHELES.   A good thought that!   The

      purest maiden's soul

Yields to the treacherous lure of glittering stones.

I know a hidden treasure hereabouts,

Left by a miser who went mad and died.

We'll pick and choose from out his buried store.

   [*As he speaks a* COMPANY OF PRIESTS *come*

      from the Church, the foremost bearing a

      cross, at sight of which MEPHISTOPHELES

      shrinks and cowers, half in fear.

There's something here I like not.   Come away!

SCENE II

SCENE. — *A small, neatly kept chamber.*

Enter MEPHISTOPHELES, *beckoning* FAUST.

MEPHISTOPHELES. Doctor, come on, but
gently; follow me!

FAUST. [*After a pause.*]   Leave me alone!
Depart, I beg of thee!

MEPHISTOPHELES.   [*Peering round.*]   H'm!
'Tis not every girl keeps things so neat.

[*Exit.*

FAUST. O welcome twilight, soft and sweet,
that fills

This virgin shrine! What peace and order
breathe

79

Around me! In this penury what plenty,

And in this cell what bliss!

> [*He draws aside the bed curtain.*

How am I thrilled!

Here could I pass long hours. Here Nature

shaped

The angel blossom from the holy bud.

Ah, Faust, what dost thou here with heavy

heart?

I who in lust's mere madness hither stole,

Now lie o'erwhelmed in the pure trance of love.

MEPHISTOPHELES. [*Returning.*] Quick! She

is coming!

FAUST. I return no more!

MEPHISTOPHELES. Here is a casket not

unserviceable;

It came from — somewhere else — quick, place it

    here !

The gewgaws stored within will turn her head.

  FAUST. Ah, but I know not — Shall I?

  MEPHISTOPHELES.   Ask you that?

Perhaps you'd keep the treasure to yourself.

I trust you are not growing avaricious;

If so, I beg you spare me further trouble;

I rub my hands in tender expectation.

                [Places casket in press.

Now, quick! away! You'll have her at your

    pleasure;

And there you stand as in the lecture-hall —

You with a sweet young girl within your grasp, —

As grim as Physics and Metaphysics! Come!

      [Exeunt FAUST *and* MEPHISTOPHELES.

    G

Enter MARGARET *with lamp.*

MARGARET.   How close, how sultry here!

[*Opens window.*

And yet without

It is not warm.

[*Begins to braid her hair.*

I wonder who he was,

That gentleman I saw to-day.   He seemed

Gallant and of a noble family.

Besides, he would not else have been so for-

ward.

I tremble strangely, I am silly, timid —

Ah! but I wish my mother would come

home!

[*She sings as she undresses herself.*

Song

A king there lived in Thule

    Was faithful till the grave,

To whom his mistress, dying,

    A golden goblet gave.

Before all things he prized it,

    He drained it at every bout,

The tears his eyes o'erflowing

    Whene'er he drank thereout.

And when he came to dying,

    His towns he reckoned up,

All to his heir he left them —

    But not the golden cup!

He sat at the royal banquet

    With his knights of high degree,

In the proud hall of his fathers,

In his castle by the sea.

There stood the old carousers!

As he drank life's parting glow,

He hurled the hallowed goblet

Into the surf below.

He watched it filling and sinking;

Deep into the sea it sank;

His eyelids closed, and never

Again a draught he drank.

[*She opens the press and perceives the casket.*

How comes this lovely casket here, I wonder!

I am quite sure I locked the press.   How

   strange!

What can there be inside it?   And a key

Hangs by a ribbon! I should love to open it!

[*She unlocks casket.*

Ah! what is this? Was anything ever like it?

Heavens! never in all my days have I seen the

   like!

Why, ornaments and trinkets such as these

A noble lady might wear on holidays.

I wonder how this chain would suit my neck!

[*She steps before the mirror.*

Oh! were those earrings mine! At once they

   give one

A different air. Youth, beauty are well enough,

But who cares? People praise one half in pity —

But all depends on gold! Alas! we poor ones.

SCENE III

SCENE. — *Garden of* MARGARET'S *house.*

[MARTHA *enters.*

MARTHA. [*Calling.*] Margaret! Alack! 'tis a hard fate to have lost a husband! Yet that might be borne; but to have no certainty of widowhood — why, 'tis enough to break the heart of any woman! No man hath a right to die unless he send home word he is decently buried. How else should his widow grieve for him in due fashion, or put away her weeds at the fitting time? Truth, 'tis a hard world!

Enter MARGARET, *agitated.*

Ah! thou art there!

MARGARET. Oh, Dame Martha! Dear Dame Martha!

MARTHA. Why, what ails thee, child?

MARGARET. This morning, as I woke I found within my press this second casket like unto the first, yet stored with richer gems. I know not what to do!

MARTHA. Then I'll tell thee. Say nothing to thy mother. She would but give them to the priest, as she did the last.

MARGARET. Look, how beautiful they are!

MARTHA. Oh, you're a lucky girl!

MARGARET. And yet I dare not wear them in the street.

MARTHA. Why, then we'll hide them, and now and then you shall put them on before the mirror. For the first let that content you. As time goes we'll choose some holiday when you may wear, perhaps, a chain or ring — then something more. Your mother will never know, or if she should, we'll forge some pretty tale of how you came by them.

MARGARET. Who could have brought them? I fear, yet know not why, that I do wrong to keep them.

MARTHA. Tut, tut, child! [*A knock.*

MARGARET. Is that my mother, think you?

[MARTHA *peeps through a little grille in the gate.*

MARTHA. No, 'tis some strange gentleman. Pray you walk in.

MEPHISTOPHELES *enters*.

MEPHISTOPHELES. Forgive me, ladies, but I sought for Dame Martha Schwartlein!

MARTHA. I am she, sir. May I enquire your errand?

MEPHISTOPHELES. [*Aside to* MARTHA.] Nay, that can wait. I see you entertain a lady of quality. Another time shall serve.

MARTHA. Hear you that, Margaret? He takes thee for a lady!

MARGARET. Nay, sir, I am only a poor maid. These jewels have deceived thee. They are not mine.

MEPHISTOPHELES. No, I took no thought of the jewels. It was rather the look, the manner, the air, that struck me.

MARTHA. And now, sir, your business, if I may?

MEPHISTOPHELES. I would I had a cheerier note to sound. Your husband's dead and sends you loving greeting.

MARTHA. Dead! O dear, true heart! My husband dead! Then I must needs die too!

MARGARET. Courage, dear Martha!

MEPHISTOPHELES. I feared the shock. A very pitiful case!

MARGARET. Indeed 'tis terrible! What use is love when death can shatter all! I would choose to die unwed.

MEPHISTOPHELES. Yet joy follows swiftly on the heels of woe. That's life!

MARTHA. Tell me, I pray you, how he met his end?

MEPHISTOPHELES. Very prettily, Madame. He lies in Padua beside St. Antony. A very cool and comfortable grave in consecrated ground. A temperate home for one who loved his glass!

MARTHA. Were there no last words? — no message for his fond and loving wife?

MEPHISTOPHELES. He did command thee to buy three hundred masses to save his soul.

MARTHA. And sent the wherewithal? Good, generous heart! A very worthy man!

MEPHISTOPHELES. No, Madame, no! He must have clean forgot it.

MARTHA. What, not a trinket even? Was there no little hoarded fund to leave to his wife?

MEPHISTOPHELES. True penitence was all he died possessed of. His cash he had expended on himself. A very worthy man!

MARTHA. Worthy, forsooth!

MARGARET. Day and night I'll pray for his soul, dear Martha!

MEPHISTOPHELES. So pitiful a lady should well deserve a husband of her own.

MARGARET. I dream not yet of that, sir.

MEPHISTOPHELES. Well, then, let's say some gallant to love and cherish. There's nothing makes life sweeter.

MARGARET. 'Tis not our custom here.

MEPHISTOPHELES. And yet it sometimes happens so, I'm told!

MARTHA. Pray you, sir, and at the last?

MEPHISTOPHELES. Ay, he much desired that all his sins against his wife might be forgiven.

MARTHA. Poor soul, he was forgiven long ago!

MEPHISTOPHELES. And yet, he added, "She was the more to blame."

MARTHA. Oh, what a liar! On his death-bed too!

MEPHISTOPHELES. Maybe his mind was wandering at the close. "I had no home," he said, "no peace, no quiet." Those were his very words. 'Twas sad to hear him.

MARTHA. And I who slaved so hard to make him happy!

MEPHISTOPHELES. Ah! he didn't speak of

that. It seems that after he left his home, he made a bit of money by fair means or foul.

MARTHA. We will not judge too strictly of the means. Where think you he hath hidden it?

MEPHISTOPHELES. 'Twere hard to tell. He told me that in Naples, where he was friendless, a fair young maid had taken pity on his hard case. They're sometimes costly, those fair young pitiful maids.

MARTHA. The villain! Oh, the villain! He was ever a shameful man! Wine and dice and —— you understand me, sir?

MEPHISTOPHELES. Perfectly, Madame. Mourn him for a year, and meanwhile keep a sharp look-out to find another.

MARTHA. Oh, I couldn't, sir! I could never love again!

MEPHISTOPHELES. A hopeless case, eh? A pity! Otherwise I should be almost tempted ——

MARTHA. Oh, sir, you're not in earnest!

[*Approaches him.*

MEPHISTOPHELES. Umph! I'd best make off, or, who knows, she might take the Devil at his word! [*Turning to* MARGARET.] What's in your thought, fair lady?

MARGARET. I know not, sir.

MEPHISTOPHELES. Sweet innocent! Ladies, farewell!

MARTHA. One moment, sir! Perhaps 'twere wiser, in view of what you've said, that this death should be duly attested.

MEPHISTOPHELES. I had thought of that.
A noble friend of mine who travels with me, can
add his deposition. I'll bring him here.

MARTHA. Oh, do sir, pray!

MEPHISTOPHELES. A very gallant youth,
and noble too. [*To* MARGARET.] All ladies
love him!

MARGARET. I should not know how to
greet so great a lord!

MEPHISTOPHELES. There is no king thou
art not fit to greet.

[*Door opens at a gesture from* MEPHISTOPH-
ELES, *and* FAUST *appears.*

MARTHA. Here in this garden this evening
we'll wait you here.

SCENE IV

SCENE. — *A garden.*

Enter FAUST *and* MARGARET.

MARGARET. Ah, sir, but I know you are only trifling with me! You put up with me, as travellers do, out of good nature. How can I hope to entertain you who have seen the great world?

FAUST. But a glance, but a word from you, is sweeter to me than all the wisdom of the world.

[*He kisses her hand.*

MARGARET. How can you bring yourself to kiss a hand like mine, so coarse and hard?

H 97

But then I am obliged to —— well, mother is really too close.

[*Exeunt.*

Enter MARTHA *and* MEPHISTOPHELES.

MARTHA. So you, sir, are always travelling about hither and thither?

MEPHISTOPHELES. Alas! business and pleasure! And many a place one regrets to leave, yet one cannot stay.

MARTHA. In the wild years of youth of course to move about is well enough; but the evil day must come, and then to sneak into one's grave a solitary old bachelor — that cannot be right for any one.

MEPHISTOPHELES. I shudder at the mere prospect.

MARTHA. Then think better of it, sir, while there is time.

MEPHISTOPHELES. I am beginning to already.

[*Exeunt.*

Re-enter FAUST *and* MARGARET.

MARGARET. Ah yes! Out of sight, out of mind! It is easy for you to be polite; and you have many friends more sensible than I am.

FAUST. People one calls sensible are more often only mean and narrow-minded — but you!

MARGARET. Will you think of me, then, just for one brief moment? Ah! I shall have time enough to think of you!

FAUST. You are alone a great deal?

MARGARET. Yes; our household is small, but one must look after it. We keep no maid;

everything falls to me. I must cook, knit, sweep and run here and there — and mother is so particular. Not that there is such great need to stint. However, just now my days are passably quiet. My brother is a soldier. I had a little sister, but she is dead. I loved her so much.

FAUST. If she was like you, an angel!

MARGARET. My mother lay so ill, she could not suckle the poor little mite; so I brought it up with milk and water. It thus became mine; on my arm and on my bosom it smiled and sprawled and grew.

FAUST. What a pure joy for thee!

MARGARET.   Ah yes! indeed. Yet many an anxious time. Beside my bed Its cradle stood; and if it merely stirred

I was awake to soothe it ere it cried!

And then for many an hour, night after
   night

I'd pace the room, warming it next my breast

Till sleep should come again.

FAUST.   Oh, gentle heart!

Hast thou forgiven me yet?

MARGARET.   Forgiven thee?

FAUST. Ay, for those downcast eyelids as
   I came

Told me thou hadst not forgotten.

MARGARET.   Did they so?

Why then, sir, it was true!

FAUST.   I did thee wrong

To stay thee on the threshold of the Church;

Yet 'twas thy beauty made me over-bold.

MARGARET. I'll own it hurt me, at the first, to think

I might have given thee warrant.

FAUST. Nay, 'twas I

Who dared too much!

MARGARET. And yet, I know not why,

I could not be as angry as I would!

Something there was within me still would plead

For thee against myself; till I felt sore

I was not sore with thee.

FAUST. Thou hast forgiven me!

[*They go up and off, hand in hand, as*

Re-enter MARTHA *and* MEPHISTOPHELES.

MARTHA. Ah! it is not so easy to convert

an old bachelor — but I should not call you old!

MEPHISTOPHELES. I am getting on, you know; but it only needs some one like you to teach me better.

MARTHA. But tell me, sir, have you never felt an inclination for any one?

MEPHISTOPHELES. Well, I am very difficult to please. I am more attracted by the soul than the body.

MARTHA. Of course, good looks are not everything.

MEPHISTOPHELES. But I am rather partial to the plump.

MARTHA. And your heart has never been really touched?

MEPHISTOPHELES. Not yet; and yet you would hardly believe the variety of women I

have come across here — and there. Charming,
I assure you: I have always been at home to them.
I wonder if it is too late for me to be constant
to one?

> [*He puts his arm round her.*

MARTHA. It is growing dark.

MEPHISTOPHELES. Yes, we must be going.

MARTHA. I would ask you to stay here longer,
but you have no notion what a place this is for
scandal.

MEPHISTOPHELES. It can't be worse than the
place I come from.

MARTHA. Is that very far away, sir?

MEPHISTOPHELES. A good distance, but they
make the journey there as comfortable as possible.

MARTHA. I have to be most careful here, I

assure you. If I were to be seen alone with you it would be news everywhere in the morning.

MEPHISTOPHELES. Surely they wouldn't mind — if they knew who I was!

MARTHA. Yes; but you see they don't. They would suspect you.

MEPHISTOPHELES. How extraordinary! I would not compromise you for the world.

MARTHA. And besides, I would not trust myself with you for long.

MEPHISTOPHELES. I assure you you need have no fear.

MARTHA. And our love-birds — where are they?

MEPHISTOPHELES. Flown up the garden path — naughty butterflies!

MARTHA. He seems fond of her.

MEPHISTOPHELES. Of course, and she of him.

Ah, dear lady, it is the way of all flesh!

[MEPHISTOPHELES *and* MARTHA *pass out
by the upper path as* MARGARET *comes
lightly down from the gate.*

MARGARET. Now ere he comes —

[*She plucks a star flower as* FAUST *follows her.*

FAUST. [*Aside.*] And would'st

thou hide again?

Nay, but I have thee now!

MARGARET. I'm half afraid

To put thee to the test; yet so I will!

[*She begins to pull the leaves.*

He loves me — loves me not! . . .

FAUST. What's in thy thought?

To bind a nosegay ere the sun be down?

MARGARET. No! 'Tis a foolish sport that
children love!

FAUST. Teach me that sport.

MARGARET. Thou would'st but laugh at me.

[She moves away.

He loves me not! — he loves me! . . .

FAUST.   Angel soul
Thou need'st not slay a flower to tell thee
    that.

MARGARET. Nay, wait! there's more to
    come. He loves me not! —
And now the last! — He loves me!

*[She drops the last petal to the ground as he
    takes her in his arms.*

FAUST.   Ay, he loves thee!

[*She sinks on his breast as he kisses her.*

Lord of the world, for so in truth I am

In owning thee: there is naught else to win.

[MEPHISTOPHELES *has peeped in at the garden*

gate during the last speech.

MEPHISTOPHELES.   Lord of the world, I fear

'tis time to go!

SCENE V

SCENE. — *An interval, during which the orchestra plays a stormy melody, gradually subsiding and ending in a peaceful strain reminiscent of the Chorus of Easter Angels which in Act I. prevented* FAUST *from taking his life. The Curtain then rises on a desolate scene of strewn boulders, black pines, and a lurid sun setting.*

[FAUST *is discovered lying prone on the earth: slowly he raises himself.*

FAUST. Spirit Sublime! thou hast given me what I asked.

Hither have I retired to Nature's breast

To ease me of this fever. Here to lose

'Mid air and water and the silent wood

My wild unrest.   Whatever stirs the bush

Or wings the air or troubles the dark pool,

With these am I acquainted.   Thou hast given

No cold amazéd knowledge of thyself,

But hast revealed thy countenance in fire.

Alas! yet nothing perfect comes to man!

Thou hast assigned me as a comrade one

Who cancels with a sneer thy loving-kindness

And ever fans within my heart a flame

Unwearied for one fair, delicious form.

I fly from her, but ever would return.

Enter MEPHISTOPHELES.

MEPHISTOPHELES.   Have you not led this life

   now long enough?

The wilderness awhile, but not for ever.

FAUST. Find other work: to plague me thou

returnest.

MEPHISTOPHELES. Thou sitt'st here like an

owl: or like a toad

From sodden moss thy nourishment deriving.

FAUST. I find a pleasure in the wilderness.

MEPHISTOPHELES. Enough of this! Yonder,

alone, she sits;

Her thoughts and yearnings all go out to thee,

And miserably long the hours delay.

She haunts her window, pacing to and fro,

Watching the clouds roll off the city wall.

Now she is lively, but more often sad —

Sad, sad and mad for thee.

FAUST.   Serpent, be still!

MEPHISTOPHELES. Ah! do I trap thee now?

FAUST. Bring not again

Desire of that white bosom to my mind.

I envy even the body of the Lord

When touched by her sweet lips.

MEPHISTOPHELES. Back to her then!

FAUST. No! no! I will no more assail her

peace;

She shall return to her old simple life,

Take up again the tranquil tasks of home.

MEPHISTOPHELES. Fool! She shall ne'er re-

cover that old peace;

She cannot now return to simple tasks.

FAUST. Cannot?

MEPHISTOPHELES. She hath seen thee.

FAUST. Am I so vile

That sight of me hath shattered all her peace?

MEPHISTOPHELES.   Thou art her only peace:

 return to her;

Never can she be glad but on thy breast.

FAUST.   All this may be; but I'll return no

 more.

If I have troubled so her serene days,

I trouble them no more.   Have I disturbed

Her virgin soul, then I no more disturb it;

I leave her.

MEPHISTOPHELES.   Leave her now?   Is that

 quite fair?

You bring the trouble, then refuse to ease it.

Go back to her.

FAUST. What would'st thou have me do?

MEPHISTOPHELES.   Finish what is begun.

FAUST.   Away, thou pimp!

 I

I'll not seduce her body and her soul!

MEPHISTOPHELES. Her soul thou hast se-
　　duced — why hang on here?

She is no longer virgin in her thoughts,

Thou hast corrupted every wandering whim.

Think you she lieth now so still of nights?

She turns in darkness to the form of thee

And round thy image throws her burning arms.

What is the body's touch between you two?

Now her imagination is deflowered:

Thou hast defiled her, Faust, for evermore.

　FAUST. Ah no! Ah no!

　MEPHISTOPHELES.　　　The only recompense

Is now to sate the craving thou hast waked;

To-night!

　FAUST. To-night!

MEPHISTOPHELES.   Ay, sir, the silvering moon

Heralds the dawn of love.   Yet have a care!

Her mother sleeps but lightly!   This shall serve

To smooth her restless pillow.

FAUST.   [*Taking phial.*]   What is here?

MEPHISTOPHELES.   A sweet decoction that shall

     swiftly link

Sunset and dawn in one.

FAUST.   Not poison?

MEPHISTOPHELES.   No!

Sleep is no poison though it last for ever.

FAUST.   Then let us both in ruin fall together,

And one damnation quickly seize us both.

MEPHISTOPHELES.   Now Hell seethes up in her

     again.   Away

Into her room, and leave it not till dawn.

SCENE VI

SCENE. — *Margaret's garden*

[MARGARET *spinning in the doorway.*

MARGARET

Gone is my peace, and with heart so sore

    I shall find it again nevermore.

If he be not near me, the world is a grave

    And bitter as is the sea-wave.

Ah! my poor brain is racked and crazed,

    My spirit and senses amazed!

Gone is my peace, and with heart so sore

    I shall find it again nevermore.

At the window I stand only to greet him,

    I leave the house but to meet him.

Ah! the smile of his mouth and the power of his

    eye

    And his noble symmetry!

What a charm in his speech, in his touch what

    bliss!

    The rapture of his wild kiss!

My bosom is aching for him alone —

    Might I make him my very own!

Might I kiss but his lips till my mouth were fire,

    And then on his kisses expire!

Enter FAUST

Ah, dearest! thou hast been so long away,

I almost feared . . . What it would be to lose

    thee

Thou know'st not!

FAUST. [*Kissing her.*] Margaret, once more

    I am happy.

I fled away into the wilderness

To commune with my God.   I lived alone

With mighty trees and waters and wide air,

With wild and wingéd things, creatures and birds;

But all availed not.   Oh, the very desert

Was haunted by thee; solitudes were filled

Suddenly with thy presence, silences

Murmured thee in my ear.   From thee to fly

Is but to bring thee doubly near to me.

    MARGARET.   And I all day lonely at yonder

    window

Have stood, and listened for a single step;

Now would I fall to singing, now would cease,

Now took my work up, and now set it down;

And now I loved in rapture, now in gloom.

Ah! leave me nevermore.

FAUST.   Nay, nevermore.

MARGARET.   Oh! the deep bliss descending on

me fast,

Like steady rain on an unfolding flower.

Yet one thing troubles me.

FAUST.   What troubles thee?

MARGARET.   Dearest, dost thou believe?

FAUST.   In what?

MARGARET.   In God.

FAUST.   Darling, who dares say "I believe in

God"?

MARGARET.   Oh! but we must!

FAUST.   I feel the living God

Trembling in starlight, surging in the sea,

And rushing by me in the wind; I feel Him

Approach me close in twilight without word.

He shakes my soul with thunder — oh, to feel

It all! I have no single name to give it —

Bliss, Love, God, what you will, the name is

    smoke

Obscuring all the serene glow of Heaven.

  MARGARET. And, dear, long has it been a

    grief to me

To see thee in such company.

  FAUST.   How so?

  MARGARET. Thy comrade, who is ever at thy

    side;

His face with a deep horror fills my soul,

And my heart shudders at his voice.

  FAUST.   Yet why?

MARGARET.   I know not; but believe me I can

tell

He is not a good man. O God forgive me

If I speak ill of any; but I feel

He is not good. I am so happy here,

So yielding and free, and warm upon thy arm,

But if his face peer round the garden wall

I am struck cold, and cannot love, or pray.

But I must go.

FAUST.   Ah! will there never come

A quiet hour when we two, heart to heart

And soul to soul may cling; when we two may

Drive down the stream and headlong greet the

sea,

The full ocean of bliss?

MARGARET.   Now am I thine

So wholly, thine in every thought and hope,

In my outgoing and returning, night

And day, by sunlight or by moonlight thine;

So utterly am I given o'er to thee

In spirit, that what else thou dost desire

Can have no strangeness in it, only bliss.

I have yielded — then do with me what thou

    wilt.

FAUST.   Oh, if to-night —— I burn for thee!

MARGARET.   And I

For thee!

FAUST.   To-night then!

MARGARET.   If I slept alone

I would undraw the bolt for thy desire;

But mother sleeps so light of late, and if

She should discover us I could but die.

FAUST. Thou angel, fear it not. Here is a

phial:

Pour but three drops into her sleeping cup

And she will sleep on deeply thro' the night.

MARGARET. It will not harm her: thou art

sure?

FAUST.   Would I

Give it if there were danger?

MARGARET.   O belovéd,

I can refuse thee nothing thou dost wish,

I will refuse thee nothing. I will open

That window when she is fallen quite asleep;

Listen for that — and then I'll unlock the door.

How heavy come the roses on the air

To-night! Kiss me — I must go in.

[He kisses her passionately.

FAUST. 'Tis hard
To part but for a moment.

MARGARET. Only wait!

[*She goes into the house. As* FAUST *stands*
expectant, the door of the garden opens and
MEPHISTOPHELES *appears.*

FAUST. Who's there?

MEPHISTOPHELES. A friend.

FAUST. A fiend!

MEPHISTOPHELES. Ay, both in one!

FAUST. Monster, begone!

MEPHISTOPHELES. I have no need to stay,
My work is done.

[MARGARET'S *hand is seen opening the lattice*
as FAUST *makes a threatening gesture to*
MEPHISTOPHELES.

Softly!   The rest is thine!

[FAUST *halts: his eyes turn toward the cottage,*
the door of which slowly opens. FAUST *is*
drawn towards it.   He looks back as he
enters.

FAUST.   And thine!

MEPHISTOPHELES.   [*As the door closes on*
FAUST.]   Ay, truly thine and mine in one!

ACT III

ACT III

ACT III

SCENE. — *Outside the Cathedral, with Martha's house to R. The nave and choir of the Cathedral set across the stage, leaving space for a narrow street that runs up stage between it and Martha's house. Down stage L.C. a fountain. Above it, beside a buttress in the Cathedral wall, stands an image of the Virgin. It is close upon Vesper time, and a group of* GIRLS *are gossiping by the fountain as they fill their pitchers.*

[ELSA *enters down street R.*

ELSA. Hast heard the news?

LAINE. Old Katrine's cat is dead!

LISBETH. We heard that yesterday.

1ST GIRL.   Ay, that's no news!

At dawn the cobbler slit his thumb in twain

In mending Sach's shoe!

2ND GIRL.   I saw it done.

LISBETH.   Hast thou naught else to tell?

ELSA.   In truth I have!

A mighty throng is gathered in the Platz,

'Tis cried the war is ended, and to-day

Our troops draw toward the city.

LISA.   News indeed!

Then Valentine comes with them?

ELSA.   At their head!

He hath won such glory that he now returns

As captain of his band!

LAINE.   Poor Margaret!

I wonder hath she heard?

LISA.   'Tis likely not,

For since her mother's death three months gone by,

She seldom goes abroad.

LAINE.   Both day and night

The shuttered windows of her house are closed,

And there she sits alone.

LISA.   'Twas late last night

I had tended poor old Anna who lay sick,

And as I hurried homeward, here she stood,

Filling her pitcher 'neath the darkened moon

Whilst all the city slept!

LAINE.   I'll go to her;

Her brother's home-coming will cheer her heart.

LISA.   Hush! here she comes.

     [MARGARET *enters and sits wearily on the*

        edge of the wall.

LISA.   Dear Margaret, hast thou heard
The war is at an end?

MARGARET.   Hither as I came
They cried the news along our narrow street.

LAINE. And Valentine returns a captain now!
Shall that not make thee glad?

MARGARET.   I must be glad
That he is safely home.

LISA.   Not every girl
Can boast so proud a brother.

LISBETH.   Some there are
Who are lucky to have none!

LISA.   Ay, true enough!

LISBETH. 'Twould be no joy for Mistress
    Barbara
Had she a brother homeward bound to-night.

LAINE. Nay, nor for him who brought her to

this pass.

LISBETH.   The fault was hers, not his!

No man's to blame

Who takes the gift a wanton flings to him.

MARGARET. [*Clinging to* LAINE.]   What is it

that they say?

LISBETH.   Dost thou not know?

MARGARET. I've been too much indoors for

three months past,

I have heard nothing but the bell that tolls

From hour to hour.

LISBETH.   Oh, 'tis a pretty story!

But now she's got her due, and serves her right.

What else could she expect? Both day and

night

She hung upon his kisses. Now she knows

What comes of too much kissing.

MARGARET.   Oh, poor thing!

But is it so indeed?

LISA.   Indeed it is!

LISBETH. Ask through the city! Every gos-
    sip's tongue

Is wagging of her shame. Why pity her?

Whilst honest girls would sit at home and spin

She'd steal away o' nights to meet her swain,

Who leaves her for reward a sinner's shift.

MARGARET. Nay, surely he will take her for
    his wife?

LISBETH. Not he! And who can wonder?
    There are more

Like proud Miss Barbara who only wait

Till he shall have a mind to kiss again.

He'll meet them on his journey.

MARGARET.   Has he gone?

Oh, 'tis not fair!

LISBETH.   Why, think you he would wed

A maid who could not wait to claim a ring?

Not he! Come, girls, 'tis late, and I've no mind

To furnish food for gossips!

1ST GIRL.   Nay, nor I!

[*They take up their pitchers and move off in
different directions. MARGARET is left weeping. LISA, who is just going out, returns
to her.*

MARGARET. Poor Barbara!

LISA.   Dear Margaret, grieve not so!

Thy gentle heart is all too pure to know

The sin that tempted her. Yet thou canst weep

While others speak in scorn!

MARGARET. Oh, leave me — go!

LISA. See then, I'll take the pitcher to thy door

And come again for thee!

[LISA *goes out.*

MARGARET. In days long flown

I too have scorned each sinner as she fell!

Sure of myself, there were no words too hard

To paint the thing I deemed I ne'er could be —

The thing I am to-day — a living sin!

And yet — and yet — that one who drew me down

    down

Seemed then, dear God, so true, so good, so dear!

[*She throws herself at the feet of the Virgin.*

O Mother of all sorrows, thou alone

Canst pierce my sorrow; thou alone canst cure

The ceaseless pain that bows me to the earth.

The prayer I dare not utter thou canst hear!

And those vain tears that washed thy stainless

    feet

Night after night, hast thou not seen them

    fall?

I have no help but thee! no hope but here.

As thou wert once a maid, be pitiful,

Take in thy hands my breaking, bleeding heart

And save my ruined soul from death's last stain.

    [*There is a pause. The organ sounds from
        the Church, the windows of which show
        the candle-light within. A few* CITIZENS
        come from L. *and enter the porch. They
        are followed by* LISA.

LISA. Dear Margaret, you are weary. Let
us go.

MARGARET. Ay, let us go within. Lend me
your hand;

To-night we'll pray together, if I may!

[*As* LISA *supports her into the Church,* FAUST
and MEPHISTOPHELES *come down the dark
alley from the right.* MEPHISTOPHELES
peeps round the angle of the Church and sees
MARGARET.

FAUST. Who was it entered there?

MEPHISTOPHELES.   Some aged crone
With crooked, twisted limbs — no dish for
thee.

FAUST. I thought 'twas Margaret!

MEPHISTOPHELES.   Nay, that lonely bird

Sits in her wicker cage waiting for him

Who clipped her wings.

FAUST.   Why, then I'll go to her!

MEPHISTOPHELES. What! doth that poorer

fancy still endure?

Doctor, you shame my trade! For this mean

feast

The merest prentice pander might have served!

Have I not cured you yet? What find you there?

FAUST. A fluttering flower that lures me like

a star.

MEPHISTOPHELES. I love them not, these

flowers that scent the air

I was not born to breathe. In these past months

Since first that bud was plucked, we have seen

the world.

FAUST. Ay! and not once her equal in the
world.

MEPHISTOPHELES. Nay! there are worlds on
worlds unfolded yet
Whose treasured store of beauty still awaits us.
As children strew the hedge-blooms they have
gathered
Along the dusty highway — cast her off
And let us on our road.

FAUST.　　　　　There is no road
That leads not back to her.

MEPHISTOPHELES.　　　　Well, as you will!
Meanwhile I have some business of my own
That needs my presence here.

FAUST.　　　　　　I need thee not!

　　　　　　　　　　[*Exit* FAUST.

MEPHISTOPHELES. This comedy must end,

and swiftly too.

Beside that purer soul my spirit flags;

I have no scythe to shear a harebell down,

Its weakness masters me. Till that hour come,

When all engulfed in sin she sinks and drowns,

My power is powerless. Once that hour is past,

Then, Faust, thou art mine again!

[*Music heard from Church.*

She kneels within

Yet knows not how to pray. I'll go to her.

Unseen, yet seeing all, beside her chair

I'll breathe a whispered poison in her ear

Shall draw her soul down to the verge of Hell.

[*As he speaks the stage darkens and the wall*

of the Church becomes transparent, showing

the dimly lit interior where MARGARET *kneels*

among the worshippers, MEPHISTOPHELES

bending over her.   The opening lines of the

Latin hymn are being chanted.

CHORUS

Dies Irae dies illa

Solvet saeclum in favilla.

MEPHISTOPHELES.   It is not with thee now as

once it was,

When as a prattling child those innocent lips

First learned by rote the words of Holy Writ

From out the well-worn book thy mother held.

MARGARET.   I cannot pray!   Across my dark-

ened soul

Hither and thither in a tangled flight

Come thoughts that drag me down.

Chorus

Judex ergo cum sedebit,

Quidquid latet adparebit,

Nil inultum remanebit.

MEPHISTOPHELES.   Where tends

thy thought?

What hidden crime within thy bosom dwells?

Would'st pray for mercy on thy mother's soul,

Who slept nor woke again through thee! through

thee!

Her blood lies at thy door.

Chorus

[With third verse.]

MARGARET.   Oh, woe is me!

I dare not look toward Heaven: the gate is shut,

My heart sinks to the dust.

MEPHISTOPHELES. Beneath thy breast

Canst thou not feel the pulse of that new life

That stirs and quickens there? Dost thou not know

Whither thy sin shall drive thee?

CHORUS

Quid sum miser tunc dicturus,

Quem patronum rogaturus,

Cum vix justus sit securus?

MARGARET. Oh! no more!

The pillars close me in; the roof falls down

To crush me to the earth. I cannot breathe!

Dear Mary Mother, turn thy face once more.

MEPHISTOPHELES. Her face is turned away, she heeds thee not;

The light of Heaven goes out.

MARGARET. [*To* LISA.] Thy cordial! Oh!

[MARGARET *half swoons as, with the final repeat of the* CHORUS, *the vision fades and the exterior view of the Cathedral is restored. In the darkness* MEPHISTOPHELES *creeps stealthily from the door and is about to go off as* ALTMAYER *and* OTHERS *enter R. He hides behind a buttress.*

ALTMAYER. They've reached the city! We'll drink deep to-night.

1ST STUDENT. [*To* FROSCH, *who comes with* OTHERS *down the alley.*] Where are they now?

FROSCH.   Within the Western gate.

ALTMAYER. And Valentine?

L

FROSCH.   He marches at their head.

ALTMAYER.   That serves as fit occasion for our

cups.

FROSCH.   The crowds draw round him shouting

Victory!

But he, scarce heeding them, still presses on

To greet his sister Margaret.

[BRANDER *and* SIEBEL, *with* OTHERS, *have*

entered L.

BRANDER.   Say you so?

Why, then he hath not heard?

MEPHISTOPHELES.   [*Aside.*]   Nay, sirs, not yet!

The Devil takes his time.

FROSCH.   What should he hear?

BRANDER.   The sorriest news, if what is said be

true.

SIEBEL. Ay! and the foulest slander if 'tis false,

As here upon my soul I vouch it so.

MEPHISTOPHELES. [*Aside.*] Be thrifty with

your soul; you have but one.

BRANDER. To-night 'tis whispered that her

mother's death

Came not at Nature's call. Within her room

A poisoned phial was found.

FROSCH.   Is that enough

To brand as murderess the gentlest maid

That dwells within our city?

SIEBEL.   Nay, there's more;

So slander grows on slander! Now 'tis said

She slew her mother to conceal her sin.

STUDENT. Oh, shame! I'll not believe it!

2ND STUDENT.   Nay, nor I!

MEPHISTOPHELES. [*Aside.*] The world grows

charitable! No fault of mine!

SIEBEL. Is there one here who would dare

breathe this lie

To Valentine her brother?

VOICES. Nay, not one!

SIEBEL. If this foul gossip needs must reach

his ears,

It shall not be through us.

Enter STUDENT.

Well, sir, what now?

1ST STUDENT. The Burgomaster with the city

guard

Keep watch on Margaret's house.

2ND STUDENT. Ay, and 'tis said

A warrant's out against her.

SIEBEL.   Nay then, friends!

At such a time 'tis fit that we who love her

Should speak on her behalf.

ALL.   Ay, so we will!

                                        [*They go off L.*

MEPHISTOPHELES. Oh, faithful hounds! be-

    fore the dawn is here

Your tongues shall learn to sound another

note.

Enter FAUST.

What, Doctor, back so soon?

FAUST.   She is not there;

The house is closed; there is no light within;

I have sought her through the city all in

    vain.

MEPHISTOPHELES. Have you no tidings of her?

FAUST. Ay, the worst!
The whisper grows against her. Every tongue
Breathes slander on her name.

MEPHISTOPHELES. I feared as much!
Some gossip hath made mischief. Gossips will.
Doctor, we'd best make off.

FAUST. No, I will stay
Till I have seen her face, and at her feet
Have prayed for pardon.

MEPHISTOPHELES. Well, I'm still your slave.
An ancient pet of mine dwells hereabouts;

[*Striking his guitar.*

These strains may wake her; she is still romantic;
We'll gather news of her.

FAUST. I care not how,
So that these eyes may greet her once again.

MEPHISTOPHELES. Doctor, to-night I'm in a
frolic mood

And, like some old Tom cat upon the tiles

Who stalks his love behind each chimney-stack,

I'll thread this alley, mewing as I go!

> [*They go off and up, the Song dying away as*
> *shouts are heard and*

> [*The* CROWD *enters,* VALENTINE *marching*
> *through them at the head of his* TROOP
> *amidst the shouts of the multitude.*

VOICES. All hail to Valentine!

VOICES.   All hail! all hail!

3RD STUDENT. Come, bear him to the tavern;
'tis not far!

The city hath decreed good wine for all,

And at the city's charge.

4TH STUDENT. Come then, let's on!

5TH STUDENT. Ay, set him shoulder high!

Our backs shall serve

In place of that stout steed that carried him.

[*They approach* VALENTINE, *who checks them.*

VALENTINE. Good comrades, wait awhile.

Ere that shall be

There's one I needs must greet the first of all,

My sister Margaret. There at her feet

I'll lay this sword, so hacked and carved with war,

And then we'll drink till dawn!

[SIEBEL, BRANDER, *and* OTHERS *have entered*

and stand in a silent group.

Ah, Siebel there!

Brander! and thou, old Altmayer!—ay, and

Frosch!

Well met, old friends! It seems an age and
    more

Since last I grasped your hands! So long, in
    truth,

I've grown a stranger to our city lanes.

Come, lead me on my way!

    BRANDER.   Where, Valentine?

    VALENTINE.   Where else but home to
    Margaret?

                          [SIEBEL *intervenes*.

    SIEBEL.   Go not there!

    VALENTINE. Why not?

    SIEBEL.   I dare not tell thee!

    VALENTINE.   Dare not? Speak!

Are ye all dumb? I am no more than man,

Yet being man, must school me to endure

What Heaven shall please to send. She is not dead?

SIEBEL. No, Valentine, not dead!

BRANDER. Would Heaven she were!

VALENTINE. What is it then that strangles all your tongues?

SIEBEL. Speak, Brander, for I cannot!

FROSCH. Nay, nor I!

BRANDER. 'Tis said thy mother died by Margaret's hand.

VALENTINE. My mother dead, and slain by Margaret!

Liar! I could choke thee!

BRANDER. I'd forgive thee that Could I unsay what's said, undo what's done!

VALENTINE. This is some villainous slander.

If God willed

In sudden wrath to change an angel child

Into a fiend, there would be cause for it.

What cause was here?   She loved her mother well

And was as well beloved.   Why should she take

That mother's life?

BRANDER.   Nay, that is worst of all!

She took that mother's life to hide her shame.

VALENTINE.   Liar!   I'll go to her!

Enter BURGOMASTER.

BURGOMASTER.   Stay, Valentine!

We all had hoped to give thee public greeting

And a triumphant welcome from the town,

But this must stand aside till happier hours:

Our duty now gives no excuse for joy.

VALENTINE.   Art thou, too, in this treachery,

this plot

Against my sister's honour?

BURGOMASTER.   If 'twere so,

The wrong were quickly righted. 'Tis not so.

Upon approved witness of her crime

Thy sister Margaret stands accused of murder,

And here I hold the warrant of the law

To arrest her as my prisoner.

VALENTINE.   Is that all?

Does not your parchment publish some excuse

To inform the world why she, a maid so pure,

Should on a sudden turn a murderess?

BURGOMASTER. 'Tis known and proved that

   night thy mother died

An unknown gallant, stranger to our town,

Was seen to enter Margaret's chamber door,

Nor left it till the dawn.

ALTMAYER.   Sure that was he

Whose comrade tricked us as we sat at wine!

FROSCH. 'Twas he, I'll warrant it!

VALENTINE.   Enough! Enough!

We'll think of him hereafter. For the time

This must seem all — that all I loved is lost.

Now, comrades, turn those torches to the ground;

Oh! that I had found death in glorious war!

Or any stroke but this! But yesterday

Round the camp fire we sat and talked of home,

And as each comrade with a brimming cup

Toasted in turn the maid he loved the best,

I let them all run on, till at the last

With lifted glass I did but breathe her name,

And all were dumb. "'Tis true, 'tis true!"

     they cried,

"In all our town there's but one Margaret,

The fairest, best of all!" — And now — and now —

Let every braggart spurn me as he will,

I have no answer, for her shame is mine.

> [MEPHISTOPHELES *and* FAUST *are seen*
>
> *coming down the alley,* MEPHISTOPHELES
>
> *singing to the guitar, with* FAUST *beside him.*

SIEBEL. Why, here he comes! That knave

who ruined her!

FROSCH. Ay, and that juggling villain by his

side!

VALENTINE. Then stand aside. This issue

must be mine,

And mine alone.

> [*He draws his sword and approaches*
>
> MEPHISTOPHELES, *who still sings.*

Thou whining rat-catcher,

Whom now wilt thou allure? That blow's for
thee!

[*He dashes the guitar to the ground.*

MEPHISTOPHELES. The lute is broken, so
the song must cease.

VALENTINE. And thou who lurk'st behind,
I've more for thee.

MEPHISTOPHELES. He knows thee, who thou
art, yet stand thy ground.

VALENTINE. Draw, or I'll spit thee!

FAUST.   Thou shalt have thy will!

[FAUST *draws.*

MEPHISTOPHELES. Lunge on now, have no
fear; I'll parry all.   [*They fight.*

VALENTINE. Then parry that!

MEPHISTOPHELES.   Why not?

VALENTINE.   And that!

MEPHISTOPHELES.   That too!

VALENTINE.   I think the Devil's here, my arm
grows weak.

MEPHISTOPHELES.   Now is your time — thrust
home!

[FAUST *lunges at* VALENTINE, *who falls.*

VALENTINE.   O God, 'tis done!

[*The* CROWD *gathers round* VALENTINE.

MEPHISTOPHELES.   He's skewered at last!
Now quick, no word — away!

[*He throws his cloak round* FAUST *and they
vanish.*

BURGOMASTER.   There's murder here!   Go,
seize them both.

SIEBEL.   They've gone!

BURGOMASTER. Whither?

BRANDER.   I know not. As we followed them

It seemed to me that they became as air.

BURGOMASTER. Look then to him who fell!

[MARTHA'S *head appears at the window above. And other heads from other windows.*

MARTHA.   What brawl is this?

[MARGARET, *with a crowd of Citizens, enters from the Church.*

MARGARET. Who is it wounded there?

BRANDER.   Thy mother's son.

MARGARET. Almighty God! Not dying?

M

VALENTINE. Ay, I'm dying,

Yet that may count for little. Cease your

    tears

And listen while ye may; my time is brief.

MARGARET. O Valentine!

VALENTINE. Why dost *thou* loiter here?

Thou should'st be at thy trade. The night is

    young;

For what thou hast to sell there are buyers yet.

MARGARET. Dear God, have mercy!

VALENTINE. Thou wert best advised

To leave God's name alone. As yet 'tis plain

Thou art but a prentice hand — I'll grant thee

    that;

But custom starves all scruples, in a month

Thy beauty will be free of all the town,

And then when that same beauty's worn and
     spent

Thou'lt stalk the street a flaunting, painted thing,

Till at the last the flaring lights shall fright
     thee

And thou shalt lurk beneath some darkened
     arch,

A wanton to the end.

MARTHA.   O slanderous tongue,

Commend thy soul to God!

VALENTINE.   Foul hag of Hell,

If I could slay thee ere my life were spent,

I'd think that all my sins were all forgiven!

MARGARET.   Oh, speak to me!

VALENTINE.   It is too late! Too
     late!

I loved thee more than all! May God forgive
thee!

Now like a soldier go I to my God.

[*He falls back dead.* MARGARET *swoons
in the arms of* LISA, *and the* GUARD, *at
a sign from the* BURGOMASTER, *gather
round her.*

ACT IV

ACT IV

Scene I

Scene. — *The Walpurgis Night.*

[*The summit of the Brocken. The Scene represents the verge of a great chasm with mountain peaks jutting up from the depths below. Across the gulf stands a high mountain with jagged sides. On the R. in front is a path descending to rocks. On the left, an uplifted crag overlooking the depths below.*

[*In a hollow at the foot of the crag the* Witch *is seated by her cauldron. The Scene opens with thunder and lightning and a raging wind. On separate peaks that rise from the gulf* WITCHES *are posted as sentinels.*

1ST WITCH. What cry is in the air?

2ND WITCH.   Our master comes.
I saw him riding by the raven stone.

3RD WITCH. Give warning down the gulf:
 from peak to peak,
Down to the lake that fills the crater bowl,
Follow the owlet's cry.

VOICE. [*Below.*] He comes!

2ND VOICE.   He comes!

3RD VOICE. Away! Away! He is here.

VOICES.   Away! Away!

     [WITCHES *disappear as*

[MEPHISTOPHELES *and* FAUST *ascend the*
 rocky path R.

FAUST.   I'll   go   no   farther!   Whither

    would'st thou lead?

MEPHISTOPHELES.   Upward *to* yonder   crag

    whose nodding crown

Leans o'er the sulphurous vale.

FAUST.   I'll climb no more!

Through shrieking caverns and o'er desert fells,

By cliff and headland down whose shuddering

    sides

The roaring cataract cleaves its thunder-road, —

Borne upward as a feather on the gale

Still have I followed thee!

MEPHISTOPHELES.   As still thou shalt

Till I have shown thee all! Hark! 'tis the

    hour.

CHORUS

[*From below.*]

The witches ride to the Brocken top

Upward and onward they may not stop.

[MEPHISTOPHELES *draws* FAUST *to the edge*
of the abyss.

MEPHISTOPHELES. Dost see them swarming
in the mists below?

Now poised for flight, and herding in the sky

They blacken out the moon.

CHORUS

Upward and onward across the night

To the topmost beacon we take our flight!

[*During the* CHORUS *there is a flight of*
WITCHES *across the sky.*

MEPHISTOPHELES.   Far down below

They scale each slope and crag, a myriad throng.

Round gnarled roots like serpents intercoiling,

O'er rock and boulder leaping, skipping,

  scudding, —

See how they press and jostle, push and scramble

To reach their master's feet! Yet some there are

  are

That stumble on the path. Up! up! and on!

The Devil's road grows easier at the last!

> [*As he speaks, the crags and mountain tops
> gradually fill with shadowy forms whose
> voices echo across the gulf.*

1ST WITCH. Whence comest thou?

2ND WITCH.   Round by the Ilsen rock

I saw the white owl blinking on its nest.

3RD WITCH. Old Baubo rides upon a farrow sow.

4TH WITCH. Ay! Baubo first and all the flock to follow.

MEPHISTOPHELES. On then! and on! lest I should flay and score ye.

VOICE. [*From below.*] Hi! there! Ho!

MEPHISTOPHELES. Nay, heed him not, press on!

1ST WITCH. Who is it calls from the rocky lake below?

VOICE. [*From below.*] I've climbed and climbed three hundred years and more,

Yet cannot reach the top!

[*A wild laugh from the* WITCHES *as* MEPHISTOPHELES *looks down the gulf.*

MEPHISTOPHELES.   Old Dotard, no!

Hast not yet learned that towards the Devil's
porch

The lighter step of woman wins the lead?

While club-foot man a laggard even in sin

Toils slowly at her heels. Trudge on, old fool!

Thou shalt reach the goal at last. Trudge on!

Trudge on!

> [*Wild laughter again.*

CHORUS

> With a rag for a sail
>
> We soar on the gale,
>
> Then swoop and fall
>
> At our master's call.

FAUST. What are these shapes and wherefore
are they here?

Mephistopheles.   To-night Sir Mammon

    holds high holiday,

And these my vassal slaves are all his guests.

A goodly throng — see how they laugh and chatter!

Sweet witches all — they have their working

    days,

But now in wanton measure to and fro

They fill a vacant hour of liberty.

Dance on! Dance on!

    [*The* Witches *dance, singing as they move.*

Witches' Chorus

Through fog and fen, o'er broom and heather,

    From hidden caves and from hill and dell,

As leaves that scatter and drift together

    We draw to our master, the Lord of Hell.

The owlet's cry is the note we follow!

As the night-wind whistles its ceaseless tune,

We hurry and scurry o'er hill and hollow

With feet as fleet as the racing moon.

Now! the wind is hushed, the stars are falling,

The moon hath fled! The skies are bare;

Hark! Hark! in the dark 'tis the owlet calling!

The night is waning. Beware! Beware!

Dost hear her crying?

Below! Below!

The clouds are flying,

The night is dying!

We go! We go!

[*As the sound dies away, the* WITCHES

gradually disappear.

FAUST. What crazy world is this?

MEPHISTOPHELES. A world where worlds are

made — a busy hive

Of murmuring bees whose poisoned honey-bags

Yield to men's lips that bitter-sweet called Love.

Here beauty ere it takes on mortal shape

Sips at the fount of sin, then onward speeding,

Enters Life's portals, gathering as it goes

The voices and the blossoms of the Spring.

Here the rough gold first takes its glittering sheen

To sate the greedy pangs of avarice;

Here crowns are fashioned, and on yonder anvil

For every crown a beaten blade is forged

To fit the usurper's hand. Glory and Power,

Ambition and the countless painted toys

That draw men onward in the race toward Hell

Here, by deft hands are decked and garlanded

To lure the world! my world!

FAUST.   And is it here

Thou dost think to stay the memory of those

  tears

That drip and fall upon my coward soul

Like rain through ruined woods?

MEPHISTOPHELES.   Good Doctor, no;

This is but preface to the feast to come.

See, here is more.

> [*They approach the* WITCH'S *cauldron.*
>
>   Old huckster, I should know thee.

FAUST. And I too well!

WITCH.   And I, I know ye both!

MEPHISTOPHELES. What hast thou here to

  please this Lord I serve?

  N

WITCH.   Good store of richest wares of every
    fashion

Most cunningly assorted.   Scan them well!

For all have served their turn! That dagger
    there

Still bears upon it the red rust of blood!

Of all these jewelled cups there is not one

That hath not borne to lips now marble-white

The sleepy wine of death.   There is no gem

Of all this glittering heap but once hath served

To bring a maid to shame.

FAUST.   Foul hag, be dumb!

MEPHISTOPHELES.   She doth   mistake   our
    errand. — All that's done

Is done. — To-night we seek from out the past
A fairer vision.

WITCH. Master, pay me then!

'Twas on the Brocken I should claim my fee;

So stood our bargain.

MEPHISTOPHELES. Would'st thou threaten

me?

I'll pay thee naught till I shall pay thee all.

WITCH. [*Aside.*] Then ere night ends I'll earn

my fee in full,

And trick thee with a vision fair and foul

That shall affright ye both.

MEPHISTOPHELES. Cease! mumbling hag.

FAUST. Is this thy power? whose vilest min-

isters

Still mock and scoff at thee?

MEPHISTOPHELES. Would'st know my power?

I who have changed thy lean and withered age

To this new garb of youth? Stand then and
hearken

While from the void my hounds of Hell give tongue.

[*A* roll *of thunder with lightning gleam.*

CHORUS

[*From below.*]

Cling fast! cling fast!

The owlet is hiding

On the tail of the blast

Our master is riding.

MEPHISTOPHELES. Dost hear those thunder
steeds whose clattering hoofs

Tear the night's covering to a tattered sheet?

Ride on! Ride on! my lightning lamps shall
guide ye.

[*Drawing* FAUST *to the brink of the chasm.*

Look where old Chaos takes a newer fashion

As down the abyss the cloven mountains fall,

And shifting forests slide into the gulf.

Doth that content thee?

   [*During this speech the rocks have sundered
   and fallen. Uprooted trees have crashed
   into the abyss, and the mountain across the
   gulf has been so shattered as to leave a vast
   cavern in its side.*

   FAUST.   Ay! no more! no more!

I have seen enough.

   MEPHISTOPHELES. [*Laughing.*] Nay, tremble
   not, good Doctor!

The work of demolition's always noisy;

Yet here it has served our turn; for yonder cleft

Carved by the thunder, yields a fitting stage

Whereon we'll summon for thy amorous glance

From out their scattered tombs those Queens of

    Love

Whom Time hath still left peerless.

[*To the* WITCH.]   On, old Granny!

Quick! stir thy brew! and let the sport begin,

As high encamped upon this airy shelf

My Lord shall watch the pageant as it grows,

And claim of all these buried vanished lips

Whose kiss he fain would win! Lead on! Lead

    on!

    [*A group of young* WITCHES *leave the cauldron*

       and draw FAUST *with chains of flowers up*

       to the summit of the crag where MEPHISTOPH-

       ELES *is already standing. And as he*

       follows them half entranced, the CHORUS *is*

heard across the gulf and the VISION *of*

HELEN OF TROY *is gradually revealed.*

CHORUS

Once more upon the purple main

That scudding sail doth bear her home,

Troy's cindered towers are fired again

And flare across the crimsoned foam.

MEPHISTOPHELES. See how they press around

her, all her train,

She for whose lips the world was drenched in

blood,

Yet note that changeless beauty bears no

trace

Of all her countless slain.

FAUST.   Helen?

MEPHISTOPHELES.   Ay, Helen,

My loyal subject Queen who shattered Troy,

And dyed the Ægean with a Tyrian stain.

    FAUST.   Draw closer, closer, till I touch those

    lips.

    MEPHISTOPHELES.   Nay! wait awhile! I know

    an Orient bough

Whereon there hangs a riper, ruddier fruit

Embrowned by Egypt's sun.   Lead on, sweet

    hag!

The feast is not half served.

    WITCH.   [*From her cauldron.*]   Nay, Sire, there

    is more,

As thou shalt learn before the cauldron cools.

    [*The* VISION *of* HELEN *has faded as the*

      CHORUS *is renewed.*

Chorus

Down old Nilus' vacant stream

Steers, with silken sail unfurled,

She who in a golden dream

Chained the masters of the world.

Ever toying, never cloying,

Soul and body ever new,

All enjoyed and all enjoying

Ever false and ever true!

[*During the* Chorus *the* Vision *of* Cleopatra

is revealed, preceded by Egyptian Dancing

Girls.

Mephistopheles. Dost see her, Faust? The

ruin that she wrought

Lies buried deep beneath the shifting Nile,

While she whose conquering beauty laughed at

    Time

Sails o'er the centuries to greet her Lord.

Fair Cleopatra, kindred serpent soul,

I hail thee peerless still!

FAUST.   And I! And I!

MEPHISTOPHELES.   Doth that not tempt thee?

FAUST.   Let me but print one kiss

Between those breasts that cushioned Antony;

There is no more to win.

                  [The VISION *fades.*

MEPHISTOPHELES.   Wait till the close,

Then thou shalt choose at will.

[*To* WITCH.   Go back to Rome.

WITCH. Ay, back to Rome, and back and back

    again!

CHORUS

She stands by Tiber's reddened flood!

That door she guards is Love's last tomb,

Those gilded breasts are smeared with blood

Wrung from the ruined heart of Rome.

[*During the* CHORUS *the vision of* MESSALINA

appears.

MEPHISTOPHELES. Look where she stands,

passion's ungrudging slave,

Who leased a throne to wear a strumpet's

crown.

Hail! Messalina, whose enfolding arms

Caught to thee nightly all the lust of Rome,

Those crimson lips have drained the lees of

Love

In many a Stygian stew: yet drink again,

My master holds the cup.

    FAUST.   Nay, let her pass;

'Tis not so fair.

    MEPHISTOPHELES. Then count the feast as

    ended.

Where falls thy choice?

    WITCH.   My master, wait awhile.

Yet one remains, the last and best of all.

    MEPHISTOPHELES. Wretch, wilt thou trick

    me?

    WITCH. Look again and see.

    [*The* VISION *of* MESSALINA *fades as the*

    CHORUS *is repeated.*

Chorus

The Springtime comes, the Springtime goes,

The lily changes to the rose,

    Now Spring hath fled,

    And Summer is dead,

And dead the Lily! and dead the Rose!

[*During the* Chorus *the lonely figure of* Margaret *is revealed with chains about her wrists, her dead child lying at her feet.*

Mephistopheles. [*To* Witch.] Foul hag, I'll scorch thee!

Witch.   Master, I am paid!

[*With a wild yell she rises into the air and vanishes across the gulf.*

Faust. Look! it is Margaret! What to me the past?

What any queen re-risen from the grave?

I can see nothing but that lovely form.

But what is that lies frozen at her feet?

MEPHISTOPHELES. What lieth at her feet thou

should'st know.

FAUST. Those eyes are turned upon me!

Margaret, stay!

Across the gulf of Hell I'll fly to thee.

Go, bear me to that prison where she lies,

Her anguish is my anguish, all her sin

Is mine to suffer, ay, or mine to cure.

To her! to her! bear me away. On! On!

[*There is a crash of thunder, and of a sudden*

the gulf swarms with WITCHES *who shriek*

amidst the thunder as FAUST *and* MEPHIS-

TOPHELES *disappear.*

SCENE II

SCENE. — *A prison cell.*

[MARGARET *is lying in a stupor chained on a bed of straw at the back. The sound of a key in the lock is heard and* FAUST *and* MEPHISTOPHELES *enter.*

MEPHISTOPHELES. See! there she lies! Quick, rouse her! We must fly.

Drugged lies the jailer; but I cannot say

When he may wake and blunder on us here.

FAUST. [*Gazing on* MARGARET.] The woe of the whole earth catches at my heart.

And then! Ah, stand and roll thy devilish eyes:

This is thy work! Lo, in a dungeon shut,

Delivered up to torment and to night!

From me thou hast concealed this ruin, me

With hollow dissipations hast thou lulled.

MEPHISTOPHELES. She's not the first!

FAUST. Abortion! Not the first!

Did not the first in her death agony

Expiate all the guilt of all the rest?

Her single misery to my marrow pierces,

And thou art grinning at the doom of thousands.

MEPHISTOPHELES. Why dost thou make a

compact with the Devil

And canst not see it out? Did I on thee

Thrust myself? Come, confess! Or thou on me?

FAUST. Rescue her: or the curse of ages on

thee!

MEPHISTOPHELES. Rescue her? Who then

plunged her into ruin?

Whose kisses stretched her on that bed of straw?

Whose hot embraces cast those chains on her?

> [FAUST *looks wildly round.*

Wilt grasp the thunder? Lucky thou canst not.

FAUST. She shall be free!

MEPHISTOPHELES.   O maudlin murderer,

Weep over thy victim sentimental tears!

FAUST. Free her — or ——

MEPHISTOPHELES. Gently! I will watch without

And keep the jailer mazed in a deep sleep,

But not for long! Drag her away with thee.

The magic steeds are ready. Quick!

FAUST.   Begone!

> [*Exit* MEPHISTOPHELES.

> [FAUST *approaches* MARGARET, *who starts up*
>
>   *dishevelled.*

O

MARGARET. Oh, they are come for me! O

death of deaths!

FAUST. Margaret! I have come to set thee

free once more.

Come, let us fly — give me your hand, come, come.

MARGARET. [*Looking at him.*] Who art thou?

Oh, it is not Morning yet.

Sir, let me live till dawn! And I am still

So young, and fair, but that was my undoing.

[FAUST *seizes the chains, endeavouring to un-*

lock them.

What have I done to thee? Use me not roughly!

FAUST. Margaret, look on me! I am thy

lover.

MARGARET. [*Looking earnestly at him.*] I ne'er

saw thee before in all my life.

I had a lover, but he's far away.

Love, did I weary thee?

FAUST.   Can I outlive

These stabbing words?

MARGARET.   Ah, let me suckle first

My baby: but they've taken it away,

And they sing songs about me in the street.

They should not do it.

FAUST.   I love thee for ever.

MARGARET. See, he is coming! The evil one:

    Hell heaves

In thunder — see, he makes towards his prey.

FAUST. Margaret!

MARGARET.   Ah, that was my lover's voice.

Margaret! So now in the howl of Hell

Still on his bosom I shall lie again.

'Tis he! The garden once again I see

Where thou and I walked up and down in bliss.

FAUST. [*Struggling with her.*

Come! Come away!

MARGARET. Dost thou not care to kiss me?

Once didst thou kiss as thou would'st stifle me.

FAUST. Follow me, darling — oh, delay no

more!

MARGARET. But is it thou, thou surely?

FAUST. It is I.

Come, come away!

MARGARET. My mother I have killed

But out of love for thee!

FAUST. Can I endure?

MARGARET. The baby too, our baby, I have

drowned.

Faust. Oh, swiftly, swiftly! the night vanishes.

Margaret. It tries to rise, it struggles still;
quick, seize it.

Faust. One step and thou art free: I must
use force.

> [*He seizes her to bear her away.*

Margaret. Oh, grasp me not so murderously, sir.

Faust. Day! day is dawning.

Margaret.   Yes, 'tis the last day.
Hark to the crowd! They push me to the block:
Now o'er each neck the blade is quivering
That quivers over mine! Dumb lies the world.

> [*She falls back on his arm.*

Faust. God! She is dying! I shall never
free her.

> [Mephistopheles *enters quickly.*

MEPHISTOPHELES. Fast, fast! to all love-mak-
  ing put an end,

My coursers shiver in the morning air.

Away!

FAUST.   No! She is dying: cold she
  grows.

MEPHISTOPHELES. Leave her if she is cold:
  no moment more.

FAUST. I will not — cannot —— Margaret!
  Margaret!

MEPHISTOPHELES. Would'st thou die with her?

FAUST.   I can leave her not.

MEPHISTOPHELES. The living wait thee! Stay
  not by the dead!

FAUST. Leave me! I go not!

MEPHISTOPHELES.   Come to fresher faces,

Others have warm blood still.

[MARGARET *dies*.

FAUST.   Ah! she is dead!
No motion: chill all o'er!

MEPHISTOPHELES.   Faust, wilt thou come?

FAUST.   Never!

MEPHISTOPHELES.   Farewell then!

[*Exit* MEPHISTOPHELES.

[FAUST *lays her reverently on the bed, composing
    her limbs*.

FAUST.   I with thee must die.
For I am fainting with thy faintness, I
Am going with thee fast.   I ebb and sink
After thee, and my blood thy blood pursues.
Hath thy heart stopped?   Mine slow and slower
    beats.

Still is thy pulse?   My pulse is faltering!

Where'er thou goest I with thee shall go,

Whether thou catch me into highest Heaven,   •

Or I involve thee in the lowest Hell.

Margaret, Margaret! after thee I come

And rush behind thee in thy headlong flight.

Dim grows the world.

> [MEPHISTOPHELES *appears in the dress he*
> *wore in the Prologue.*

                    Is this the film of death?

Do I behold thee, Mephistopheles,

Or some superior angel?   Now no more

The sneering smile and jaunty step I see;

I feel that thou art Evil yet dost wear

Evil's auguster immortality.

Say wherefore art thou come?

MEPHISTOPHELES. Remember, Faust,

Thy compact. Though it pleased me to take on

A lighter shape more easily to lure thee,

Yet know I am that Spirit who rebelled,

With whom a million angels mutinied.

Behold the thunder-scar and withered cheek!

With me, then, was thy holy compact signed.

FAUST. Though I should die yet thou canst

fright me not.

Even from thy lips shall I believe the tale

Of burning coals and everlasting fire

And all the windy jargon of the priests?

MEPHISTOPHELES. Far other is that Hell where

thou shalt live.

As I did serve thee faithfully on earth,

Thou faithfully shalt serve me after death.

Listen! On dreadful errands shalt thou go,

On journeys fraught with mischief to the soul;

Shalt be a whisperer in the maiden's ears,

Drawing her to defilement — shalt persuade

The desperate to self-slaughter, thou shalt guide

The murderer to his work, thou shalt instil

Into the child its first polluting thought,

And bring to the world's apple many an Eve.

In taverns shalt thou drink invisibly

Urging the drinkers on, and thou shalt walk

With painted women to and fro the streets.

So, Faust, shalt thy eternity be spent

Seducing and polluting human souls,

Purveying anguish, madness, through the world.

This was thy compact: this shalt thou fulfil.

    FAUST. Horrible! horrible! Yet do I defy thee.

Hast thou fulfilled thy promise, brought an hour —

A single hour — to which I could cry "Stay,

Thou art so fair"?

MEPHISTOPHELES.   That hour shall come;

My service is not ended.   Countless years

Are left thee yet ere life's full cup be drained.

Up, then, and on!

FAUST.   Weary and stale the life

Thou gavest me; from pleasure hurled to pleasure,

And evermore satiety and hate.

Weary and stale is all that's yet to come.

Though countless years, chained ever at thy side,

Be still my doom, my spirit newly winged

Outspeeds the flight of time.   That flower I
     crushed

And trod beneath my feet, see where it springs

And blooms again in Heaven's serener air.

Beyond the night I see the final dawn

Wherein from out that ruin I have wrought,

Purged at the last, my soul shall win its way

Whither her soul hath sped.   The laggard years,

That chain me prisoner to this desert earth,

Though in their sum they should consume all
        time,

Were all too short for what is left to do.

Up, then, and on!   I shall abide the end;

Still I fight upward, battle to the skies,

And still I soar for ever after her.

I shall go past thee, Mephistopheles,

For ever upward to the woman soul!

How long?   How long?

        [*Rolling clouds ascend, obscuring the stage,*

until the First Scene, the neutral mountains,

is discovered again. During the change a

CHORUS *of invisible* ANGELS *is heard from*

above.

CHORUS

All the unnumbered years of man

    Count not against thy larger day

That flushed and dawned ere time began,

    And still runs radiant on its way.

Onward and on in ceaseless flight

    The rolling centuries race by,

Onward to where thy torches light

    The threshold of Eternity.

[*When the scene is fully revealed,* MARGARET

    is seen lying robed in white at the feet of

RAPHAEL, *the* OTHER ANGELS *attending*.

MEPHISTOPHELES *remains below*.

MEPHISTOPHELES. Lo! on this neutral ground

  I reappear

To claim of the Most High the soul of Faust.

Is not the wager won? Have I not drawn

A high aspiring spirit from his height,

Plunged it at will in lust and wantonness?

Hath not this servant of the King of Heaven,

This famous Doctor, proud philosopher,

Seduced a maiden to a grave of shame,

To drug her Mother, and to drown her Child?

While he with his own hand her Brother slew?

Have I not now reclaimed a soul for night?

Have I not now the great world wager won?

Answer!

[*An* ANGEL *alights on the topmost peak as in the Prologue.*

THE ANGEL. The great world wager thou
    hast lost,

And, seeking to confound, hast saved a soul.

When for thine own ends thou didst fire his heart

For Margaret, and inflamed his lustful blood

So that they sinned together, yet that sin

So wrapped them that a higher, holier love

Hath sprung from it; where once their bodies
    burned

Their spirits glow together, what was fire

Is light, and that which scorched doth kindle
    now.

Thou, thou hast sped him on a nobler flight,

Thou, thou hast taught him to aspire anew,

Thou through the woman soul hast brought him

home.

[ANGELS *are seen bearing the soul of* FAUST

upwards towards MARGARET.

Hither the spirit angel-wafted floats

While she her saving arms outspreads to him.

MEPHISTOPHELES. Still to the same result I

war with God:

I will the evil, I achieve the good.

CURTAIN.

PIETRO OF SIENA

A DRAMA

BY
STEPHEN PHILLIPS

CHARACTERS

PIETRO TORNIELLI	{ *Head of the ancient and exiled house of Tornielli*
LUIGI GONZAGA	{ *Head of the rival and reigning house of Gonzaga*
ANTONIO	*Podesta of Siena*
MONTANO	{ *Boon Companion and Jackal to Pietro*
ANSELMO	{ *An Aged Warrior devoted to the Tornielli*
GIACOMO	*Jailor of the State Prison*
AN EXECUTIONER	
PULCI	}*Personal friends of Luigi*
CARLO	
GEMMA GONZAGA	*Sister to Luigi*
FULVIA TORNIELLI	*Sister to Pietro*
CATERINA	*An Aged Nurse devoted to Gonzaga*

OFFICERS, MESSENGERS, ETC.

The action of the play is confined to Siena and lies between the hours of sunset and sunrise.

ACT I

SUNSET

PIETRO OF SIENA

ACT I

SCENE. — *The great hall of the ancient palace
of the Gonzaga. At either end stand armed
sentries. In the centre is the judgement chair.
On the rising of the curtain furious shouts are
heard without, and grow louder at times as
from an approaching multitude, and the
besieging army of* PIETRO. LUIGI *is discovered striding to and fro in great perplexity.
His friend* PULCI *is watching him earnestly.
The time is sunset.*

PULCI. Luigi, go forth, and show thyself
at last !

3

Still the gate holds; though Pietro Tornielli

Three times in vain hath shaken it — Go

    forth!

He makes enough of clamour and of din;

Thou liest like a rat, unseen, unheard;

Whom can we fight for, or for what? Go

    forth!

LUIGI. No, Pulci, no! Pietro Tornielli

Advancing takes the wind from all my sails.

He cows me from afar, and quells my spirit,

I know not why or how; but I am quelled,

Like English Richard before Bolingbroke.

It is not that he hath more wit than I,

It is not that he hath more will than I;

Only that on this man success attends.

Where I am foiled and thwarted, he goes free.

Such men there are, and what they will,

    they grasp.   [*A louder uproar without.*

PULCI. This is the sophistry that fears

    to act.

LUIGI. [*Pausing.*] Think with what in-

    juries this man comes armed:

He comes not merely to supplant my rule,

To seat himself where I so long have sat,

But furious memory smoulders at his heart.

Did not our father bear his mother off,

And use her for his lust? his father pined ;

And kept a dreadful silence till he died.

With all these memories this man comes

    fraught,

And thunders an avenger at our gate.

        [*A sentinel rushes in from the left.*

SENTINEL. The gate has been surrendered;

    they swarm in;

And hither are they making with loud cry!

    [*A cry louder and nearer. Enter* GEMMA

        GONZAGA, *hurriedly and terrified, the*

        nurse CATERINA *limping behind.*

GEMMA. Luigi, what can I do in this

    dark hour?

How aid and comfort? Send me not away!

For thou and I have grown together so

We may not be divided but with blood.

Your hopes, your thoughts are mine; your

    frailties mine.

Brother, let me be near thee in the storm.

I claim its lightnings and its thunder clasp.

Ah, send me not away! I put my arms

About you as of old : now come what will.

   [*Sound as of door below broken open.*

LUIGI. Sister, they come ! This scene is

 not for thee :

Go then within and quietly ; I alone

Must stand upright against the towering

 wave.

   [*Exit* GEMMA *and* CATERINA.

[*Soldiers enter and are drawn up along
the walls of the hall. Then enter the
Mayor* ANTONIO, *surrounded by citizens of Siena, a Priest, and, lastly,*
PIETRO, *his sister* FULVIA *following him.*

PIETRO. Luigi Gonzaga, I might well

 have stormed

Siena gate with fiery memories

And with the sword of vengeance sought thee

  out.

Thy father with hot lips kissed out the soul

Of her that bore me, and my father broke

Down to the ground and wrapped in mortal

  shame.

I say, Gonzaga, that I bear enough

Of private injury to spill thy blood.

On no such crimson errand am I sped,

But summoned by Siena's citizens,

Here to resume the sovereignty possessed

Erst by the Tornielli : and to purge

The city of thee and thy iniquities.

  [*He ascends the judgement chair, motioning*

    to ANTONIO.

Now read aloud the charges 'gainst this man.

ANTONIO. [*Reading*]. "It is here charged against thee, Luigi Gonzaga, that thou hast taken bribes to set aside the course of justice, whereof many instances can be proven. Further : that thou hast surrounded thee with a troop of desperate malcontents whom thou hast paid and used for purposes of private quarrel. Moreover, that two famous enemies of thine thou hast by poison taken off, having bidden them to supper here in this palace. That thou hast offered to spare the life of Paolo Gerli if his daughter would deliver herself to thee for purposes of lust ; though this man had been condemned by public tribunal over which thou didst thyself preside. And many other counts are here

set down against thee, but for the moment
let these suffice."

PIETRO.   Luigi Gonzaga, what hast thou
to say?

LUIGI.   All that is charged against me I
confess.

PIETRO.   Then, for these violent ills a violent cure

Demand, and a swift, instant medicine —

I, Pietro Tornielli, summoned here

To adjudicate upon Siena's wrong,

Hereby pronounce upon thee doom of death!

And since delays in these distracted streets

Were perilous : to-morrow thou shalt die.

[*Writing.*]   I, Pietro Tornielli, called by the
people of Siena to heal the breach and woe of

the city, do hereby commit Luigi Gonzaga,

sometime ruler of Siena, to prison this night

to the intent that at sunrise to-morrow he

may be executed. Given by me this day.

PIETRO TORNIELLI.

LUIGI. At sunrise! Ah, not death! Ah,

not so soon!

Let me still watch the sun thro' prison bars,

And manacled behold the rising moon.

Ah, send me not from glory to the grave.

I promise in my cell I will not stir

All day, and will not speak even to myself,

Or murmur an angry word until my death;

Ah, hold me, Sir, in prison till I die.

How can I trouble thee; none breaks away

Or bursts that massy fortress. Can I lead

Rebellion, fettered fast and deep immured?

Deliver me to long imprisonment!

Or banish me an exile from the shore

Of Italy for ever : Let me roam

The limits of the world and utmost isles.

Only I pray thee let me breathe !   To go

For ever from the sun !   I care not what

Of heavy misery or imprisonment

Thou mayest inflict if only I may live.

[He breaks into sobs.

PIETRO.   Luigi Gonzaga, freely thou hast
>   drunk

The purple cup of life ; now not to wince,

To beat the breast, befits thee in this hour.

Sweet was the draught, now fling the cup
>   away !

And having richly lived, so strongly die.

Bear him away.

LUIGI.   Sir ! Sir !

PIETRO.   Bear him away !

[LUIGI *is taken off between two guards, four*

others following.

PIETRO. [*Rising.*] Now for the moment
nothing more detains us.

ANSELMO. [*Coming forward.*] Sir, this man
whom you have dispatched to die,

A sister has ; and though the rabble rise

Against the brother for his many crimes,

She may untouched through all Siena pass,

For she is beautiful and still and pure.

She is a greater peril than the man,

And while she lives, thy throne will tremble
  still.

  PIETRO.   Is she within the palace?

AN ATTENDANT.   Sir, she is.

  PIETRO.   Send for her hither.

                    [*Exit Attendant.*

ANSELMO.   In this warrant add
To Luigi Gemma, to the brother's name
The sister; so we root out the whole house,
No son nor daughter of Gonzaga lives
Save these; then make an end and sit secure.

        [*Enter* GEMMA *escorted by Attendants.*

  PIETRO.   Art thou the sister of Gonzaga —
    say !

GEMMA.   I am, Sir.

  PIETRO.   He hath been so deeply charged

With public crime and private injury.

That I, called in to judge and to pronounce,

To prison have committed him, that he

May die to-morrow at sunrise.

GEMMA.   Ah, no !

Ah, do not slay him.   Wonderful has been

The love between us — and so soon to die !

Why, he hath but a few brief hours to pray ;

To reconcile him with eternal God,

Only the transit of a summer night.

Oh, Sir, at least be merciful to me !

And send me to him that I too may die.

Let me not wither out this hollow world

Alone ; but in that warrant add my name

To his ; for all his frailties I defend,

In all his acts I am associate.

I would give up the very ghost in me,

And my dear soul would put in pawn for him.

Then by the same blow let the sister fall !

I crave to die with the first light of dawn.

Ah, separate us not, here I beseech thee !

[*She throws herself at his feet.*

ANSELMO.   Enough !   By her own mouth

    she merits death.

PIETRO.   [*With slow hesitation.*]   I cannot

    — for the moment — well decide.

[*Angry murmurs from* ANSELMO'S *troops.*

That I have doomed her brother is no cause

Why her too I should doom !   Is it supposed

A maiden, but a year ago a child,

Could of his crimes and bribes be cognizant ?

I ask you all — were it not well to pause ?

To pause for a few hours, and hesitate

Finally to pronounce? What thou hast said,

Anselmo, I doubt not is wise, but I

A little leisure must demand in this.

Lead her away!   [*To* GEMMA.]   Ere dawn
thou shalt receive

My judgement. [*She is escorted within.*] Now,
Sirs, I should be alone.

      [*Exeunt all but* ANSELMO, GIROLAMO,

        FULVIA, *and* MONTANO.

ANSELMO.   Sir, if this foolish mercy to the
house

Which hath so deeply wronged you, be dis-
played,

I cannot pledge me for these faithful bands

That hitherto have followed your wild star.

c

Sparing his sister's life, you but ascend

A trembling throne, for men who hated him

Will rally to her face as to a flag.

Ah, God ! 'tis the old weakness of the blood.

What stopped us at Ancona ? what made vain

The long siege of Perugia ?   Evermore

A woman's face hath foiled us.   Now I speak

Once, and no more.   Thy followers will fall off

Being again deceived ; much have they borne,

But more they will not bear.

> [*Sullen murmurs are heard.*

Strike down the house,

Strike to the root and ere the night be passed.

> [*Exit* ANSELMO, *who is acclaimed by the troops awaiting him.*

GIROLAMO.   [*Advancing.*]   Pietro Tornielli !

Thus saith Rome :

Let none of the Gonzaga house be spared !

Nor man nor woman : end the pestilence

That brooded o'er Siena all these years.

If thou wouldst rule secure, blot out the brood

That are anathema to Holy Church !

If a fair face can shake thee from thy seat,

Look not to Rome !   Rather be thou of Rome

Outlawed, accursed.   So speak I, and depart.

[*Exit* GIROLAMO *with attendant Priests.*

FULVIA.   [*Approaching* PIETRO.]   Brother,

what hath been said by Holy Church,

Or by Anselmo speaking for the State,

Is well, and well enough.   I am a woman,

And cannot easily forget the shame

Wrought on our mother by their father ; now

Comes in revenge though late, and justice too.

These are his children, his; the man who

    wronged

Her, and brought down our father to his grave.

He hath left issue luckily, for us

To dash our ire on, let his children die!

Not one, but both.   Have we not waited long?

Have I not in my pillow set my teeth

Through the grim night to stop these mem-

    ories?

But here they are delivered to our hands.

Hast thou forgot thy mother's desperate death,

Hast thou forgot the pining of thy Sire?

Here with one blow we clear us before God

That she in that sea-tomb no longer toss

Unsatisfied ; nor he call from the ground.

Art thou the victim of a passing face,

Art thou the helpless spoil of shadowed eyes?

Art thou a man, or but a drifting leaf,

Unworthy to be served or followed or loved?

If that pale face can turn thee from thy wrongs,

Or a low voice make all thy vengeance vain?

I leave thee therefore to the blood of the dead.

This must thou expiate and swift and sure.

[*Exit* FULVIA.

PIETRO.   Give me some wine, Montano!

Oh, Montano,

The fever's in my blood and must have vent.

MONTANO.   What fever?

PIETRO.   For a face a moment since

Sprung like a sudden splendour on the dusk,

Now vanished; for a voice that stole on us

Like strings from planets dreaming in faint
skies,

With a low pleaded music ; for a form

Slight and a little bending over in dew.

This night, Montano, in this coming dark

I must possess her ; for I shall not sleep,

Knowing her breathing sweet so near to me,

Here in this palace ; no ! nor shall I drowse

Until I clasp her fast and kisses rain

Upon her lips, her eyes, her brow, her hair.

MONTANO.   Sir, you well know I serve your
every mood,

But here, is not the game too perilous ?

Here on the very first night of your rule

To seize Gonzaga's sister, he meanwhile

Purposely prisoned — ah, so they will say —

So that he may not mar, nor intervene.

Let policy propose some slower way.

 PIETRO. No! No! Such beauty must be

  stormed, not snared,

Caught up and kissed into oblivion,

To saddle hoist, and through the world away.

 MONTANO. I scent a way by which she

  might be won

And without force, and on this very night.

 PIETRO. How? how?

 MONTANO. Her brother Luigi at sunrise

To-morrow, perishes; now he to her

Is more than just a brother; they have lived

Even from the cradle a life intertwined.

Remember but the burning words of her!

" I would give up the very ghost of me,

And my dear soul would put in pawn for
　　him."

PIETRO. Well — well —

MONTANO. The dawn will come soon, all
　　too soon

For her ; but were it breathed into her ear,

That for her beauty thou wouldst spare his life,

Would not her deep love to thy arms consent ?

As slowly all the sky grows lighter still,

And Luigi's blood is on the morning cloud,

Will she not for her brother give herself

To thee, and in thy clasp forget the dawn ?

PIETRO. See, see her ; with the nurse have
　　first a word,

That she may sound her warily.   But haste !

Darkness already closes on us two,

And if I have my will 'twill be ere dawn.

Speed, speed away, Montano, be thou swift !

And I with every flower will fill the room,

With fume of lilies and raptures of the rose,

And odours that entice the drowsing brain,

And far-off music melting on the soul.

At once away till thou hast news of her.

[*Exit* MONTANO.

Come, night, and falling give her to my arms.

What fools are they that use thee but for sleep ;

Come and enfold us in the dark of bliss !

ACT II

MIDNIGHT

SCENE I

SCENE. — Midnight. A dark part of the gardens of the palace; various followers of ANSELMO *assembled with torches. To them enter* ANSELMO *with four followers, also carrying torches.*

ANSELMO.   Comrades, to this dark garden, and in night
I have swiftly summoned you : you all well know
That I have followed Tornielli's star,
Howe'er it wavered in the heavens ; and you
How often have I led to the desperate breach,

29

Or to that timely charge which all decides.

And yet you can recall that oftentimes

Here were we foiled, or here: and this the
    cause,

Ever a woman's face Pietro marred.

The weakness in his blood undid our toil.

Now at Siena, crown of all our hopes,

And destined to the Tornielli rule,

When vengeance is demanded, he falls short;

And cannot lift his hand against the face,

Too beautiful, of Luigi's sister.   Him

Easily he condemned to die at dawn,

Yet he would not complete the task imposed.

He wavers through the night, and will not act.

Now none hath been more faithful to his star

Than I, but I that star will follow not

If at the supreme hour we must be fooled.

You as you please will act : but now no more

Lean upon me to lead you as of old.

    A SOLDIER. I will speak bolder than our

        Captain. What

If he should be persuaded by this girl

To spare the brother's life ? [*Angry murmurs*.]

        How do we stand ?

Were ever soldiers on such errand fooled ?

I say that on this very night, perhaps,

While here we stand, she hath persuaded him

To cancel the decree of death at dawn.

So is our march, our battery, our spoil

Made vain for ever : who henceforth will trust

A ruler palpably to beauty weak,

At mercy of red lips and drooping eyes ?

Shall this man rule Siena ?   Never man

In all Siena will to this consent.

Pietro Tornielli can fight well,

Is not in courage backward, but this fault

Will leave him unsupported and alone.

>   [*Angry shouts and murmurs.*

ANSELMO.   Friends, let us see what darkness

>   brings to light,

If then my apprehension be revealed,

Or worse, our comrades' fear ; at least at dawn

Let us assemble here : with knowledge then

We our own way can take, e'en tho' it be

To assault the palace and slay Pietro.   Speak !

Is this agreed ? [*Shouts.   All drawing swords.*

>   Anselmo, 'tis agreed.

>   [*The scene closes.*]

SCENE II

SCENE. — *An inner room of the palace; with a door communicating with a further room, which is closed. A lamp is burning on the table. The old nurse* CATERINA *is seated near the window with bowed head and in deep grief. A knock is heard at the door. She hobbles toward it, and opening it admits* MONTANO.

MONTANO. Signora Caterina ?

CATERINA.   That is I.

MONTANO. I see that you are broken

down with grief.

Give me your hand. [*He leads her to a seat.*

                    The reason of these tears

D

Is easily guessed.   Luigi Gonzaga dies

With the first flush of day.   This is the cause?

   CATERINA.   Ah, sir, if my own son had then
     to die

I could not suffer more.   I have no son ;

But he took on him all the unborn child,

That never quickened in the might have been.

I have watched him as a gardener does a
     flower,

And seen him slowly grow into his strength.

Ah, who can say I had not pangs from him.

What he hath done I know not to deserve

So swift a death ; only that he must die

I know.   *[She breaks again into sobs.*

   MONTANO.   You know not yet.   I bring
     a hope.

CATERINA. Oh, that he may be saved, may

be released!

Sir, do not trifle with a soul so old,

Or play with cracking heart-strings!

MONTANO. I will not.

I come from Pietro Tornielli straight.

Where is your mistress?

CATERINA. Dumb, and as the dead,

Within she sits, fixed on the coming day.

MONTANO. She, she alone can save him if

she will.

CATERINA. [*Stumbling to inner door.*] Ah,

Gemma, Gemma!

MONTANO. [*Taking her arm.*] Peace, and

sit you down.

To you I'll tell the terms of his release,

You then to her; and she shall then decide.

CATERINA.   Terms! but there are no terms
She will not give.

Life even!

MONTANO.   Perhaps a harder thing is asked.

CATERINA.   Harder than life!   What is so
dear as breath?

MONTANO.   To a woman one thing only.

[A pause.

CATERINA.   Still I grope
In darkness.   What can Gemma give more
dear

Than very life?

MONTANO.   More dear? her very soul.

CATERINA.   I seem to guess more clearly
now.   You mean —

MONTANO.   I mean — for the night passes,

and already

Is little time for words — Lord Tornielli

Will spare the life of Luigi but to hold

His sister in his arms this very night.

Am I now plain enough?

CATERINA.   Aye — plain enough!

Had it been life —

MONTANO.   It is not life he asks.

CATERINA.   Oh, what a dreadful choice!

MONTANO.   Yet on these terms,

And these alone can Luigi's life be spared.

CATERINA.   She will not do it, never, never,

never!

MONTANO.   Still lay the chance before her:

see you how

Already the stars pale ; the time is short.

He from his dungeon watches how they pale.

You as a woman to another may,

With what authority and wisdom else

May prompt, disclose, and may at last persuade.

I'll leave you to her — then I will return

To know her verdict on her brother's life.

                      [*Going, then returning.*

Remember paling stars and coming sun !

                           [*Exit* MONTANO.

CATERINA.   Ah, God ! must I, this old and
shrunken voice

Use to persuade her white soul to this act ?

She hath been filled with pity for the fallen,

Yet with that pity hath so loathed the cause.

So innocent and yet so understanding,

She hath been so gentle to those sinners, yet

Sick with abhorrence but to think their sin.

But, Luigi, any sacrifice for thee !

Gemma, my child, Gemma.   [*She goes to door.*

    I must have word

A moment with you.

[*Enter* GEMMA *white and with a fixed movement.*

         One has left me but

A moment, who brought word from Tornielli.

  GEMMA.   No word can ever reach my ear

    but one,

And that one "death," "death," "death"

    for evermore.

  CATERINA.   Gemma, sit here, and I will

    kneel and lay

My old face in your lap.

GEMMA.　　　　　　　As I how oft

Have laid my face, old nurse, down in your
lap,

Dreaming, to hear thee tell of fairyland.

But, ah, no fairyland is with us now!

But life, how grey and cruel — ah, and
death!

CATERINA. Do not start from me, nor
fall swooning down,

At that I have to say — Luigi —

GEMMA.　　　　　　　O listen!

Do you not hear the stones down on him
falling?

CATERINA. It is not yet resolved that he
shall die.

GEMMA. What, what! Have I gripped

    your arm too fast? Yet speak!

This is some foolish comfort, shallow thought,

To ease me for a moment. Why, I heard

Pietro Tornielli — and to me

He spoke — declare aloud the doom of death.

    CATERINA. He did so; but he may repent

      him yet.

    GEMMA. But what hath chanced in these

      brief hours to change

A state decree? How is he sudden white

Who then so black was, — hath he been

    re-tried

All in a moment? Ah, toy not with hope.

    CATERINA. I tell you, Luigi's life may yet

      be spared.

GEMMA.   By whom then, how ?   Who holds

the scales so fine ?

CATERINA.   You !

GEMMA.   [*Starting up.*]   I !   How should I

save him ?

CATERINA.   Can you not

A little guess and save my speech o'er-rough ?

Did you not mark then Tornielli's glance ?

How in his speech he stumbled, while on you

His eyes were anchored ?   how, alarmed, his

host

Cried out against delay and for thy life ?

GEMMA.   [*Passing her hand over her brow.*]

Yes, I remember his eyes fixed on me.

CATERINA.   Now can you not conceive, and

realise ?

And I my face will turn away from you.

GEMMA. Oh, now I see, and but this

    moment since.

I have gulped down such a draught of this

    world's cup

As leaves me shivering, and to wind exposed.

This was the plan, then ; like a beast, not man,

He would ensnare me for a fleshy hour,

Baiting the trap even with a brother's life.

You know, my Caterina, well you know

How I have loved my brother. If 'twere death,

That I would gladly suffer ; to expire,

And lose the sweet and music of this life,

All joy for ever to forego — for him,

Or if I must be stabbed, or poisoned — yes.

But this — not this !   He is not such a coward

That he would put his life into the scales

Against his sister's shame. I will not do it.

Oh, all the stars that muster in the heaven

Would cry on me with voices like to beams,

More awful in their silence to the soul.

I tell you, No, No! And what more repels

My soul is this — a trap laid for my soul,

Again I say, baited with brother's blood!

I hate this man, I hate the mind that thought

This business out, this trader of the dark,

This burning merchant for a maiden's soul.

What should I be, old Caterina, what

For ever and for ever? They who went

To flame for faith, they went not for this cause,

And out of scorching flesh deserved the stars.

The girl who yields beneath a summer moon,

That I can understand, but never a true woman

Made bargain with her body such as this.

There is my answer, now and for all time.

CATERINA. Child, though I know what

sickens in your soul,

Still, when all's said or thought, is't not

enough

To bring back Luigi from the grave? At dawn

Surely he dies. I as a woman speak,

Let this man vent his riot; let the fool

Have his hot way, and suffer his embrace!

Yours is the laugh by daybreak, and for ever.

Think, then, of Luigi freed! The world is

wrong,

None catch perfection; save your brother's

life,

Spending an hour within those silly arms!

What are his kisses, if the grave is foiled?

GEMMA.   You, you persuade me to it?

　　You who nursed

Both of us; why is it, then, that a nurse holds

Dearer the boy than the girl? he must be

　　spared,

She never!

CATERINA.   What you do you do not do.

GEMMA.   Ah, woman, but our bodies are

　　our souls!

　　　　　　　　　　　[*Enter* MONTANO.

MONTANO.   Ah, Signorina? Straightway

　　from my lord,

Pietro Tornielli, I have come,

In the strong hope that you will speak to him.

GEMMA. What use so to pretend, and

gloze the truth?

You know well why this gentleman desires

To see me; on this errand you are sent.

Take back my answer, then: I will not come.

I loved and love my brother, but he must die.

MONTANO. Is he so well prepared? And

can he launch

On such a voyage? What has been his life?

His public faults this day were charged on him:

None of them he denied. His private lusts

Are through Siena sounded publicly.

You, you alone cast his immortal soul

Before the conscious Judge, unripe and crude,

You, you alone can stay that dread assize.

[*The hour strikes midnight.*

The night wears out : and hearken how the
    gong

With solemn syllables divides the night !

He hears them from the dungeon, stroke on
    stroke.

What is thy hour to his eternity ?

  GEMMA. Dead mother, tell me !

  CATERINA.   She to whom you cry

Remember was *his* mother —

  GEMMA.   I will come.

  [*She takes down an old dagger from the
    wall and hides it in her bosom secretly.*

  CATERINA. See, let me set this red rose
  on your breast.

  GEMMA. Yes, yes, it is the colour of his
  blood.

[MONTANO *motions the way out and he and* GEMMA *exeunt.*

CATERINA. Oh, only for his life! for the boy's life!

Virgin in heaven, forgive me if I sinned!

E

SCENE III

SCENE. — *Another room in the palace; distant music is heard, and various flowers are set about.* PIETRO, *turning from giving directions, meets* MONTANO, *who ushers in* GEMMA, *then immediately retires.*

PIETRO. Ah, Signorina, you are come at
    last !

GEMMA. I have come as one adorned for
    sacrifice,

Nothing omitted ; and this red flower see,

The symbol of a brother's blood !

    PIETRO.   You think

Too gravely.

GEMMA.   Oh, too gravely ?

PIETRO.   We must take

What chance we can when beauty is the goal.

GEMMA.   You think, then, that this lure is

clever ?

PIETRO.   No.

But by your face all right and wrong is

dimmed.

GEMMA.   This is the game ; the stakes, a

brother's life

And a girl's soul ; with these, then, you can

play.

PIETRO.   I see my chance but as a gambler

sees.

GEMMA.   You play with loaded dice, and

human too.

Listen !   I have come here to give myself

To you to snatch a brother's life ; but think !

Do I now for a moment give myself ?

I give you ice for fire, and snow for flame ;

Your touch I loathe, and shudder to be

    touched ;

Your kisses have no sweetness but for him.

I but endure, and listen for the dawn ;

And when you clasp me to your breast, I

    see

Behind your phantom face a rising sun.

You shadow ! murmur, kiss, do what you

    will,

I have forgotten you for evermore !

You ghost, with but the vantage of the grave,

O lover with cold murder on your lips,

Bridegroom whose gift is blood, whose dower
  is death !
Ah, what a tryst ! What moonlight ever saw
Such a forbidden rapture as is this ?
Then take me in your arms, but never me !
Or kiss these lips where lips have ceased to
  move.
Fool, can you understand in your wild blood
That never shall you reach me on these terms ?
How can you drink my beauty, if no soul
Makes the draught live ? You bargain for a
  bliss,
But no bliss from a bargain ever came.
That bliss may be too sudden, may be slow,
Howe'er it come ; but it is thoughten wise,
Not planned, not calculated ; be it sin

Or fire of angels, not this way it comes,

Nor ever hath : now to thy lips I yield

My own, but with a cold laugh in my soul,

Or else in dreadful thought thy kiss I take.

Now thou art master ; thy brief hour demand !

But had I loved thee, Pietro, not this way

Would I have clasped thee, but in sacred fire,

And then shouldst thou have tasted of deep
    life ;

Then not of flesh but of the endless soul.

But since this is so and this world endures,

> [*Taking the dagger from her breast.*

Let Luigi die ! let him cease ! and I with him.

  PIETRO. [*Snatching the dagger from her
    hand.*] Gemma Gonzaga, can you not
    believe

Your words have shaken into me a soul?

What was a furious sport proposed, is now

The mighty meaning of a changèd life.

Oh, it is true, most true, that I had planned

To use the seat of justice for thy lips.

So have I loved : not here nor there alone,

But everywhere pursuing my own prey.

So have I foiled my soldiers, and made vain

Cities besieged, for lure of some fair face.

But now your revelation breaks on me ;

Even your sneer sublime and starry scorn

Has taken from my feet the under-world.

I would be what you say I cannot be :

Not with the ape-like wooing as of old,

But as a spirit suing thee through stars.

Gemma, here I discard the "whence" we
  came,

And I pursue the "whither" we are bound.

I'll lose thee not through too much lust of thee;

Now if thou wouldst, I would not what I
  dreamed.

I see a distant pleasure deeper far,

For — if you will, I'll wed you without pause;

And with the light of children's faces we,

Not worse for this encounter, will deserve

The falling sunset and the coming star,

And you perhaps shall smilingly recall

This plunge for beauty which hath ended sweet.

Say, will you wed me — kiss me and speak not.

GEMMA.   I say no word but give to you my
  lips.

But ah, my brother ! faint the dawn comes on,

But it is dawn.

PIETRO.   [*Sounding gong and writing.*]   Release on the instant Luigi Gonzaga, imprisoned by my order in the prison of Faenza.

(Signed) PIETRO TORNIELLI.

[*A servant enters.*

Ride with this and ride fast.

[*Exit servant with the written order.*

Now comes the golden morning on us two,

And never a drop of dew that she bestows

Is like unto that dew that falls from you.

Here is my fury ended and wild hours.

GEMMA.   I love you more than if your suit had been

Pale, without fault, for I believe that he

Who once has wrongly burned can change
    that fire

Into a radiance but to spirits clear.

[*He kisses her as the curtain descends.*

ACT III

SUNRISE

SCENE I

SCENE. — *The prison of Faenza;* LUIGI *alone.*

The dawn is approaching.

LUIGI.   The dawn, the dawn !   Now when

    all wakes to life,

I wake to death.   When all revives, I die.

This freshness and the coming colour make

The faint grave worse.   Oh, but to die at dawn !

At midnight, yes ! but not when the world

    stirs,

When the Creator reassures the earth,

And reappears in balm out of the East.

Now I must give up life, now when the bird

Resumes its carol and the old music makes,

Now must I go to silence ; never there

The twitter of the brown bird in the leaves,

Nor rustle of foliage there, nor flushing sky.

      [He rises and walks restlessly to and fro.

Now the bright river-fish leaps to the light,

Now creatures of the field bestir them, and

    speak

With mellow sound in twilight of the farm,

And shrilly Chanticleer proclaims the day.

Now the rose lifts her from a weight of dew,

Or raises her red bosom from the rain,

And many a pale flower from dark ground re-

    vives.

Not far away, so little a space away,

Many a garden freshened by night's cloud,

Suspires its various odours from the earth,

And Nature sighing from good sleep awakes.

The sea is conscious of the invisible orb,

Revisiting in glory her faint flood.

The stars are gone, and balm breaks on the

world.

[He sits again.

And in this moment I must yield my breath.

[Starting up again.

And now not only Nature shakes off sleep,

But now the labourer to the field repairs

To dig the sweet earth, or to clip the hedge,

Or through the furrow follow on the plough.

Now wakes the young wife, and but half-awake

Kisses the dreaming babe beside her laid,

While all her deep heart murmurs in its ear.

The soldier starts up to the trumpet-call;

The shopman takes the shutter from the
　　shop,

And in the window carefully displays

His wares; the trim girl unto market trips;

And many a memory stares up at the sun.

And he who rides, and would the morning take,

To saddle springs, or he the morning dew

On foot meets gladly; sweetly comes the day

To the sea-weary, watchers stung with brine;

News of the absent to the bed is brought,

Letters from children in a world far-off.

And whether sad or sweet the world awake

Whirls with a million graves about the sun.

Life, life begins! And I this hour must die.

　　　　　　　　　　　[Still walking to and fro.

And who knows that we cease who seem to
cease?

If I must answer, ere the dawn is full,

For all my faults and folly, and to whom?

Haled before him who made us, or to view

A heavy river rolling amid souls,

Or to remember in an outer dark?

Life! life! I cannot die, I dare not die,

And yonder cloud is slowly reddening!

She, too, she comes not, though she heard my
fate;

I am by all deserted and bereft.

O Gemma, sister, you, you then at least

Might for the last time round me throw your
arms,

Giving the extreme kiss before my doom;

F

But I must go to what I fear alone.

> [*A knock is heard at the door.   Enter the*
> JAILOR, *accompanied by the* EXECU-
> TIONER *and an* ASSISTANT.

JAILOR.   Luigi Gonzaga, are you now prepared?

Or will you see a priest, and in his ear
Confess and with a lighter bosom die?

LUIGI.   Is not my sister here? has she not
sent

A word, a little word?   I cannot think
That she will let me die in such a silence.

JAILOR.   She is not here, and she has sent
no word.

LUIGI.   Oh, but she might!   It is not yet
too late.

Give me a little more of time to breathe;

She would not let me perish who so long

Has grown with me and loved me : I but ask

A little space to see her once, or hear

Her voice: — is this unnatural ? If 'twere

One to whom passion drew me, even thus

Leave would be given, but my sister, sure

You'll not refuse to me a brief delay?

   JAILOR. I have no order, and I have no

     leave

To grant delay : immediate is my task,

And theirs who now await you.

    LUIGI.   Grant me then

A cup of wine : this is allowed ; then, then

I'll make no more delay : a cup of wine,

The last cup !

JAILOR.   You shall have this ; but no more
Then can you tarry, or by force we bear you
To execution.   [*To* ASSISTANT.]   Fetch a cup
    of wine.   [*Exit* ASSISTANT.

LUIGI.   I cannot think why Gemma all this
    while
Holds off from me ; she surely, if none else,
Would say farewell ; ah, strange her silence is.

    [*Enter* ASSISTANT *with cup of wine, which
        he gives into the hands of* LUIGI.

Now for the last time do I taste of thee,
Juice of the grape ; I drink my final cup.

                      [*He drinks.*

Ah, but the joy of life from this last draught
Runs stronger through my veins, and takes my
    heart,

And now than ever more impossible

It seems to die; I cannot, will not cease,

With this red liquor dancing thro' my blood.

If you must kill me, it must be by force,

I'll not be tamely haled by you along.

But ah, can you not spare me a short while;

Look, I have money; you, all three of you,

Shall live at ease if only I may breathe;

Then hide me in this dungeon, and give out

That I am dead, I will reward you well.

You have no grudge against me; one of you

Hide me and take the price!

JAILOR.   Seize him at once,

Bear him without, and as the law enjoins,

Do with him : we have heard enough of speech.

I will not lose my office for soft talk.

EXECUTIONER.   Nor I.

ASSISTANT.   Nor I.

JAILOR.   Then bear him quickly out !

[*They advance on* LUIGI *and seize him,*
when there is heard approaching the gal-
loping sound of a horse's hoofs.

LUIGI.   Listen ! a horse's hoofs, and here
they stop !

[*There is a commotion outside and a*
MESSENGER *rushes in, breathless,*
with a paper.

MESSENGER.   This from Pietro Tornielli,
straight
Dispatched.

JAILOR.   [*Opening and reading.*]   Gonzaga, you
are free forthwith.

LUIGI.   Free, free !

JAILOR.   We have no further leave to keep
    you;
There is the door — and there the world again.

LUIGI.   But, but !

JAILOR.   The reason of this freedom find
Without these walls; we have but to obey.

LUIGI.   And yet I cannot —

[*A further noise without, then* PULCI *and*
    CARLO *rush into the prison.*

PULCI.   Luigi, you are freed.
So much we heard and from the horseman
    learned.

[*Exeunt the* EXECUTIONER *and* ASSISTANT.

JAILOR.   I wish you well, sir.   What I said
    I said

Because it is my office — fare you well.

LUIGI.   But I am lost in this — farewell,

good fellow.   [*Exit* JAILOR.

And you two have no joy in those your eyes;

We have been friends — how long?   Yet you

run hither,

Bringing me life and news of liberty,

With no wild word or clasp of sudden hand,

Nor steady grip, nor look of eye to eye.

Well, I am freed — ah, God! — I should

rejoice!

Thou soaring sun, I come to thee again

To revel in thy splendour!   I am given

Back once again to colour and the dew.

Well, let us quit this place; come, come, my

friends.

Yet, yet — again I say you seem to grieve

That I am snatched thus from the dismal
grave.

Is my life hateful to you, thus restored?

Speak, men, speak! There is some lurking
cause

For such a funeral greeting from the tomb.

You, Carlo, if not Pulci, speak straight
out!

    CARLO. Luigi, you cannot think we are not
glad,

We two of all Siena, to behold you

Now freed, and passing to the outer air.

    LUIGI. Yet still I say that something
lurks behind,

And I myself am not less guilty now

Than when committed — what my crimes
    were then

Are now my crimes no less — yet I am freed.

PULCI.   Luigi, the prison door is open now

Because your sister, in the deep of night,

So is it said, for your sake yielded her

To Pietro Tornielli.

LUIGI.   Ah, my God !

No, no, I'll not take life upon these terms.

I am shaken through all my being, I am
    changed ;

Where once I cowered, now I cower no more.

She, she — she knew I would not have this
    bargain.

Now I will put my freedom to some use.

Call up our friends, however few they be,

And I will storm the palace and demand

My death.   I'll ask it as a boon, as once

Life I demanded.   Ah, I loathe to breathe,

And the great sun is blackening in the heaven.

Come with me, come !

    PULCI.   Some friends we have without

Already; more will join us as we go.

    LUIGI.   On to the palace ! on !   And let

      me die !

SCENE II

SCENE. — *A hall in the palace of the* GONZAGA.
*There is a sound of mutiny outside, and as the
curtain rises* ANSELMO *breaks in accompanied
by others of the troops, while sullen shouts are
heard from outside.*

ANSELMO.   He is not here; he spends the
hours with her.

Sirs, let us force these doors and slay the man

Who has betrayed us for a woman's eyes.

My sword is drawn !

ANSELMO.   And mine.

ANSELMO.   We'll follow you.

[*Enter* PIETRO.

PIETRO.   Now, sirs !

ANSELMO. Pietro Tornielli, we

Have heard a rumour thro' Siena flying

That not alone the sister's life is spared,

But that, in hot desire for her, the brother

Too you have spared, whom we all heard

    condemned

Out of your own mouth! So, then, we must

    fight,

And follow you through peril and through

    death,

Only at last to be confronted thus;

Our swords are nothing 'gainst a lady's

    eyes,

Our faith is nothing 'gainst our leader's lust,

                  [*Angry murmurs.*

Our services as air against her kiss.

Thus then I speak, and speaking speak for
    all —
Either we slay thee or we leave thee here
To riot and to passion and to wine.
But if I cannot for old memory
Plunge in thy heart this sword, I'll never draw
In such a cause again. I'll not be fooled,

[Angry shouts.

To fight and find all lost at last for lust.
So, Tornielli, fare you well for ever.

[He is about to exit when LUIGI, *after much*
commotion, bursts into the hall, followed
by a retinue of followers.

LUIGI. Now, Pietro Tornielli, face to face
We stand. I owe my freedom to your will;
I am set free — no cause assigned, but freed.

Why then ?   My sister's honour !

> [*Pointing to his sister.*

And do you think

That for the madness of a night with her

Whom I have worshipped like the blessed saint,

Whose very tears were holy water, her blood

The very wine we drink not if we sin —

You think I'll take my life for such a fee ?

Oh, I was craven, I deny it not ;

Here was the chance, then, here the basest lure

Ever proposed within a woman's ear —

She should submit to you and I go free !

No, death a thousand times, and death again !

I'll not contaminate the air henceforth,

And all shall cry " See, Luigi walks abroad

Freed by his sister's soil !"   If you will fight,

Then let us fight and without pause, and
    now ;

If not, I give myself again to death.

    [*A door is thrown open and* GEMMA *comes
        in,* PIETRO *taking her hand.*

You, Gemma, though some may applaud this
    act,

I loathe you for it and for evermore.

Ah ! but perhaps it was no martyrdom !

Perhaps the sacrifice came easily,

Perhaps —

    PIETRO.   Enough is said.   Now I will
        speak.

Luigi Gonzaga, and Anselmo there,

It is most true that what you here have
        charged

G

Against me I did plan and did intend.

                                  [Murmurs.

That fault is in my blood.　But here I make

A holy oath, before all saints in heaven,

That she, this lady, stands by me untouched,

That she is pure as ever without spot.

Rather would she have killed me or herself

Than so submitted even for such a cause ;

But I, who have so played the game of love,

Am won to something nobler at the last :

To-day I make this lady my true wife.

    GEMMA.　Luigi, I should have died ere this

        I did.　　　　*[Murmurs of astonishment.*

    PIETRO.　Her brother, who has thus refused

        his life,

Knowing the truth will not refuse it more.

A golden morning on us all descends,

And I foresee a golden morning wax

Into a deeper life between us two,

Bringing not bloodshed nor old enmity,

But on our houses and Siena peace.

CURTAIN